The Politics of English

2001 05211

The Politics of English

A Marxist View of Language

Marnie Holborow

SAGE Publications
London • Thousand Oaks • New Delhi

First published 1999

P
119.3
H65
1999

 SAGE Publications Ltd
6 Bonhill Street
London EC2A 4PU

SAGE Publications Inc
2455 Teller Road
Thousand Oaks, California 91320

SAGE Publications India Pvt Ltd
32, M-Block Market
Greater Kailash – I
New Delhi 110 048

British Library Cataloguing in Publication data

A catalogue record for this book is available
from the British Library

ISBN 0 7619 6017 1
ISBN 0 7619 6018 X (pbk)

Library of Congress catalog record available

Typeset by Mayhew Typesetting, Rhayader, Powys
Printed and bound in Great Britain by Athenaeum Press, Gateshead

Contents

Acknowledgements   vii

1   Introduction   1

2   In the Beginning was Society: Marx, Volosinov and
Vygotsky on Language   13

3   Money Talks: The Politics of World English   53

4   Women, Language and the Limits of Feminism   97

5   The Politics of Standard English   149

6   Conclusion   189

Bibliography   197

Index   213

Acknowledgements

I would like to thank all those in the School of Applied Languages and Intercultural Studies in Dublin City University for making my sabbatical leave possible, and particularly Dermot McMahon, Veronica Crosbie and Maurice Scully who covered my teaching while I was away. I am also very grateful to Deirdre Beecher in the Library for her unstinting help with Inter-Library Loans.

I am grateful to Julia Hall and Kate Scott at Sage Publications for their valuable assistance during the process of getting the book to print and to Norman Fairclough for his generous encouragement.

I am indebted to many socialists, in Britain and in Ireland, who, over the years, have set me thinking in this direction, and particularly to Sheila McGregor for a talk that she gave at Marxism 97 in London on Language and Consciousness, to John Molyneux for his invaluable article on the political correctness debate and to Chris Harman and Alex Callinicos whose writings on the origins of human society and the cul-de-sac of postmodernism provided the starting point for this book. Particular thanks also go to Jeannie Robinson for her detailed (and very cheering) reading of the draft and to James Eaden for his suggestions. Thanks, too, to Paul Holborow and Jan Nielsen for providing me with some of the political landmarks that started me off on this route. I'd also like to thank my father and mother, John and Cicely Holborow, who have always encouraged me, even from afar.

Finally, most of all, I would like to thank Kate Allen for her incredible and much appreciated patience with me and Kieran Allen for his valuable criticisms of the drafts, and a lot of other things besides.

1   Introduction

> They declare they are only fighting against 'phrases'.
> They forget, however that they are in no way combating
> the real world when they are merely combating the
> phrases of this world.
>   Life is not determined by consciousness, but consciousness
> by life. (Karl Marx, *The German Ideology*)

There is little disagreement that language and politics are connected. Traditionalists may claim that language itself stands free-floating above politics but they consider attitudes to language as intensely political. These they see as dominated by a radical leftist current that has infected teachers, social workers and, worse still, university professors. At the other end, postmodernists, and others, see language as the nucleus of political life, steeped in power and defining people's role in the world. Why has language come to be so politically contentious? In what sense can one speak of language being political? Why is English at the centre of the political controversy? Does language determine people's ideas of the world? How much can language shift political realities? These are some of the questions that are the concern of this book.

The politics of English runs along many axes. At one level, the sheer extent of the use of English around the world brings into sharp linguistic focus the effects of globalization. It is by no means an exaggeration to say that the language of capitalism at the turn of the twenty-first century is English. Not surprisingly therefore, reactions to English are shaped accordingly. English is either the modernizing panacea or the ruthless oppressor, depending on your place in the world.

At another level, because of its dominance and its social spread, English has also been the language that has most eclectically absorbed political changes and tensions. So it was with the 'politically correct' controversy at its height in the early 1990s with

English, more than other languages, feeling the effects. While the issues may have seemed like so many storms in university teacups, at its core the debate concerned wider ideological questions, drawing lines on either side of the radical legacy of the 1960s. At a time when the struggles against oppression of women and minorities seemed to have achieved rights for only a few and even these were under attack, politics seemed to become displaced into language. Language became a political battleground. Political correctness was condemned as the closing of all liberal minds by the right and the necessary political opening of them by the left. It seemed as though language had come to signify everything politically.

Another dimension of the politics of English was about which variety of English should be recognized. Paradoxically, while English has increasingly become a world language, it has also become infused with different social and political experience. In Rushdie's words, 'English, no longer an *English* language, now grows from many roots'. *Whose English*? and *which English*? has been raised in cultural and educational debates. Internationally, more and more English-speakers speak English as a second, or third, language with non-native speakers probably now making up the majority worldwide.[1] Also within English-speaking societies, particularly the US and Britain, the issue of persistent educational underachievement shifted into the question of language differences. Coinciding with a right-wing offensive on both sides of the Atlantic, Standard English was raised as the cultural and educational rampart against other Englishes, Black English, Caribbean or Cockney English, Chicano English, and on other continents Indian, Nigerian or South-East Asian varieties of English, all of which continued to flourish. Orwell who, in the crisis of post-war Britain, sensed intuitively the relationship of language to politics, noted that for the upper classes and empire-builders, somehow history had not gone according to plan (Orwell 1970: 217). The same might be said for some of the last-ditch advocates of Standard English. Behind their shrillness lurks a deeper anxiety about Britain, about class and about ideology.

These three issues show that the politics of English reflects the shifting sands of today's world. Older certainties seem less secure, and in language as in social questions, the governing class, as

Gramsci noted in an earlier period of crisis, attempts to reassert its dominant role, reemphasize its distinctive ideology, reorganize its cultural hegemony (Gramsci 1985: 183–184). While many of these debates about language have been set in motion by the right, they have arisen from a position of weakness and self-doubt, not self-assurance.[2] The desire to fix language in the face of change bears witness, paradoxically, to the profound unfixedness of the present world and the extent of social change. For linguistic models to hold, whether they are Standard English, World English, or calling a person a man, the social world has to seem, however tenuously, to correspond to the example – yet the example seems out of date.

From a historical perspective, this is not the first time that pleas for linguistic stability have enfolded the search for social stability. The Académie Française was founded to fix French in the seventeenth century, the most turbulent, war-torn period of French history. Its attempts lay in shreds amid the flourishing of dialects until the more stable and prosperous period of Napoleon. In Italy too, keen young nationalists, amid the inter-state rivalry of the sixteenth century, proclaimed Tuscan as the national language in a Florentine academy, but only after national unification would Italian begin to become a historical fact across the peninsula. Standardization in Britain gained its greatest impetus under the solid industrial and imperial expansion of the nineteenth century and this provided the background to its promotion in mass education. The success of such a project rests on the power and political confidence of its promoters. Macaulay's absolute certainty about the role of English and things English in India, or Arnold's profound sense of British culture as 'the best that is thought and known', reposed on the fruits, and extirpations, of the Age of Empire. Today, however, the material and ideological roots are shallower, and society more divided. An orderly Standard World English, amid the diversity and social disparity of today's world, seems more like a forlorn cry after the horse has bolted than a robust, forcible ideology.

In a very real sense, then, language questions reformulate political questions. But the politics of language impinges at a deeper level. Language, as a part of human consciousness, is also the practical way in which humans grasp the world around them, make sense of it, interact with each other and contribute towards changing that world. Language is not just ideological because it is a political issue but because it is the stuff of political consciousness. This intimate connection between language and ideology means that theories of language are also political theories, as the Russian Marxist Volosinov writing in the 1920s pointed out with so much foresight. Volosinov's polemic took issue with a strand of idealism, namely structuralist linguistics, as represented by Saussure. His argument was that by creating a distinction between *langue* and *parole*, between what is general, systematic and stable in language and that which is momentary, interactive and unpredictable, the essential social nature of language was lost. Such a distinction was not ideologically innocent. It refocused the study of language – later to become linguistics – on an abstract system whose actual connections with society had been cut. It created an artificial discontinuity between language system and language history. Language became thus 'a stationary rainbow' arched over living utterances, giving language an over-determining role by making its speakers mere conformers to its intricate rules. Language was made into an object, reified, and thus somehow outside the speakers who produce it.

How Volosinov saw the ideological nature of language, as well as his arguments against 'abstract objectivism', is relevant for defining what is meant by the political nature of language today. The prison-house of language, from structuralism to postmodernism, has cast a long shadow. It has infused much of the writing on the political aspects of language and its sometimes uncritical acceptance is another reason for examining the politics of English in different terms. Language as a key aspect of social reality has eclectic sources, from Whorfian language determinism to social constructivism, with different strands providing different emphases. Nevertheless, seeing the world through discourse has become the dominant theme. 'Discursive practices', 'dominant discourse', 'discourse as a site of struggle', 'the subjection of discourse': such terms have become commonplace in writings on the political dimensions of language. An influential figure in this landscape has unquestionably been Foucault. I examine some of these views in Chapter 3, but since his influence has been prodigious, I will outline briefly here the key themes of Foucauldian discourse and indicate some of the difficulties that they present.

Foucault's Shadow

Foucault's writings are concerned with many things – the history
of ideas and how sexuality and madness have been socially judged
– but a central strand to his work is his understanding of the term
discourse. This term, rather than *language*, is significant. Discourse,
for Foucault, is not simply linguistic expression but also the various
social props around language that are its 'conditions of possibility'.
Discipline is an organizing concept for Foucault and discourse
itself is both disciplined by social pressures and disciplining for its
users. *Order of Discourse*, the title, significantly, of his defining
inaugural address to the Collège de France in 1970, is about rules
and constraints, inclusionary and exclusionary procedures which
determine who can say what. It is a 'regulated practice' defined by
society at particular points in time, setting boundaries to areas of
knowledge. These practices determine how subjects are catalogued
into areas of study, into a 'single system of formation', such as
clinical discourse, economic discourse, the discourse of natural
history, psychiatric discourse (Foucault 1972: 107–108).

But Foucault is talking about more than subject boundaries.
Crucially, discourse is about what is constructed as truth. Discourse is how knowledge is represented, which is the source of its
social power. Truth and power are not located ontologically and
socially, but in the formation of discourse itself. It is this that
constitutes the overwhelming power of Foucauldian discourse.
Types of discourse become thus 'regimes of truth':

> Each society has its regime of truth; that is the types of discourse which it
> accepts and makes function as true; the mechanisms and instances which
> enable one to distinguish true and false statements, the status of those
> who are charged with saying what counts as true. (Foucault 1979: 46)

Foucault is deliberately vague about where the power for his
discursive practices arises. In the foreword to *The Order of Things*
(which in French was entitled more pertinently *Les Mots et les
Choses*) he explains that it is the exercise of power, not its causality,
which interests him (Foucault 1970: xii). Notwithstanding, he does
provide a certain view of history. Indeed Foucault's work has been
the inspiration for what some in cultural studies have seen as the
'new historicism'. Foucauldian history also concerns discourse.

The 'genealogy' that he proposes for various intellectual eras – the Renaissance, the Classical Age, the Age of Positivism and the Modern Age – is demarcated partly according to discursive features, and how representation of the world is understood. Each era is characterized by an 'episteme', from the Greek word for knowledge, by which Foucault means the accepted guiding principles of everyday knowledge, science and philosophy.[3]

Discourse in Foucault's account is pivotal. Foucault's discursive formations share with structuralism the methodological procedure of providing definitions within an enclosed system. Like Saussure's *langue*, it is self-referential in so far as discourses are defined in relation to other discourses. But its idealism goes all the way down; discourse swallows up all other phenomena, social, political, ideological. As Eagleton points out, the power of discourse grasps language as an obstacle, not as a horizon, and is, strangely, culturally reductionist (Eagleton 1996). Discourse and discursive practices become, as one recent admirer of Foucault puts it, 'the only way we have to apprehend reality'. The only order of the world is 'the order which we impose on it through our linguistic description' (Mills 1997: 52–54). Whether Foucault himself would put it in such stark terms is unclear because his writings are hedged with evasions, and his interviews even more so. Nevertheless, what one can say is that Foucault's abiding, even morbid, conviction was that discourse seemed to him to be everywhere. As he explained in an interview, it 'hangs over us, leading us forward in our blindness', the meaning melting away into other discursive meanings, 'its face inclined toward a night of which we know nothing' (Miller 1993: 123). Discourse is everything and everywhere.

This view poses serious difficulties for the seizing of the political aspects of language. If reality is only grasped discursively, where does that leave real oppression, real suffering and pain, the very things that make politics so important? A discursive rendering of the world, even if it talks about power regimes through which it is practised, obfuscates the recognition of actual oppression. If language is just another discursive practice, if there is no truth outside it, then everything is relative, including oppression. As Geras has remarked about postmodernism, if there is no truth then there is no injustice (Geras 1995). There is just multiplicity, and duplicity, in the discursive renderings of reality. Some have argued that such relativism is not the necessary outcome of postmodernism and that an ethical judgements are still possible. Foucault himself did not shy away from making value judgements and was involved in various political struggles. Nevertheless, placing discourse at the centre of interpreting reality, denying an objective reality, discounts epistemologically taking any one discursive practice as any truer than any other. Yet ironically, it is precisely through language that we gain a greater awareness of undeniable objective realities. For example, claims on the part of those who have brutally suffered that they need 'to tell the world' of their experiences are no mere discourses. Accounts of slavery like Frederick Douglass's, accounts of suffering like Arthur Koestler's, accounts of survivors of the Holocaust like Primo Levi or its victims like Anne Frank, leave us in no doubt. Their impact and value is that we instantly recognize them, not just as accounts, but true accounts, proof themselves of the secure link between language and reality.

Yet there is another intractability about making discourse sovereign. If discourse is the prism through which reality *is* grasped, indeed *is* reality, how do you get out of language? What decides whether you can contest a *discursive practice*? At what point and for what reasons do you break the linguistic chain? Furthermore, if linguistic representation is everything, then politics becomes simply the rephrasing of language. Politics is just about speaking. Real content falls out and politics becomes a question of style. Systematic oppression in a social world, in this discursive framework, becomes collapsed into frames of mind and politics transferred on to a plane of individual attitudes. Mills, for example, tells us that 'the discursive framework of femininity may determine the type of clothes she chooses to wear, the type of bodily stance she adopts and ways of thinking about herself and others in relation to power (Mills 1997: 18). This is a far cry, it would seem, from the deeper harsh reality of women's oppression in this society and a sadly tame version of women's liberation.

Language, Ideology and Society

At this point, it is useful, both philosophically and politically, to make a distinction between ideas and reality, between ideology and the specific social and economic foundations of society. Foucault was quite explicit that discourse, despite its apparent political dimensions, was not ideology. In one interview he expressly rejects the category of ideology and the reasons he gives are instructive. He rejects ideology because it presupposes in some way an opposition to truth. For Foucault, there are only truth effects produced by discourse which are not in themselves true or false. Secondly, ideology presupposes a subject. And thirdly, Foucault insists, ideology is related to some material determinant of it (1979: 36). In other words, Foucault's rejection of ideology rests on cutting loose material reference points.

Ideology, however, is the only way that one can apprehend the politics of language. The term is spurned by some discourse theorists as being Marxist and crudely reductionist, although these interpretations are more often asserted than explained.[4] Yet ideology is a crucial concept because it provides a framework for understanding that ideas and language constitute a different order of things than the material world. Descriptions of starvation are not the same as being hungry. The discourses of imperialism are different to the devastating consequences for the actual lives of countless Indians, Africans or Irish, wrought by the power of colonial capitalism. The discourse of racism is different to being physically attacked, or to the gas chamber. Marx rightly observed about the idealists, who believed that phrases were everything, that there was a difference between phrases and the real world and that 'Life is not determined by consciousness, but consciousness by life' (Marx and Engels 1974: 41–47). This distinction is cast aside in Foucault's order of things. To imagine that phrases and life are interchangeable, other than perhaps revealing something of the writer's more comfortable position, says little about the world itself.

Understanding that ideas and the material world are of a different order, is not to be reductionist. It is difficult to see how any reading of Marx could arrive at that conclusion. Marx was at pains to point out that consciousness was an active agent in the making of history, that while humans do not choose their circumstances, they do themselves make history (Marx and Engels 1969: 398). Marx was acutely aware of the pressure of dominant ideas which weighed like a nightmare on the brains of the living. But he also saw that within society there were contradictions and contending forces that could overturn them. His remarks about language fit into the understanding that consciousness and the social world, while being of different orders, are dialectically related. No outcome is determined in advance, and language as one of the primary elements of human social interaction is a vital part of what he called 'practical consciousness'. Language as part of ideology makes the crucial distinction between ideas and reality, interpretation and social transformation.

Language and Politics

Ideology is also different to discourse as regards the notion of power. Power for Foucault, as it was for Nietzsche, was irrational, a will to power and an almost transcendent category. Power and knowledge are fundamental themes in Foucault and both are interwoven with his understanding of discourse. Discourse is a manifestation of 'regimes of truth' and, as such, it is a constraint on human beings. Underlying his critique of these ways of ordering the world is his rejection of rationalism. At the end of *The Order of Things* Foucault rejects the 'grand narrative' of the Enlightenment, and pushes its humanism to one side in his now famous prediction: he questions knowledge as it has hitherto been accepted and wagers that 'man would be erased like a face drawn in sand at the edge of the sea' (Foucault 1970: 387). Foucault attempts to tear down the certainties of rationalism with the unstable category of discourse.

It is important to point out that Marx, too, saw the limits of bourgeois rationality. He pointed out that rationalism rested on exploitation and social division of labour, without which progress would not have been possible. Marx's critique was not of rationalism itself, but that there were limits to bourgeois rationalism. When rational investigation came up against class interest it was abandoned. Bourgeois rationalism is, in other words, 'one-sided and inadequate'.[5] It was historically situated in the way that one class turned it to its own ideological purposes to justify the exploitation of the vast majority. Power was not an elusive human characteristic, but a force with material roots which was constantly contested by the very class on whose exploitation the bourgeoisie depended for its wealth. This contradiction offered a challenge to bourgeois rationalism, not by negating it but by defying its limits. The alienation of individuals, so well described by Foucault, but whose source he shifts to the realm of irrationality, is thus an unfathomable Nietzschean 'social straitjacket', human psychological impulses that individuals play their own part in maintaining.[6] Marx, by contrast, locates powerlessness, and the source of alienation, in class society which then becomes the basis of social revolution; only then can the narrow horizon of bourgeois right be crossed and 'the free development of each is the condition for the free development of all' (Marx and Engels 1973: 61). Marx's identification of power in social class provided a historical and social basis for power in society and, simultaneously, the means of overthrowing it. Power was not something strangely irrational and pervasive but a specific set of social relations. In contrast to Foucault's 'insurgence of knowledge', Marx saw social revolution.

Finally, one might ask how it was that the shrinking of politics into discourse came about and how it came to be so widely and often unquestioningly accepted. This can best be explained, as others have done, by understanding how Foucault's ideas fitted with the dominant political mood of the time. Those academics who articulated discourse at the centre of politics were also those who had come to the brink of social change in the late 1960s only to see it recede into conservatism in the late 1970s and 1980s. Such dashing of political hopes left its mark on a whole generation. As Callinicos has correctly observed, 'the term postmodern would seem to be a floating signifier by means of which [a socially mobile] intelligentsia has sought to articulate its political disillusionment and its aspiration to a consumption-orientated lifestyle' (Callinicos 1989: 171). It was this disillusion, experienced within the relative comfort of academia, that allowed discursive practice to become mistaken for political practice. The shortcomings of this approach, already obvious then, have become more so today. The persistence of the issues that so enraged the generation of the 1960s – oppression, social inequality, imperialist wars – makes the political irrelevancy of an exclusive concern with discourse all the more glaring.

This book approaches language from a Marxist standpoint in which language is seen as 'practical consciousness' of social reality with all the contradictions and possibilities that such a view implies. Neither language nor English is everything nor determining. Humans are not prisoners of language nor are they, through language, creators of reality. Language is both a social product and a component in the social process of how humans interact and act on the society in which they live. English, for good or for ill, is what history has handed down to large numbers of people but people, in different social circumstances, have also transformed it. Therein lie both the limitations and the potential of language. It is this perspective that I adopt in looking at the politics of English with the hope of setting language back on its feet, as it were.

Notes

1 Crystal's figures estimate non-native speakers at 350 million, just above native speakers, although this is probably an underestimate (Crystal 1997: 60–61).

2 'A dwindling body of linguistic reactionaries' is how Roger Scruton describes his political camp (Scruton 1990: 118). Other arch-conservatives see themselves as an embattled minority weighed down by the New Orthodoxy (Marenbon 1987).

3 See Fink-Eifel (1992) for a useful account of Foucault's view of knowledge and power.

4 Mills dismisses Marxist views of ideology as vulgar, simplistic and negative with no further reference or explanation (Mills 1997: 30).

5 Marx writes this about Ricardo, who had pursued the labour theory of value only up to the point where it did not clash with the bourgeoisie's justification of pursuing profit (Marx 1976: 306). In *The Grundrisse* Marx writes of the bourgeoisie: '[t]he universality towards which it is perpetually driving finds limitations in its own nature' (Marx 1971: 95).

6 For an illuminating account of the overlap between Nietzsche and Foucault see Miller (1993), Chapter 7.

2   In the Beginning was Society: Marx, Volosinov and Vygotsky on Language

'People know how to talk in more or less the sense that spiders know how to spin webs.' Stephen Pinker's observation in his 1990s bestseller on language reformulates a theme that has dominated linguistic theory since the beginning of the twentieth century. Language is an autonomous system that happens on its own, whose very uniqueness and complexity reinforce its position as an independent structure, and which has no necessary frame of reference in the social or cultural world. For Pinker, the autonomy of language arises from its physiological roots in 'a distinct piece of the biological makeup of our brains'; language is an instinct subject to its own spontaneous impulses (Pinker 1995: 18). Previous well-known figures in linguistics have thought along the same language-independent lines. Chomsky, possibly the most influential figure in contemporary linguistics, holds that language arises from an innate mechanism in humans which enables the production of grammatical sentences. Chomsky's language process is purely mental, and grammar is seen as independent of general meaning let alone extra-linguistic contexts (for example, Chomsky 1972: 15). At the beginning of the century, Saussure, the founder of modern-day linguistics, prioritized language-as-system over evolving language and thereby endowed language with a self-referential status. He likened language to a piece of paper with thought on the front and sound on the back; you cannot cut the front without at the same time cutting the back (Saussure 1971: 157). Language is apparently a movement back and forth between *signifié* and *signifiant*, but the paper floats free of the world. Post-structuralists, more recently, have taken this linguistic limbo to its logical conclusion and declared that there is nothing outside text.

While some of these radical relativists have begun to have second thoughts, the self-reflexive nature of language, expressed by Pinker in biological terms, nevertheless states a theme that has reverberated far and wide across linguistics and philosophy.[1]

This chapter seeks to redress the balance in favour of the social nature of language. Many of the issues surrounding the politics of language hinge on the precise nature of the relationship of language to society. A social view of language might be expected to run counter to the autonomous view of language, an assumption that Newmeyer makes automatically (1986, 1991). However, things are not quite so straightforward. A social interpretation of language can still give language an independent status by holding that language is not just part of society but is *constitutive* of it. In this way of thinking, the direction is from language to the social, and thus language is held to possess reality-creating powers quite as formidable as those who claim that language is autonomous. Foucault's 'discursive practices', which are claimed to constitute and reproduce power relations in society, articulates this strain of thought. His influence has not been insignificant in matters related to the politics of language, as Fairclough confirms somewhat critically (Fairclough 1995). Foucault and postmodernist interpretations have also left their mark in the work of commentators on the role of English in the post-colonial world (as in, for example, Pennycook 1994a, Ashcroft et al. 1995).[2] These views concur in according cultural practices, including language, the full weight and dynamism of social forces as if language has as much material weight as wars, plunder or disease. The widespread acceptance of these ideas highlights the need for a theory of the relationship between language and society which avoids the circularity of language determinism.

With the aim of providing just such a theoretical framework to the discussion of some of these issues, we will first look at what Marx and Engels had to say about language. Many commentators on the social nature of language refer to Marxism, indirectly, or obliquely, or critically; a re-examination of what they actually wrote is therefore necessary. Second, we will examine the contribution of Volosinov. His work on language, in the view of one, 'is remarkable because what [he] wrote . . . appears to anticipate some of the directions of contemporary thought' and because it suggests some innovative ways of approaching the social nature of language (Dentith 1995). For others, Volosinov was a lone, pioneering figure who stood out against the trend of a historical formalism in linguistics (Jameson 1974, Crowley 1996). His work remains, it is argued here, a key Marxist text for the social understanding of language not least because the political nature of language arises from the fact that it is part of ideology. Further, we will briefly examine some aspects of the view of language put forward by Vygotsky, a contemporary of Volosinov, whose theory regarding the social formation of language is strikingly relevant today, particularly the interrelationship of language and thought, the evolution of language and the role of context. In conclusion, we will bring together these different strands and evaluate their relevance in the context of the politics of language.

The Origins of Language and Consciousness

Direct references to language in the writings of Marx, particularly in his *Economic and Philosophical Writings of 1844*, and in *The German Ideology*, are fragmentary. One of the few contemporary linguists to have commented on what Marx wrote, has claimed that his few remarks on language are self-contradictory and that the subject was of little concern to him (Newmeyer 1986). Other commentators in the disciplines of politics and philosophy, as well as standard reference books on Marx, tend to disagree.[3] I will argue that, even from the fragments left by Marx, a coherent view of the nature of language emerges. Taken in the broader context of consciousness, ideology and superstructure, of which Marx saw language as a constituent part, it is difficult to see how the assertion that Marx simply had little interest in language can be sustained. Marx's theory of dialectical materialism, as Jones has pointed out, centrally involves questions of language (Jones 1991: 5). Even in the ostensibly more economic texts, like *Capital*, Marx refers to ideological questions which have a bearing on language. Perhaps the fact that philosophers and political scientists have devoted more energy to reviewing Marx's view of these matters than have linguists, itself reveals the often narrow purview of linguistics.[4]

In determining the nature of language and its role in society, the question of how human language emerged must surely be an essential one. Marx identified *the origins of language* as being inextricably linked with *the emergence of consciousness*. In the 1844 Manuscripts he had already asserted that language is the element, 'the vital element', of consciousness (Marx 1975: 356). In *The German Ideology*, written in 1846, he sketches a fuller context of the materialist basis of historical development and how human relations are determined by their own needs and by the mode of production. Marx describes, first, the emergence of consciousness and the emergence of language as sound, in its material sense:

> From the start, the 'spirit' is afflicted with the curse of being 'burdened' with matter, which here makes its appearance in the form of agitated layers of air, in short, of language. (Marx and Engels 1974: 50–51)

From these beginnings, language develops among humans in response to problems posed by their material life and is essentially, not just contingently, social:

> Language is as old as consciousness, language *is* practical conscious- ness that exists also for other men, and for that reason alone it really exists for me personally as well; language, like consciousness, only arises from the need, the necessity, of intercourse with other men. Where there exists a relationship, it exists for me: the animal does not enter into 'relations' with anything, it does not enter into any relation at all. For the animal its relation to others does not exist as a relation. Consciousness is, therefore, from the very beginning a social product, and remains so as long as men exist at all. (Marx and Engels 1974: 51, original emphasis)

In so far as both language and consciousness involve the ability to generalize beyond the particular and the present and to process abstract thought, they overlap and are interconnected. Language is the mode of being of thoughts, 'practical consciousness', as Marx puts it. For Marx the practical nature of language is self-evident. For example, he describes social relations using the metaphor 'the language of life' (Marx and Engels 1974: 47). Language and con- sciousness share an inherently social dimension, which originates in the social nature of human activity. Newmeyer claims that

Marx's running together of language and consciousness as social entities is over-simplistic. 'Consciousness is a social product; language is practical consciousness; therefore language is a social product. The syllogism could not be more straightforward', is how Newmeyer dismisses the identification (1986: 105). But Marx does not proceed in this way: consciousness and language are intertwined because of the social basis of the origins of both. They are not compared as abstract essences but looked at historically from the point of view of how the specifically human attributes of consciousness and language came into being, and evolved, in specific conditions. As Marx wrote in 1859, in the *Preface to the Critique of Political Economy*:

> The mode of production of material life conditions the social, political and intellectual life processes in general. It is not the consciousness of men that determines their being, but on the contrary, their social being that determines their consciousness. (Marx and Engels 1969: 503)

The development of language and consciousness were linked because both were aspects of the process of modern humans coping collectively with the material world around them.

This decisive social dimension arises from the unique relationship that humans have with nature and that manifests itself in the form of human labour. 'Labour is, first of all, a process between man and nature, a process by which man, through his own actions, mediates, regulates and controls the metabolism between himself and nature' (Marx 1976: 283). Labour is an exclusively human characteristic which sets humans apart from animals. It allows humans to establish a relationship with nature, rather than be dominated by it. Nature then becomes something that humans, unlike animals, can change.

The process of human labour is qualitatively different even to processes in the animal that seem similar. Human labour occurs as a result not of instinct, but of reflection. Marx explains in *Capital*:

> A spider conducts operations which resemble those of the weaver, and a bee would put many a human architect to shame by the construction of its honeycomb cells. But what distinguishes the worst architect from the best of bees is that the architect builds the cell in his mind before he constructs it in wax. At the end of every labour process, a result

emerges which had already been conceived. . . . Man not only effects a
change in form in the materials of nature; he also realizes his own
purpose in those materials. (Marx 1976: 284)

Marx returns to the bee analogy elsewhere in his writings. A
beehive may be a highly organized place where allotted tasks take
place, even where complex patterns of coded behaviour develop,
but the activities have not changed for many millions of years. What
a bee can do is limited in advance to a very narrow range of activities
dictated by its genetic make-up.[5] Human labour, by contrast, is not
programmed but inventive, and is creatively adapted to different
and unpredictable situations. Human labour has to change constantly to meet new needs and this is only possible because humans
are able to stand back from the task and reflect, looking back and
forward in time, on what they do. Human language makes this
process possible. This uniquely human ability to represent events
removed in time and place, what has been termed *displacement*,
allows experience to carry its full weight in human existence.[6] The
result of this ability is that humans can change the conditions of
their existence and make their own history; in this process, furthermore, they also change themselves (Marx 1976: 283). The pivotal
role that language plays encapsulates the larger two-way process of
historical materialism that Marx is describing. Language both *arises*
from the social demands and needs of the material world and,
through human cooperation and activity, *contributes* to the transformation of that world. It is then itself transformed as human
society changes. The dialectical relationship between language and
society that we can draw from Marx here will be important to bear
in mind when we examine the specific aspects of the connections
between language and society, in later chapters.

Marx makes it clear that the development of consciousness, and
therefore language, was evolutionary. Consciousness did not just
emerge in one biological quantum leap, one evolutionary saltation,
with developed language coming together all at once. Marx indicates
that language and consciousness evolve continuously over time.
He distinguishes between a lower level of consciousness and higher
consciousness involving abstract thought (Marx and Engels 1974:
51). At first, human consciousness is merely an immediate awareness of the physical environment, a mere 'herd-consciousness',

distinguished only from animals in so far as humans are aware of themselves, 'conscious beings' as Marx says elsewhere (Marx 1975: 328).[7] This barely distinctive human characteristic then develops alongside humans' ability to enter into relations with other humans, a process which, Marx implies, involves the use of sounds at this early stage. The later development of productivity, the increase in needs and a growing population then begin to transform primitive consciousness through increasing collective cooperation. At a further stage, alongside an increased division of labour, the distinction between 'material' and 'mental' labour appears. Thus abstract thought, 'consciousness emancipated from the world', capable of transforming material life, not just experiencing it, emerges alongside social production. From these developments in human society, the formation of '"pure" theory, theology, philosophy, ethics etc.' becomes possible (Marx and Engels 1974: 52). The evolutionary aspect of language and consciousness parallels the evolution of human society itself.

Engels in his *Introduction to Dialectics of Nature* written in 1875–6 makes the same substantial point although he defines, in more detail, human development, and the development of language, as a number of *interrelated stages*. Although his work echoes Darwin whose *Origin of Species* was published some sixteen years before and whose *Descent of Man* only four years before, Engels makes some significant changes to the stages described by Darwin, as Harman (1994) points out. Darwin while stressing the continuum between some animals' use of tools and sounds, held that it was higher mental powers, 'improvement of our reason', which enabled humans to develop elaborate tool use and articulate language (1930: 92–106). Engels by contrast stresses the significance of upright gait and the freeing of hands for human labour in the development of speech.[8] 'When after thousands of years of struggle, the differentiation of hand from foot and erect gait were finally established, man became distinct from the ape and the basis was laid for the development of articulate speech and the mighty development of the brain that has since made the gulf between man and ape unbridgeable' (Marx and Engels 1970: 52).[9] Engels locates the development of mental abilities in the emergence of social cooperation through tool use, not in the development of the brain *per se*. Like Marx, Engels saw language as part and parcel of the development of consciousness, and resulting from the dialectical process of the interaction of human labour on nature. Engels, too, sees this transformation as marking the beginning of human history. The ability now of humans to impress their stamp on nature means that 'with man, we enter history. . . . [T]he more they make their history themselves, the less becomes the influence of unforeseen events and uncontrolled forces on this history, and the more accurately does the historical result correspond to the aim laid down in advance' (1970: 53). In a memorable passage in 'The part played by labour in the transition from ape to man', Engels shows the interdependence of labour and language:

> the development of labour necessarily helped to bring the members of society closer together by increasing cases of mutual support and joint activity and by making clear the advantage of this joint activity to each individual. In short, man in the making arrived at the point where *they had something to say* to each other. (1970: 68–69; emphasis in original)

Engels notes here the unity of material social activity and language. The genesis of language is in human labour – 'the point at which humans have something to say to each other'. Communication is not therefore just one of the functions of language; on the contrary, language presupposes both logically and *de facto* the interaction among people. Language only arises from the need to communicate with other humans. It is quintessentially social.

Language and Ideology

In their description of the evolution of language from social production, both Marx and Engels are aware of the qualitative change that the appearance of this language-consciousness represents. 'We ascend from earth to heaven,' Marx sardonically puts it (Marx and Engels 1974: 47). The sheer power that consciousness confers produces another effect: that ideas seem cut loose of reality, as if free-standing, floating above the constraints of the material world. Engels describes how this impression can lead to a distorted view of human mind over matter, to an overblown view of mental power over reality. Instead of history being seen as part of a dialectical process *between* humans and the material world, mind comes to be seen as the prime mover of historical change. With the development of society, the growing complexity of human labour and the rise of industry, as labour became more perfect and more diversified, and tribes developed into nations and social organization became codified into law and politics, the human mind came to be seen as the supreme organizer of these things. 'Men became accustomed to explain their actions as arising out of their thoughts instead of their needs' (Marx and Engels 1970: 72).

Marx's comments on this aspect of language were made in an explicitly political context. *The German Ideology* was written as a polemic with the Young Hegelians, who had an elitist view of ordinary people and whose philosophical and political traditions had led them to be ruled by the world of ideas. Marx uses the occasion to stress once again the relationship of language to thought as well as making an unapologetic attack on 'pure' philosophy:

> For philosophers, one of the most difficult tasks is to descend from the world of thought to the actual world. *Language* is the immediate actuality of thought. Just as philosophers have given thought an independent existence, so they had to make language into an independent realm. This is the secret of philosophical language, in which thoughts in the form of words have their own content. The problem of descending from the world of thoughts to the actual world is turned into the problem of descending from language to life. (Marx and Engels 1974: 118; emphasis in original)

Marx, like Engels, sees how language becomes the means by which abstract thought seems to take on a life of its own, with all links with the material world broken. This constitutes the idealistic world outlook that Marx is referring to in the passage above. This enthronement of language and abstract thought is seen by Marx as an ideological act – a theme we shall return to with Volosinov. Marx is quite explicit about the social source of this world view: it stems from the class position of its advocates, who have an interest in rejecting materialism.[10] Marx does not specifically mention the still influential German linguist, Wilhelm von Humboldt (1767–1835), although Humboldt's concern to raise language above everything else in the quest for 'self-cultivation' is part of the same

German Romanticism of a rising bourgeoisie (Dumont 1994).[11]
Again and again, Marx returns to the theme that 'neither thoughts
nor language in themselves form a realm of their own', but 'that
they are only manifestations of actual life'. Obscuring this fact only
reveals the extent to which language thus becomes 'the distorted
language of the actual world' (Marx and Engels 1974: 118).
Language is, according to Marx, doubly ideological: first, as part of
consciousness of society, and secondly as a philosophy of language
which sees language as separate from the material world.

At this point it is useful to make some general points about
Marx's overall view of ideology and what aspects of it are relevant
to language.

First, Marx's view of the relationship between the economic base
and the ideological or political superstructure was far from being
crude or simplistic, as is often held, and was in fact highly subtle
and qualified. Marx is clear that the relations of production constitutes the economic structure of society, 'the real foundation on
which rises the legal and political superstructure and to which
correspond definite forms of social consciousness'. 'The mode of
production of material life conditions the social political and
intellectual life' (Marx and Engels 1969: 503). But conditioning
something is not the same as determining something in a mechanical fashion, as Engels was at pains to point out in a letter to
Bloch, written soon after Marx's death. Because the same misap-
prehension lingers among detractors of Marx today, it is worth
quoting what Engels had to say on the subject:

According to the materialist conception of history, the *ultimately*
determining element in history is the production and reproduction of
real life. More than this neither Marx nor I have ever asserted. Hence if
somebody twists this into saying that the economic element is the *only*
determining one, he transforms that proposition into a meaningless,
abstract, senseless phrase. The economic situation is the basis, but the
various elements of the superstructure – political forms of the class
struggle and its results . . . and even the reflexes of all these actual
struggles in the brains of the participants, political, juristic, philosophical theories, religious views and their further development into
systems of dogmas – also exercise their influence upon the course of
their historical struggles and in many cases preponderate in determining their form. (Marx and Engels 1970: 487; emphasis in original)

Marx never argued that the cultural and political spheres passively reflect the economic base. As the passage here makes clear, while the social relations of production set limits to developments in the superstructure, there is an interaction of all elements. Social consciousness is historical, like the relations of production from which it emerges.

> Consciousness can never be anything else than conscious existence. . . . If in all ideology men and their circumstances appear upside down as in a *camera obscura*, this phenomenon arises just as much from their historical life-process as the inversion of the objects on the retina does from their physical life-process. (Marx and Engels 1974: 47)

This is not a one-dimensional, determinist account of how society influences ideas, culture and, from our point of view, language. On the contrary Marx refers to the relationship between material production and 'spiritual' production as being uneven, and 'the reciprocal influence of one on the other' (Marx and Engels 1963: 285). As we have seen with his historical account of consciousness, the relationship is not predetermined or simply reflective, but dialectical.

Because of this relationship between the economic base and the superstructure, the ruling social class will also dominate in the superstructure.

> The ideas of the ruling class are in every epoch the ruling ideas, i.e. the class which is the ruling *material* force of society is at the same time its ruling *intellectual* force. . . . Insofar, therefore, as they rule as a class and determine the extent and compass of an epoch, it is self-evident that they do this in its whole range, hence among other things rule also as thinkers, producers of ideas, and regulate the production and distribution of the ideas of their age. (Marx and Engels 1974: 64)

The ruling class have at their disposition the means – institutions and wealth – to bolster their world view. This does not mean that ruling ideas always or uniformly hold sway. Marx merely makes the point here that dominant ideas, including ideas about language, will often reflect a ruling-class world view. This has relevance, as we shall see later, for the view of English promoted internationally by various interested parties, and also within English-speaking countries concerning which version of English is considered acceptable.

This brings us to the third aspect of ideology that is relevant for our purposes, and one that Volosinov expands upon. Marx saw that ideological forms were terrains to be contested, arenas 'in which men become conscious of . . . conflict and fight it out' (Marx and Engels 1969: 504). This ideological battleground operates at two levels concerning language. First, interpretations of the philosophy of language and of its social role despite the appearance of being mere academic questions, actually represent clashes of ideology. Second, language use itself reflects ideological questions because it encompasses wider social questions of class and social identity. This latter terrain sees language as dynamic and stresses its expression of 'practical consciousness' deriving from its role in social life. On both counts, Marx was the first to note, language is ideologically highly charged.

'Wherever a Sign is Present, Ideology is Present Too'

Volosinov's *Marxism and the Philosophy of Language*, first published in Russia in 1929 (and in English only in 1973) expands considerably on Marx's view of language and ideology.[12] The second and third decade of the twentieth century in Russia, in and around the most remarkable event of that period, the Russian Revolution, experienced one of the most lively intellectual climates this century. It is perhaps by virtue of the impact of the ideas of this time that, as one scholar of Volosinov pointed out some sixty years later, they speak with such force and resonance (Dentith 1995: 11). The 'superb interpretation of linguistic problems' that linguist Roman Jakobson was one of the first to recognize in Volosinov, cannot be separated from the social turbulence and creativity that Volosinov himself experienced in Russia before, tragically, he disappeared into the abyss of the gulags. Indeed it has been claimed that it was Volosinov's disagreement with the linguist Marr, representative of official Soviet linguistics, that first brought him under suspicion (Matejka and Titunik 1973: 173). The interconnectedness of language and society, stressed so much by Volosinov himself, applies poignantly to his own work.

Volosinov's starting point is the *ideological nature of all signs*, including language. He defines a sign as that which 'represents, depicts or stands for something outside itself' (Volosinov 1973: 9). This correspondence is an essential feature of all signs. Signs can be highly symbolic in one context but remain simple objects in another. Bread and wine – mere objects of consumption in one setting, but invested with religious significance in another – Volosinov used as an example of the inherent dualism in signs. Sign systems exist side by side with material reality, not independently of it.

> A sign does not simply exist as part of a reality – it reflects and refracts another reality. Therefore it may distort that reality or be true to it, or it may perceive it from a special point of view . . . every sign is subject to the criteria of ideological evaluation. . . . The domain of ideology coincides with the domain of signs. They equate with one another. Wherever a sign is present, ideology is present too. *Everything ideological possesses semiotic value.* (1973: 10; emphasis in original)

The quality of signs to represent, 'to reflect and refract another reality', to interpret, is what gives them their conceptual potency and makes words the very stuff of ideology. '[T]he word is the ideological phenomenon par excellence' (1973: 13).

For Volosinov, this signing process is the means by which consciousness takes shape and is socially constructed. Signs emerge in the process of interaction between one individual consciousness and another; not just any two human beings but between two who are 'organized socially', and part of a social group (1973: 12). Consciousness, then, does not arise spontaneously from nature, nor as the external coating of some inner spirit; it materializes through signs created by humans in the process of social intercourse. There is a constraint and creativity in the formation of consciousness which reveals the relationship between individual and society. Volosinov pinpoints it with a memorable aphorism: 'individual consciousness is not the architect of the ideological superstructure, but only a tenant lodging in the social edifice of ideological signs' (1973: 13).

Like Marx, Volosinov sees the connection between the relations of production and the ideological superstructure as a highly complex one. But Volosinov expands on Marx's insights and describes in more detail the way in which language is at the centre of ideology and how it reveals aspects of ideological formation and change. For Volosinov, the social ubiquity of language and its sensitivity as an index of social change makes it a crystallization of the ideological process. We will return to this later; but to fully grasp the ideological dimension of language that Volosinov sets out, we must first examine his critique of contemporary linguistics and his own elaboration of the social nature of language.

Language Made, Not Inherited

Seeing language as part of human consciousness, Volosinov stresses the changing and generative nature of language. However he sharply distinguishes this view of language from the earlier Humboldtian trend in linguistics which he terms *individualistic subjectivism*. Humboldt had professed an essentially Romantic, subjective view of language and had located linguistic creativity in individual psychology. This was then taken up by Vossler, the German linguist and the Italian literary scholar, Croce, to mean that language was primarily a question of individual style. These purely subjective views of language creativity defies scientific study, according to Volosinov, because they rely on such subjective terms as 'linguistic taste' (1973: 51) and aesthetic appreciation.

But Volosinov attacks more forcefully another dominant trend in linguistics, what he calls *abstract objectivism*, as represented by Ferdinand de Saussure. By prioritizing the synchronic dimension (language at a fixed point in time) over the diachronic dimension (language in a historical perspective), Saussure effectively converts language into 'an inviolable, incontestable norm which the individual can only accept'. This view robs language of its creative dynamism; it becomes like a 'stationary rainbow' arched over living language (1973: 52–53). Yet it is precisely a speaker's potential to supersede the synchronic dimension, and select a new form over a recognized one, that makes language what it is (1973: 56).

Volosinov uncovers the weakness of Saussurean linguistics on two counts. He points to the arbitrariness of a methodology that sets up self-contained categories of language system (*langue*) from utterance (*parole*), and which then casts aside the latter as being too randomly individual to merit scientific study. Yet the fact remains (conceded by Saussure, as Volosinov notes) that utterance 'returns as an essential factor in the history of language' since it is this aspect of language that is the origin of language change (1973: 61). Language looks both ways: to tradition and to innovation, to what has already been established in language and, because of the speaker's unique needs of the moment, to what can be changed. A child does not just inherit a language which she then has to learn. She uses language in a social context and thereby fashions it. Language is socially distinctive because each speaker brings his or her social experience to it. The *langue/parole* distinction artificially breaks up the linguistic whole, and fails to capture the interaction of both aspects in the actual practice of language.

Second, Volosinov declares, echoing what Marx had noted earlier, Saussure's abstract objectivism is not without ideological overtones. 'What interests the mathematically minded rationalist is not the relationship of the sign to the actual reality it reflects, nor to the individual who is its originator, but the relationship of sign to sign within a closed system already accepted and authorized' (1973: 57–58). Abstract objectivism places language on a pedestal removed from its users. It displaces actual speakers, specific situations, the contexts of language, relegating these to insignificance outside the perfectly tuned linguistic system. It makes the subjects of language into their objects. On a larger scale, it writes history out of language. History is seen as an intrusive, untidy, irrational force upsetting the logical purity of the language system. Abstract objectivism is thus an ahistorical view of language and one which, Volosinov points out, leads to a focus on dead languages and an 'over concern with the cadavers of written languages' (1973: 71). As Barker notes regarding the Saussurean view, 'the system always comes first' (Barker 1994: 256). Volosinov's critique of this aspect of Saussure, in which speakers become the mere acquirers of language, is a highly relevant critique for Applied Linguistics today, which has tended, as we shall see, to focus on language devoid of its historical and social settings and to downplay the role of speakers, both native and non-native, in the making of language.

Verbal Interaction

A fundamental element of Volosinov's critique of abstract objectivism is his view of language as being able to generate new meanings, that it is in a constant state of becoming. 'What is important for the speaker about a linguistic form is not that it is a stable and always self-equivalent signal, but that it is an always changeable and adaptable sign' (1973: 68). This generative quality arises from the fact that language is inseparable from its context and its users. The actual context for any particular word is not self-contained, but, via the social experience of the speakers, overlapping with other contexts. 'Contexts do not stand side by side in a row, as if unaware of one another, but are in a state of constant tension or incessant interaction and conflict' (1973: 80). The meanings and different connotations for a word or a piece of language are constructed by the speakers, who give each utterance their particular *evaluative accent*.

Let us take an example to illustrate the way in which Volosinov touches on the essential element of context. *I'm hungry* conjures up a general concept. When, however, we look at different contexts in which the phrase might be used, we see how the evaluative accent changes everything. *A child saying this to her mother* might be indirectly a request for the mother to get her something, an enquiry about what there is to eat, or a statement that she just feels like something to eat. *One adult saying it to another* might mean that it's time for lunch and be a suggestion that they go somewhere to eat. A third situation might be *a homeless person on the side of the street* bearing a piece of card with this written on it because he desperately wants passers-by to give him money. In each case the context is not merely the gloss on the meaning but constitutes different meanings – different in every aspect, in what is being referred to, the intensity of hunger, and what is often called the illocutionary force of the statement (what effect it has on the addressee). This possibility of an infinite amount of different shades of emphasis

Volosinov calls the 'multiaccentuality' of language. Volosinov captures in this concept the powerful quality of language which makes it at once so creative and infinitely unstable and elusive.

Volosinov, in an essay called 'Discourse in life and discourse in art', gives an example that shows how even the significance of the simplest word is embedded in its social context. 'Two people are sitting in a room. They are both silent. Then one of them says "Well!". The other does not respond.' To outsiders the word is meaningless; to the two speech participants, it made perfect sense (Volosinov 1976: 99). They were looking through the window as it began to snow, although it was May, and late in the year for snow. Both, as it happens, were sick and tired of spring not arriving and so were bitterly disappointed to see the snowflakes fall. The tone of the utterance and the extra-verbal context gave it meaning. Volosinov finds the sense of this 'Well!' lies not within the word or within one person's mind but *between* the speakers, in what is common to them. This common ground he lists as (1) the physical space, (2) the common knowledge and understanding of the situation and (3) their common evaluation or assessment of the situation. Language does not thus reflect reality; rather, meaning occurs at the point where the 'real conditions of life' and the 'social evaluation' of them come together.

His explanation here throws into sharp relief the social nature of language and how the language occurs as part of social relations between human beings within society. Volosinov's view of language and its different elements – the ideological, the social, the unstable and the creative aspects – gains theoretical unity through his concept of *verbal interaction*. This goes to the heart of the social nature of language which, for Volosinov, is not just one dimension of language, but its *sine qua non*. Language is made for an addressee (a listener or a reader); there is no such thing as language into a vacuum. Even when we think we are speaking to 'the world at large', as for example in some written texts, in fact our imagined reader is historically and socially quite precisely identifiable. A word is a two-sided act and a product of the relationship between speaker and listener:

> I give myself verbal shape from another's point of view, ultimately from the point of view of the community to which I belong. A word is a

bridge thrown between myself and another. If one end of the bridge depends on me, then the other depends on my addressee. A word is a territory shared by both addresser and addressee, by the speaker and his interlocutor. (Volosinov 1973: 86)

Language is shared territory. Its meaning takes shape on the uncertain ground between people and is moulded by the specific time and place of the language participants, but also by a broader aggregate of conditions under which that particular community of speakers operates. It is around these elements that language acquires life and historically evolves (1973: 95). Volosinov later identifies this uniqueness of meaning of utterances as *theme* – which he defines as the overall indivisible significance of the whole utterance in a specific context. He recognizes that smaller elements of language – what he terms *meaning* – are consituent parts of the whole theme and are reproducible. But he makes a qualitative distinction between these elements and the whole. 'Theme' is not merely a combination of smaller 'meaning' units but something whose whole is more than its parts because of its formation in verbal interaction and in a social and historical context.[13] Theme is an instance of the generative process of language. It is verbal interaction in operation.

In the theme concept we can see how ideological meanings take shape and are contested. Themes are meanings which have come to be accepted but they can also be called into question in different social circumstances. The same words come to have different interpretations. *Democracy* in America meant something different to those involved in civil rights than it did to those in the White House. It is taken to mean something different today in Harlem than it does in Beverly Hills or, come to that, in Brixton or in Bayswater. Sometimes the choice of word is an ideological act on the part of the speaker. Choosing to say *downsizing* rather than *redundancies*, *peacekeepers* instead of *armies* is an ideological, class-based choice. A strike is *settled* or it is *won*, there are *surgical strikes* and there are *bombings*. There is the *unborn* child and the *foetus*. All these different emphases are what Volosinov means when he writes that meanings are not given or fixed; they are 'an arena of class struggle'. As Barker points out, this is because languages do not coincide with classes and people from different social classes have to be able to communicate. 'But sharing a language does not mean agreeing on its uses' (Barker 1994: 260). As we speak, in all the different contexts of social life, we are saying something about social life.

Inner Speech

For Volosinov, the social nature of language permeates even the innermost recesses of consciousness. It makes its appearance even in supposedly solitary situations, like silent thought, when words, 'the semiotic material of inner life – of consciousness (inner speech)' are as socially charged as ordinary speech (Volosinov 1973: 14).

The theme of inner speech is recurrent in Volosinov because for him it brings together both the identification of language with consciousness and the social element of both. The term reappears in Vygotsky.[14] Where Vygotsky approaches the issue of consciousness as a component of psychology, Volosinov examines the phenomenon from a linguistic standpoint. For him, words are the building blocks of thinking. Consciousness is 'bathed by and suspended in, and cannot be entirely segregated or divorced from the element of speech' (1973: 15). Words are the means by which consciousness is accessed and signs are part of the inner psyche and inner speech is thinking, 'the skeleton of inner life' as Volosinov terms it. (1973: 29). The piecing together and distilling of experience takes place through signs, and signs are the means of mental processing (1973: 85).

The workings of this inner speech are not just social in the sense that they take the form of signs and words but they are also social in the sense that they have a social audience (1973: 86). Consciousness is not something emanating from the self, as bourgeois ideology would have it. Rather, consciousness is 'a social event on a small scale', an 'inner word embryo of expression' turned on the outside world, a dialogue in the making, 'set toward fully actualized outward expression, and not just an inner act on the part of the individual (1973: 90). Only the inarticulate cry of an animal can be said to be organized from the inside because of its nature as a behavioural reflex. By contrast the organizing centre of human utterances is not within but outside – the social context. The social context is both the immediate situation of the utterance and the broader aggregate of conditions in which the speakers are living (1973: 93). Volosinov thus expands on Marx's view of social consciousness by analysing the nature of that consciousness in linguistic terms: by reference to *signs* as its constituent parts and *inner speech* as its process.

Volosinov's identification of language as part of consciousness, not just loosely, but as the very stuff of thinking, is of considerable significance when we consider the questions of how and which language is involved, a first or a second language, and identification with a particular language. Questions of language and consciousness are not just general philosophical considerations but questions which force an appraisal of the specific social context of the language concerned.

Reported Speech and the Evolution of Grammar

Volosinov's criticism of traditional linguistics is that it views language as a static monologue that fails to take account of the fact that language occurs as dialogue. Participating in a dialogue is actively 'understanding' what someone says. Reporting what they say represents a measurement of how their speech has been received and for this reason Volosinov chose to study reported speech in some detail.[15] In recounting what another has said, the speaker simultaneously makes evaluative judgements about what and how it was said, which is then focused on a new hearer. In this way the phenomenon of reported speech pinpoints the dynamism between speaker and situation and brings out the process of reception and interpretation of another's speech. It is 'speech about speech', 'utterance about utterance', 'words reacting on words' (1973: 115). It is this multilayered and multiaccentual aspect to reported speech, which represents, in microcosm, the dynamism of language as a whole, that makes it of special interest to Volosinov.

But Volosinov is interested in reported speech forms for another reason: for what they can reveal about grammatical forms and how they vary and change. Grammatical terms associated with indirect speech are as paradigmatic as they are different across languages. In Latin, strict concordance applies; in Russian it is less rigid. Reviewing these, Volosinov describes how reported speech has historically changed from strict syntactic enclosing of reported speech to a more fluid approach where the boundaries of the message are weakened and where reporter and reported overlap. Grammarians have pointed out that Russian forms for indirect speech are underdeveloped because they do not incorporate tense agreement. But Volosinov sees in such a judgement a failure to appreciate that the more flexible Russian forms allow for a more vivid, pictorial rendering of the original discourse which can bring new interpretations to bear. To illustrate what he means he shows that a piece from *The Brothers Karamazov* brings out the literary forcefulness of this flexibility:

> Though filled with the profoundest respect for the memory of his ex-master, he nevertheless, among other things, declared that he had been negligent toward Mitja and had *'brought the children up wrong. The little child without me would have been eaten alive by lice'* he added. (1973: 132; Volosinov's emphasis)

This and other examples illustrate the fluidity between direct and indirect speech. These quasi-direct discourse forms, which escape rigorous grammatical description, reveal how overlapping contexts are brought in and out of focus. Direct discourse is prepared for by indirect discourse and emerges as if from inside it, 'like those sculptures of Rodin's in which the figure is left only partially emerged from stone' (1973: 132). Such features also bring into relief the context of literature and the expansive narrative effect.

Through this examination of the development of one grammatical form, Volosinov reveals a fundamentally important aspect of the process of language itself: that grammatical forms are in a constant state of adaptation and change. Volosinov picks the weakest axis of this change since his examples are in literary texts which are less susceptible to change than are spoken texts. But his literary examples allow him to reveal the difficulties of categorizing style and grammar as separate entities, thus revealing at the same time the shifting sands of grammar itself. A demarcation between grammar and style for Volosinov is spurious since '[t]he borderline is fluid because of the very mode of existence of language, in which, simultaneously, some forms are undergoing grammaticization while others are undergoing degrammaticization' (1973: 126). Elsewhere, Volosinov notes that style and grammar overlap. In the case of highly elaborate categories of address in Japanese, for example, compared to relatively few in English, he notes: 'We might say that what is still a matter of grammar for the Japanese has already become for us a matter of style' (Volosinov 1976: 110). In other words, regarding grammar in general, Volosinov is saying that it is in a state of becoming; not given, but evolving. This is not just a secondary question regarding the social nature of language. If language arises from and is infused with social activity, then it must follow that the workings of language – grammar and syntax – are also subject to social change. This is a premise that is not accepted by those who hold that language follows its own logic, and is an innate product of the human mind separate from social formations. The question about the degree to which grammar changes, if at all, is the subject of some controversy today. We should note two important contributions that Volosinov is making. First, the inclusion of grammatical change in his overall view of language again places speakers at the centre of the making of language instead of being mere receivers of grammatical form. Second, his identification of grammatical change provides a fundamental addition to the social nature of language and contributes to the theoretical unity of his analysis.

Speech Genres and Alien Word

In his writing about the relationship between base and superstructure, Volosinov outlines the nexus of language and society:

> Every sign . . . is a construct between socially organized persons in the process of their interaction. Therefore *the forms of signs are conditioned above all by the social organization of the participants involved and also by the immediate conditions of their interaction.* When these forms change, so does the social life of the verbal sign. And it should be one of the tasks of the study of ideologies to trace this social life of the verbal sign. Only so approached can *the problem of the relationship between sign and*

existence stand out as a process of genuine existence-to-sign transit, of
genuine dialectical refraction of existence in the sign. (Volosinov 1973:
21; emphasis in original)

Social organization is distilled in language, both as a point of
reference that situates meaning and as the specific social relationship of participants in any speech event. Social changes are
discernible in language and Volosinov thus outlines in novel form
a truly historical linguistics, which is not an enclosed linguistic
account of language change but which is the interconnection of
language change and social change. It is in this context that
Volosinov outlines the need for a topology of what he terms the
repertoire of concrete forms or *speech genres*. By these, he means
typical forms of utterance that abound in any given society and
represent specific social relations at any given historical moment.
These are established ways for people to talk to each other. The
methodological assumptions for such investigation are (1) the
recognition that ideology and signs are interconnected, (2) that
utterances arise from specific forms of social relations and (3)
that language cannot be separated from the economic structure of
society and the relations of production. These are fundamental
questions concerning the politics of language, for Volosinov's
speech genres describe the extraordinary sensitivity of language to
fluctuations in the social atmosphere and to the various manifestations of social relations. However, Volosinov's description of
speech genres has been interpreted in terms of seeing genres as
quite contained and formalistic categories. Hymes, for example,
has seen genres as categories: for example poems, myths, tales,
proverbs, lectures and sermons, each a distinct component of our
ways of speaking (Hymes 1986: 65). Yet from Volosinov's brief
account of speech genres he did not see them as mere formal
properties. Barker expresses it more subtly when he describes
speech genres as 'the way we link our material and social lives'
(Barker 1994: 10). Conditioned by the social organization of the
participants and by the immediate conditions of their interaction,
speech genres also have a social life. 'When these forms change so
does the sign' (Volosinov 1973: 21).

But it is Volosinov's concept of the *alien word* which has been
rightly acknowledged as one of his most original contributions

(Jameson 1974: 539). Volosinov refers to 'alien word' on two levels, as *language oppression* and *alienating views of language*.

The first is in the literal sense of imposed, 'alien' languages whose historical weight Volosinov declares, is difficult to over-state. The foreign word, 'a dialect accompanied by an army and a navy',[16] down through the Roman and the Byzantine Empires and Slav expansionism, brought cultures, religion, new forms of social organization. The alien word became synonymous with 'authority, the idea of power, the idea of holiness, the idea of truth', and 'dictated that notions about the word be preeminently orientated toward the alien word'. This 'grandiose organizing role of the alien word' became another vehicle of oppression and the bearers of it exerted their influence as controllers of education, and were very often priests (1973: 74–75). In contrast, a native language is '"one's kith and kin"; we feel about it as we feel about our natural attire or, even better, about the atmosphere in which we habitually live and breathe' (1973: 75). The sensitivity with which Volosinov writes about language imposition might reveal one of the few insights into his own life and his awareness of the legacy in his day of language oppression under Russian expansionism. Volosinov however also recognizes that even a shared mother tongue does not guarantee unity. Class divides even speakers of the same language: it can seem alienating in the mouths of those who dominate (1973: 75).

In Volosinov's description of the alien word, the example closest to his own experience was Russian; in other contexts, it is English. Volosinov's description of the alien word recalls the way that Joyce, through Stephen Dedalus, captured the feeling of an 'acquired speech' that English represented in Ireland:

> The language in which we are speaking is his before it is mine. How different are the words *home, Christ, ale, master*, on his lips and on mine! I cannot speak or write these words without unrest of spirit. His language, so familiar and so foreign, will always be for me an acquired speech. I have not made or accepted its words. My voice holds them at bay. My soul frets in the shadow of his language. (Joyce 1992: 205)

Joyce's portrayal of the 'smart of dejection' that Stephen felt was an expression, in linguistic terms, of social division. The English of the

English Dean of Studies lorded it over Stephen's own Dublin English. Volosinov has an awareness of the same alienating sensation. It is 'an expression of the enormous historical role that the alien word has played in the formation of all historical cultures . . . from the sociopolitical order to the behavioural code of daily life' (Volosinov 1973: 75).

It is worth noting, also, that Volosinov's assessment is strikingly similar to what Gramsci would write later about how language can become an instrument of exclusion. Volosinov's 'priests-philologists' and 'the last residues of the dictatorial and culture-creating role [of alien speech]' touches on the same phenomenon of linguistic alienation described by Gramsci. He describes how people *see* religious rites, *hear* sermons, but cannot follow or participate in what is being said because the rites are monopolized by a caste. Gramsci's writings understand historical linguistics in the way that Volosinov outlined: not as the recording of the iron laws of linguistics but as the way in which social relations enter the linguistic sphere. Gramsci sees language change as the process in which one dominant speech community is challenged by subordinate ones. Dante's use of the Italian vernacular, medieval Tuscan, was a revolt against 'Latinized mandarinism'. It then became adopted politically by Manzoni, spread by the Risorgimento and later became an ideological instrument in the hands of those who were to become the dominant class. Later still, the 'standard' would be used to dominate over the 'dialect'. Gramsci saw each language as 'an integral conception of the world', with Italian dialects representing linguistic sediments of earlier social formations and standard Italian as representing the domination of the city over the countryside (Gramsci 1985: 167–188).

A further aspect of this historical view of language is that it is not the linguistic forms *per se* that are oppressive but their social content. Alien word is not conceived by Volosinov as some form of language determinism or language forms dominating people. Volosinov is clear that the signs themselves are ideologically neutral. Signs are ideologically laden in their context of use but words are not in themselves bearers of an ideological function (Volosinov 1973: 14). Different classes will use the same language with different ideological meanings, different 'accents', and it is this fact that allows signs to become an arena of class struggle

(1973: 24). The dominant class attempts to appropriate meanings and interpretations of words as if they cannot be contested, but meanings are constantly being subverted by the accent and interpretation that all their speakers place on them. Signs thus make and remake themselves in terms of ideological content. In periods of social crisis these changes of meanings become more generalized and beyond the confines of individual interpretation and serious shifts in meanings occur (1973: 24). Again Volosinov is stressing the unstable and changing nature of language in which its speakers leave their ideological mark.

The observation that it was not the language itself that determined its ideological baggage but its use in social relations allowed Volosinov to counter the crude linguistic determinism of Marrist linguistics which held that languages of themselves had a class character. To return to the English in Ireland analogy, it was not English *per se* that was the problem but who was giving it its ideological coloration and in what circumstances. Joyce, while aware of the historical legacy of English, rejected the idea that language itself formed social identity. As Eagleton has noted, Joyce, through his revolt against English conventions in his writings, used English 'to give voice to a non-English experience', 'subverted English for his own egregiously non-English ends' (Eagleton 1995: 265). It is this paradox that Volosinov's understanding of how ideology operates in language fully grasps.

The other way that Volosinov sees the 'alien word' is as the way in which language is presented as a dead thing. Seeing language as the sum of various internal laws and rules makes language something that is passively inherited intact, down through the generations:

> In reifying the system of language and in viewing living language as if it were dead and alien, abstract objectivism makes language something external to the stream of verbal communication. . . . Language cannot properly be said to be handed down – it endures but it endures as a continuous process of becoming. (Volosinov 1973: 81)

Seeing language as handed down makes language into a dead weight imposed from above. It takes little account of how speakers themselves, however alienating the experience of imposition, can transform the language themselves. The relevance of these remarks for the spread of English as a world language, as well views of presenting that language, we will take up in later chapters.

Vygotsky – Thought and Language

Lev Semenovich Vygotsky was a contemporary of Volosinov and part of the flowering of scientific, literary and linguistic innovation that so characterized post-revolutionary Russia. Vyogotsky did not begin his systematic work in psychology until 1924 and only ten years later he died of tuberculosis at the age of thirty-eight. In that period in collaboration with Leontiev and, particularly, Luria who oversaw later translations of his work, he launched a series of investigations into developmental psychology whose approach and conclusions earned him the reputation of a revolutionary scientist.[17] Wertsch attributes Vygotsky's originality to the socio-historical milieu of those turbulent times in Russia and sees his vision as a product of his time (Wertsch 1985). Vygotsky's *Thought and Language*, suppressed in 1936, two years after its appearance, did not reappear until 1956. Luria points out that the 'battle for consciousness' during the late 1920s and 1930s consisted of breaking free from both vulgar behaviourism, as promoted by official Russian ideology, and the introspective subjectivity to be found so often in academia in the West (Vygotsky 1962: iv). Vygotsky rejected both these and, from a Marxist perspective, reaffirmed the role of history in human consciousness and intellect. He avoided the fawning Marxist sycophancy which was to become the hallmark of so many under Stalin and rejected the crude over-quoting from Marx that became *de rigueur* in later Soviet texts.[18] Vygotsky's rediscovery of the dialectical relationship between social activity and language became his method. He explained it thus:

> I don't want to discover the nature of mind by patching together a lot of quotations. I want to find out how science has to be built, to approach the study of mind having learnt the whole of Marx's method. (Vygotsky 1978: 8)

His work is a pioneering attempt to investigate the complexity of human consciousness from a social perspective.

Vygotsky elaborated on Marx's theme of language as 'practical consciousness' and described the organic interconnections of thought and language. Contemporary debates on this subject have stressed that thought and language progress along parallel tracks (Pinker 1995) or that language as thought is essentially individual and representational (Bickerton 1995).[19] Vygotsky, however, demonstrated that language is the means by which reflection, generalization and thought processes take place and that these cognitive processes are socially formed. Theoretical questions about the relationship of thought to language and the degree to which both arise from social interaction are core questions concerning the relationship of language to society and how language coincides with the formation of social identity. Vygotsky's writings uncover from a social psychological perspective both the highly personal and at the same time profoundly social facets of language. Many of Vygotsky's writings cover experiments in child development and approaches to education, and some of these have relevance for political and ideological questions surrounding the teaching of language. But he also wrote in broader more philosophical terms, as in *Thought and Language*, and these writings are a necessary complement to his overall view of the social nature of language.

Vygotsky believed that in order to reveal the nature of human social and psychological processes their origins and development had to be traced. Vygotsky, like Engels before him, located the origins of human consciousness in the process of social cooperation and human labour but he singled out Engels's reference to the use of tools in the process as being particularly significant. Tool use was the mediated activity by which humans changed nature and the world around them. This was externally orientated activity that produced effects in the material world. Vygotsky saw parallels between physical tools and humans' psychological tools, or signs. Both mediated human activity, but one was orientated externally and the other internally; one was a means of managing nature, the other aimed at mastering humans' own behaviour. While qualitatively different, nevertheless the two sets of tools overlap and together produce new forms of behaviour. Tools and speech lay the basis for the meeting of human's needs and thereby underpin humans' unique intervention in nature.

The development of the use of signs paves the way for the development of higher mental processes and internalized abstract thought. An example of a pre-speech sign that Vygotsky gives, the gesture of pointing, shows clearly the continuum of these processes and how social relationships intervene. A child attempts to grasp an object beyond her reach; reaching towards it is one of the child's movements, nothing more. Her parents' arrival on the scene transforms the meaning of her movement. Reaching for herself now becomes a gesture, a sign for others. If it achieves the desired goal of getting the object for the child, then pointing becomes internalized, in the mind of the child, as a meaningful sign. Meaning and function has been created first by an objective situation and then socially by people who surround the child (Vygotsky 1978: 52–57).

Vygotsky's mapping of this process presents an interactive and developmental approach to the development of signs in human behaviour. It reveals the genesis of human speech and how at root language is social. It inverts the rationalist formula, from thought to action, and challenges the idea that the human brain itself procures mental functions. Instead it shows that mental function is created through social activity. As the Vygotskian scholar, Kosulin, puts it, '[d]evelopment is therefore not an unfolding or maturation of pre-existing "ideas"; on the contrary it is the formation of such ideas – out of what originally was not an idea – in the course of socially meaningful activity' (Kosulin 1990: 114).

The example shows at a simple level something fundamental for Vygotsky: that signs have both communicative and intellectual functions. When signs become speech, the more signs become the 'psychological tools' of higher mental processes. Vygotsky does not, however, crudely equate language with thought. Intellect and speech have different origins both on a wider evolutionary basis (phylogenesis) and in child development (ontogenesis). What distinguishes humans from animals is that gradually thought and speech become intertwined when thought becomes verbal and speech, intellectual. Vygotsky distinguishes four stages of this development: the first where speech and intellect operate primitively and independently; the second, during which a child begins

to master basic problem solving where speech develops syntac-
tically but where it may not correspond to the concrete operations
of the intellect; the third when problem solving is aided by symbolic representation and egocentric speech; and the fourth stage
when the child internalizes intellectually and verbally (Vygotsky
1986: 68–95). Gesture 'in itself' becomes gesture 'for others'.

Vygotsky's description runs counter to the wired-in version of
language which presents cognition and language as ready-formed
in the structure of the brain. By stressing the developmental role of
language and thought, Vygotsky thereby accords context, not just
an adjunctive role but a formative one. Thought and speech are, in
this model, literally moulded *from the outside in*, as the child adapts
and reacts to the society around her. Vygotsky rightly notes the
epistemological importance of this fact:

> [t]he nature of the development itself changes, from biological to socio-
> historical. Verbal thought is not an innate, natural form of behavior, but
> is determined by historical-cultural process and has specific properties
> and laws that cannot be found in the natural forms of thought and
> speech. Once we acknowledge the historical character of verbal
> thought, we must consider it subject to all the premises of historical
> materialism, which are valid for any historical phenomenon in human
> society. (Vygotsky 1986: 94)

Furthermore we see here the very opposite to the view of language
determining or constituting reality. Language is not the prism
through which all things pass. Language and thought come
together in different stages and for different functions. By separating the roots of language and thought, Volosinov reveals both the
dynamic relationship of the two and how, in the development of a
child, they evolve. One interacts with the other through social
activity and together in this dialectical process they constitute a
qualitative leap forward in terms of consciousness.

Inner Speech and Context

It is in his description of the features of inner speech that Vygotsky
develops further the thought–language relationship. In a similar

way to Volosinov, Vygotsky saw meaning in a sociohistorical perspective. In an essay entitled 'Thought and word', he notes that word meaning is an instance of the unity of thought and word – one cannot be separate from the other. 'The meaning of word represents such a close amalgam of thought and language that it is hard to tell whether it is a phenomenon of speech or a phenomenon of thought' (1986: 212). But central to a word meaning is that word meanings change. 'They are dynamic rather than static formations' (1986: 217). This mutability springs from the very relationship back and forth between thought and word. To grasp the interconnection of thought and word, Vygotsky probes deeper than Volosinov into the workings of inner speech. Where Volosinov stressed the social signs and the dialogic element that make up inner speech, Vygotsky stresses its contextual features, again along a developmental axis.

Instrumental to his investigation into inner speech is how the latter develops in children from *egocentric* speech (or speech to oneself). Vygotsky discovered that this transitory stage enabled the child to mentally orientate herself, to regulate her behaviour towards overcoming difficulties. Far from egocentric speech being a mere accompaniment to the child's activity with no apparent function, as Piaget held, Vygotsky revealed that egocentric speech occurred with the assumption that it was understood by others. It was a way of developing thought processes out loud. Egocentric speech was not something that withered away as the child became more socially adept. Rather, as a crucial transitory stage from speech-for-others to speech-for-oneself, egocentric speech went on to become entirely internalized in the form of inner speech. This distinction was important because it showed at every developmental stage that speech had a social function and a social audience. Furthermore, Vygotsky argued, the regulative function of egocentric speech was carried over into inner speech. Vygotsky touched on a key insight that inner speech too, rather than being simply speech addressed to oneself, had a decision-making and concept-formation role. Inner speech, Vygotsky concluded, could not be regarded as simply speech without sound but was an entirely separate speech function (1986: 224–235).

In examining the abbreviated, truncated forms of inner speech, and taking parallels from 'external speech', Vygotsky shows how context is indivisibly part of language. Vygotsky makes the distinction, similar to that made by Volosinov, between 'meaning' in a general term (in Russian *znachenie*) and 'sense' in a more restrictive way (*smysl*).[20] The senses of a word are both more and less than its general meaning and more fluid because of their dependence on a particular context. For Vygotsky, the structure of inner speech was highly context-dependent, 'sense' orientated rather than 'meaning' orientated. To explain this, he showed that what appeared the peculiar syntax of inner speech – its disconnectedness and incompleteness – was in fact to be found in various forms of external speech. Pure predication (the omission of the subject) occurs very frequently in spoken speech; the subject is tacitly understood by the participant and the shared context rules out confusion. Equally, in cases where the thoughts and experience of speakers coincide, verbalization is reduced to a minimum. The persuasive example that Vygotsky gives is from Tolstoy's *Anna Karenina*. Kitty and Levin share so much that they need only say the first letter of a word for the other to know exactly what word is meant (1986: 237–238). Another aspect of this semantic condensing, referred to by Vygotsky, is when names – Hamlet or Don Quixote – become overlaid with symbolic meaning, over and beyond their reference to a specific character. All these ways of abbreviation reach a height in inner speech so that a kind of internalized idiom develops that is a distinct plane of verbal thought. What is striking about Vygotsky's explanation of inner speech is how context gives it shape because it provides the missing links of its abbreviated forms. What in external speech allows participants to reduce verbalization to a minimum, in inner speech becomes the connecting thread. Although appearing a monologue, in Vygotsky's perspective inner speech has the same dialogic ground rules as spoken speech. Far from inner speech floating free of context as Humboldtian individualism would have it, it is intensely contextualized, and progresses as if a dialogue. 'When we converse with ourselves we need even fewer words. . . . Inner speech is speech almost without words.' With this seeming paradox Vygotsky lays bare the fundamental formative role of context in both thought and language.[21]

Kosulin notes the extent of the contribution that Vygostky has made to what has become one of the central concerns of modern philosophy, the relationship between thought and language, and how his concept of inner speech is fundamental to the social nature of language (Kosulin 1990: 268). What is distinctive about Vygotsky is his refusal to reduce either language or thought to a mechanical category. Rather he retains the dynamic notion of language as practical consciousness first articulated by Marx:

> Consciousness is reflected in a word as the sun in a drop of water. A word relates to consciousness as a living cell relates to an organism, as an atom relates to the universe. A word is the microcosm of human consciousness. (1986: 256)

Conclusions

I have attempted in this chapter to provide a theoretical basis for the study of language in society and thereby highlight certain political questions surrounding language. I have done this by examining aspects of language provided in the writings of Marx and Engels, Volosinov and some of the more relevant writings of Vygotsky. I shall now draw together some of the theoretical themes relevant to aspects of the politics of English, themes which will be further developed in later chapters.

The first concerns the question of *origins of language*. In various ways applied linguists and linguistics have attempted to capture the essence of language by concentrating on its formal properties, or more recently, by claiming that language is a genetic product of pure biology. These views share the starting point of isolating language from human society and thus seeing language in ahistorical terms. The question of origins of language has a crucial bearing on which view of language a linguist adopts and goes to the heart of the nature of language itself. Establishing how a phenomenon comes into existence tells us something fundamental about its nature. The same goes for language. Applied Linguistics, however, has ignored the question of the origins of language, and until recently the question of the history of language, and has left these for more 'theoretical' disciplines to tackle. This does not mean that linguists have no view about the nature of language, but Applied Linguistics has favoured the view that isolating language is the way to study language. But Marx and Engels's writings on the emergence of language in early human society show that language arises as part of human development of cooperative labour as part of humans' growing mastery of their environment. What Marx noted for human consciousness in general, Vygotsky reformulates at the level of the individual. The development of child language, Vygotsky powerfully demonstrates, carries the same social components that are present in the development of language at the beginning of human society. Questions of exactly how language arose, the role of gestures, the development of the vocal cords, the beginning of signification and concept formation are complex ones that have given rise to many theories.[22] What is key for Marx and Engels, however, is that form cannot be separated from social content and that the curve of an early tool, the shape of a cave drawing, or the structure of language, bears the imprint of the human social activity out of which it emerged. It is this essentially social view of language, its historical dimension and more precisely its link to a particular mode of production, that has to be the backcloth to the examination of the role of English today.

Second, and as a consequence of its social rootedness, as explained by Marx and Volosinov, *language is located within the realm of ideology*. The generalizing potential of signs, from which language is built, the way that signs in Volosinov's terms *refract and reflect* reality, makes them a critical aspect of the ideological process. While the weight of the dominant class in society can skew ideological significance, including language, towards their world view, there is nothing predetermined about the outcome of these ideological accents. They are constantly contested by speakers. Alongside the ideological nature of language itself, however, are views of language which are in themselves ideological, and the value of Volosinov's contribution was to highlight the ideology of idealist and 'abstract objectivist' trends of thought in linguistics.

Volosinov's view of ideology in language contains a number of points that are relevant to the focus of our study. First, English is not ideologically unencumbered as some have claimed. It does carry specific ideological baggage from its historical and colonial roots and from the economic and cultural contexts in which it is promoted today. Second, what Volosinov has to say about ideo-logical views of language, particularly, abstract objectivism, is almost directly applicable to views of language within Applied Linguistics, and indeed the various offshoots of structuralist linguistics. Thirdly Volosinov's additional concept of alien language, with all its ideological overtones, provides an apt starting point for the spread of English today, as well as raising questions about linguistic oppression. All these questions will be examined in Chapter 3.

Volosinov's pioneering study of an aspect of *grammatical change* raises fundamental questions about the politics of language. The view of grammar as an unstable entity subject to change, and itself a socially specific product, is a view not particularly widely held, either in Applied Linguistics or in linguistics in general. An evolutionary view of grammar overturns assumptions about the hard-and-fast rules of grammar that even recent more interactive approaches to language have not managed to challenge success-fully. In general linguistics, the view is widespread that language structure is something apart, a law unto itself. Bickerton, for example, while fully admitting the close interconnection of human consciousness and human language, takes for granted that grammar is non-evolutionary. He argues that languages do not change according to social complexity and that syntactic structures transcend social conditions. When it comes to language, as he puts it, Sapir was right: 'Plato walks with the Macedonian swineherd and Lao-Tze with the head hunter of Assam' (Bickerton 1995: 35). Yet such assumptions see language running loose of society. The evolution of language, ongoing grammatical change, as Volosinov rightly pointed out, is the corollary to a social view of language. Timeless language, whose mechanisms remain immune to changing societies, is at odds with a view that sees language as a social product. The politics of English polarizes around the question of language change, as is examined in Chapter 5, on Standard English.

But the evolution of grammar has wider implications for our subject. It is evidence of a different interpretation of non-standard and non-native versions of English – examples of language change in process – both within English-speaking societies and within those where English is widely spoken. Much of the emphasis in educational settings is on a standard and fixed view of language which, I shall argue, writes out the makers of the language themselves. In the case of English spreading across the globe, the ways in which different speakers bring their social experience to their use of the language is not just a secondary consideration. It is part of the language itself. Volosinov grasped this inherently generative view of language as emanating not just from individual creativity but from the shifts and alterations in society. 'In the vicissitudes of the word are the vicissitudes of the society of word-users' (Volosinov 1973: 157). The acceptance of language varieties as part and parcel of the process of language change is something that is central to the freeing of oppressive strategies of language imposition but is an assumption seldom made in the institutional promotion of English worldwide.

Finally, in the area of language and thought as outlined by Vygotsky we gain insights into how language and mental processes are socially formed. Vygotsky's view is the antithesis of a determinist view of language, whereby language becomes the mould through which all perception forms. Vygotsky, in his emphasis on the role of context in both external and inner speech, captures how meaning is constantly shifting and how language and thought are both aspects of consciousness but with neither being reducible to the other. This dynamic view of meaning provides a welcome antidote to the linguistic quagmire which so engulfed the post-structuralists and postmodernists and restores language to society and social relations to language. It is a useful theoretical perspective on the question of language reform and the 'political correctness' debate, which we examine in Chapter 5. As Vygotsky put it: 'The word is a thing in our consciousness . . . that is absolutely impossible for one person, but that becomes a reality for two. The word is a direct expression of the historical nature of human consciousness.' It is this dialogic and historical nature of human language that explains why language is such a political question.

Notes

1 Jacques Derrida, once a proponent of the idea that there is no knowledge of the world except that of language, has recently retreated from linguistic relativism (see Derrida 1994).

2 These authors are explicit about their debt to Foucault for their view of language as forging reality. This debate will be taken up more fully in Chapter 3.

3 'Marx and Engels dealt with the question of linguistic theory sporadically though in a fairly systematic way' is how some political scientists have put it (Bottomore et al. 1983: 281).

4 There have been, of course, exceptions to this trend. One such was Leonard Bloomfield who, notwithstanding his later position as doyen on the American structuralist school, claimed to be much influenced by Marx's *Capital*, and was particularly struck by the similarity between Marx's approach to social behaviour and that of linguistics (see Metejka and Titunik in the introduction to their translation of Volosinov's *Marxism and the Philosophy of Language*, 1973).

5 Marx's analogy with bees is particularly interesting, since bees, it has been widely claimed, also make use of language. Yet recent research into the 'dance language' communication of bees has begun to question further the degree to which bees can be said to 'communicate' at all. Odour and wind direction seem to play a more significant part in the successful location of nectar-bearing flowers (Wenner et al. 1991). Another study explains why the dance language hypothesis is unconvincing and the authors seriously question the reasons why scientific researchers have so adamantly maintained the dance–language case (Wenner and Wells 1990). Despite the findings of these studies, bees' language is still often widely referred to as if it were fact, and often with the inference that some aspects of human language are also genetically driven (see Wilson 1991).

6 This process first mentioned by Marx and Engels is fully elaborated on by Woolfson (1982: 56), who also sees this as a uniquely human ability.

7 'Conscious life activity directly distinguishes man from animal life activity. Only because of that is he a species being. Or rather, he is a conscious being, i.e. his own life is an object for him, only because he is a species being. Only because of that is his activity free activity' (Marx 1975: 328).

8 Darwin's reluctance to concede the role of human labour in the development of the human brain may reveal his own attachment to the idealist view of the human mind prevalent in Victorian England. For a full discussion of the ideological pressures surrounding Darwin see Gerratana's article on Marx and Darwin (Gerratana 1973).

9 Marx saw much in common between his theory of dialectical historical materialism and Darwin's revolutionary discovery of evolution. Interestingly, Darwin automatically drew parallels between his approach to evolving species and contemporary philologists' approach to evolving language and languages (pointed out by Dennett 1996: 138).

10 Philosophizing for its own sake becomes an aspect of their own acceptance of the status quo since the Young Hegelians believed that their only task was to liberate people from mistaken ideas (Marx and Engels 1974: 41).

11 Humboldt has been a point of reference for many in linguistics, including Chomsky (1970: 25).

12 In recent times there has been much dispute about the authorship of *Marxism and the Philosophy of Language* and *Freudianism: a Marxist Critique*, works first ascribed to Volosinov. Clark and Holquist (1984) declare that Mikhail Bakhtin wrote Volosinov's (and Medvedev's) texts. Volosinov and Medvedev were both members of the same intellectual circle with Bakhtin in Nevel, Vitebsk and then Leningrad from 1924 to 1929. Clark and Holquist's claim springs from

their wish to distance themselves from Volosinov's Marxism. They maintain Volosinov's texts were 'Marxist' only in so far as they needed to get past Stalin's censor. Fredric Jameson, in his review of Volosinov's book (1974), would also appear to have accepted Bakhtin's overall authorship. Because so little is known of Volosinov's life, particularly during the 1920s when these works were written, and afterwards when he disappeared some time in 1934 during Stalin's purges, a definite answer as to the true authorship may never be known. Bruss and Titunik, editors and translators of Volosinov's book on Freud (Volosinov 1976) remain unconvinced by the flimsy evidence in support of the Bakhtin thesis. Parrington (1997) notes the significant fact that Bakhtin never officially denied or accepted that he wrote the original texts. Dentith points out that the dispute has arisen exclusively from ideological motives and thus sees the value in distinguishing between the three different authors (1995). Because the Marxist framework is such an important part of the two books of concern to us here and because I believe that it cannot be so easily smoothed away for whatever reason, I have kept to the names which originally appeared over the writings. That is Volosinov, with the spelling as it first appeared in English.

13 One might be tempted to see in Volosinov's distinction between theme and meaning an attempt to reinvent a variation on the *parole/langue*, diachronic/synchronic distinction. Volosinov, however, is categorical that theme and meaning are of a different order: 'Theme is the upper actual limit of linguistic significance; in essence, only theme means something definite. Meaning is the lower limit of linguistic significance. Meaning in essence means nothing; it only possesses potentiality – the possibility of having meaning within a concrete theme' (1973: 101).

14 Matejka in an appendix to her translation of Volosinov also observes striking similarities between Volosinov and Vygotsky, not only as regards inner speech but also in their shared use of a particular anecdote from Dostoevsky to illustrate the force of intonation (1973: 171). Kosulin points out that a relative of Vygotsky was in the same Leningrad circle as Volosinov and Bakhtin (Kosulin 1990). While there is no hard evidence that any of the three met each other, the overlap of approach and even terminology indicates clearly much common ground and, in the case of Volosinov and Vygotsky, a shared Marxist view of language and consciousness.

15 *Chuzaya rech* in Russian has more dimensions to it than the English rather rigid reported speech, the translators point out. They tell us that it can mean technically reported speech but it can also mean another person's speech and also alien speech. We are taking the narrower interpretation here as Volosinov does at this point, although we shall return to the concept of alien speech later.

16 Actually this expression is taken from the linguist Max Weinreich (quoted in Pinker 1995: 28) but Volosinov describes it in much the same way: 'this grandiose organizing role of the alien word, which always entered upon the scene with alien force of arms and organization' (Volosinov 1973: 75).

17 See Newman and Holzman (1993) for an overview of his contribution.

18 See Vygotsky (1978: 8) for his views on this subject.

19 Pinker holds that there is a processor of thought separate from language, which he calls mentalese. He claims that knowing a language is about translating this mentalese into a language (Pinker 1995: 55–82). This is a logical outcome to his view of human thought as given, an innate, fully formed ability. It leads him

to conclude that this special endowment enables humans to learn a language rather than seeing the delayed arrival of language two or three years after birth as a sign of the presence of development, and that thought processes themselves undergo transformation and refinement. This distinction between innate ability and developmental processes is an important one, because the first obviates the influence of social factors in both language and thought formation. Bickerton, although closely interweaving thought and language, and convincingly demolishing Pinkerton's separate thesis writes out of the picture both the evolution of language and the communicative social function of language. We shall return to this point at the end of this chapter (Bickerton 1995: 41–84).

20 For Volosinov's distinction between meaning and theme, see above, p. 30.

21 Interestingly enough, recent studies on the grammar of speech identify similar features to Vygotsky's. Brazil (1995) not only starts from some similar premises – purposeful activity, interactive speech, meaning a shared understanding between speaker and listener – but also indicates similar instances of abbreviation. This point is explored more fully in Chapter 5.

22 For an examination of these interpretations see Woolfson (1982) and Beaken (1996), whose pioneering introduction to the question provides one of the clearest overviews, from a Marxist perspective, of the origins of language and the social nature of language.

3   Money Talks: The Politics of World English

The unprecedented spread of English across the globe, intensified over the last forty years, poses in stark fashion the questions of language and social change, of language and power. Fervent Empire-builders in the last century were quite open about English being part of the imperial project. States were centralized and ruthlessly brought into line with the needs of imperial trade. Civil services, school systems and armies stirred to the sound of English. For the most part, they continued to do so after the imperialists had left. Later state-builders in the twentieth century, sometimes reluctantly, took on the linguistic inheritance, for motives similar to their colonial predecessors. English, after independence, pro-liferated not declined. Now, as Ahmad notes for India, it pene-trates more deeply administration, the professions, commerce, schooling and the media (Ahmad 1992: 74). For the Kenyan, Ngugi wa Thiongo, the brutal blinkering of the African by English shows how language still remains a central issue, and an aspect of social conflict (Ngugi 1985).

But the reach and spread of English across the globe raises the question of language and power beyond former colonial contexts. In parts of the Middle East, in East and South-East Asia and even in Europe, English is spoken in places without a British colonial legacy. Few dispute the dominance of English, but reactions to it differ widely. The British Council, with bland optimism, claims the pro-cess is inevitable and unstoppable, a question of merely apprehend-ing the facts and participating, like Pangloss, in this most positive of worlds (British Council 1995). With centres in 118 countries world-wide, it has an interest in doing so. Some see the dominance of English as the attainment of a linguistic pinnacle which states and individuals ignore at their peril. Some cautiously welcome the development. Others are resolutely opposed to it. For these, the spread of English has been seen as a new kind of imperialism. Social inequality, discrimination and cultural imperialism has been laid at its door. English is seen to be the main bearer of American economic and technological hegemony (Naysmith 1987, Flaitz 1988, Phillipson 1992a, Pennycook 1994a, Graddol 1996).

Manifestly, the spread of English is, as Kachru pointed out over a decade ago, a highly charged political issue (Kachru 1986a). Previous enthusiasts of English often covered over its political traces. Their efforts were not ideologically innocent, as Phillipson and others have shown. Presenting linguistic matters as part of the inevitable tide of history, neutral and above the mire of social conflict, as we noted in the last chapter, often masks the social and ideological struggles attached to language. That those involved with the teaching of English have, in the 1990s, begun to voice uncomfortable realities, is itself politically significant since Applied Linguistics has hitherto tended to studiously avoid overt political references.

This chapter will examine the political and ideological aspects of English as a world language. First it will survey the spread of English and examine its impact. Second, it will review critically some quite widely held views which purport to explain the spread of English from specific ideological standpoints, from the first imperialists to the expedient promoters of English today, both linguists and others. Third, it will examine critical responses to World English, and in this context re-examine notions of language and power: what has been termed 'linguistic imperialism' and postmodernist interpretations of linguistic power. Fourth it will argue for a need to affirm the historical in language, to reappraise the spread of English in social and historical terms and thereby highlight the contradictory elements of English in an international context. Through these accounts, this chapter aims to define the political parameters of English as a global language, and reveal the degree to which the development of a language is rooted in its social and historical context.

English across the World?

World-wide there are over 1,400 million people living in countries where English has official status. One out of five of the world's population speak English to some level of competence. Demand from the other four fifths is increasing. . . . By the year 2000 it is estimated that over one billion people will be learning English. English is the main language of books, newspapers, airports and air-traffic control, international business and academic conferences, science, technology, diplomacy, sport, international competitions, pop music and advertising. (quoted in Graddol 1996: 181)

Thus read a British Council press release issued to coincide with the launch of their *English 2000* report in 1995. The findings were that English was set to become the global language, and there was an unquestioned assumption about the importance of English for 'economic and social advancement', as well as 'personal development' (British Council 1995: 12). Some members of the British Council have been even more emphatic: 'The English language is fast becoming the only language for global communication in the following six "worlds": transnational companies; Internet communication; scientific research; youth culture; international goods and services; and news and entertainment media' (Seaton 1997: 381).

Crystal has updated and expanded previous data on the extent to which English is used across the world (Crystal 1987, 1997).[1] Eight-five per cent of the 12,500 officially listed international organizations make official use of English. Ninety per cent of international bodies in Asia and the Pacific carry on their proceedings entirely in English. English has special status in seventy-five territories across the world and one-third of these publish newspapers in English. Crystal estimates, from British Film Institute figures, that 80 per cent of all feature films released in 1996 were in English and, from the 1990 *Penguin Encyclopaedia of Popular Music*, that 99 per cent of popular music was predominantly or entirely in English. Tourism worldwide is mediated mainly through English with notices, maps, safety instructions and menus provided in English from Tokyo to Montreal. English is the main language of the Internet. As one commentator has put it, 'the Internet and World Wide Web really only work as great unifiers if you speak English' (quoted in Crystal 1997: 107). As much as three-quarters of the world's mail is reckoned to be in English and, according to statistics from computer sales, possibly 80 per cent of the world's electronically stored information is recorded in English. The number of people learning English would seem to be ever on the rise, though the British Council's figures, quoted above, may be somewhat over-optimistic.

Crystal's estimates on numbers who speak English worldwide are striking. Those who have learnt English as a first language (L1) he estimates at 337 million. He gives the total of 235 million for those who have learnt English as a second language (L2), but if those with some command of English are included, the number of L2 speakers rises to 350 million. The third category, of those who have learnt English as a Foreign Language, is far more difficult to assess, given the varying degrees of competence covered. Crystal estimates this to be anywhere between 100 million and 1,000 million. Overall Crystal settles for a grand total estimate of 1,200–1,500 million. Crystal points out that no other language has spread around the globe so extensively, nor with such recent speed (1997: 57–61).

Looking over a longer historical span, English's present-day role would have been scarcely conceivable. At the time of the Romans, when Latin seemed set to dominate, English as an identifiable language did not exist. Five hundred years after the fall of the Roman Empire, an early form of English was spoken by no more than a few hundred people. In Elizabethan times, perhaps 7 million people spoke English within a very confined area, 'of small reatch, it stretcheth no further than this Iland of ours, naie not there over all', in the words of Richard Mulcaster in 1582 (quoted in Bailey 1991: 96). Half a century later it was still believed that English was of no more than local value and of use abroad only for filling the linguistic gaps left by other more useful languages. English was invaluable for 'stopping holes', as one contemporary put it (quoted in Bailey 1991: 98). French, Spanish and Dutch were considered of much greater international value. Commentators of the time endowed French with the universal, modernizing qualities that are often attributed to English today (Bailey 1991: 98–101). English was spoken only in England, and even there some places were still Cornish- or Welsh-speaking. Only half the people in Scotland spoke English, and in Ireland even fewer.

The increased spread of English represents a powerful expression of the bond between language and social change. The dominance of English today is the continuation of a process started in the earliest days of capitalism, deepened by the expansion of the

British Empire and given further impetus by the commanding position of American capitalism in this century. Many commentators have tended to stress the sudden, recent surge of World English: Crystal sees its spectacular rise as having occurred particularly in the last fifty years, and talks of 'a massive change of stature' that has been achieved in a 'mere eye-blink in the history of language' (Crystal 1997: 63). We should, however, be sceptical about interpretations which foreshorten its development. Bailey points out that by the mid-eighteenth century English was already in a strong position, through the expansion of British markets, and its corresponding military conquests. In 1767 the philosopher and historian, David Hume, pointed out, with some glee, that the colonization of America enabled English to challenge French linguistic hegemony (Bailey 1991: 100).[2] In his historical analysis of the development of the telegraph, first established between Britain and India in 1865 Graddol shows that by the early twentieth century English was already the increasingly dominant language. He also points out how commentators then were as overwhelmed by the effects of the telegraph to 'annihilate time and space' as any commentator on information technology today (Graddol 1996: 207). His account lends a sobering, historical perspective to similar present-day rhapsodic descriptions of the role of English and of the onslaught of economic globalization. Graddol shows that both have a somewhat longer history. Telescoping the dominance of English into the period which saw the development of certain aspects of it – namely information technology and related media – ignores the fact that its dominance well precedes these developments and has it roots, not in one recent technological innovation, but in the power of capital.

Locating the cause in economic factors is important for another reason. It explains the disparity of contact with English. The extent of the English-speaking phenomenon has been neither uniform nor even. Indeed, precisely because those who comment on worldwide English are, for the main part, involved at first hand with the process itself – language planners, Applied Linguists and English teaching agencies – they may exaggerate its reach and believe that their encounters are more representative than in fact they are. For, while English at the end of the twentieth century is more widely scattered, more extensively spoken and written than ever before, the economic process that gave impetus to its development has also left its mark. The spread of English has been as uneven as the spread of the global economy. Pattanayak parallels the widening inequality on a world scale with the widening inequality within national states. In India, where he claimed in the mid-1980s 'out of 30 per cent literates, only two percent have anything to do with the printed word', English is the preserve of the elite (Pattanayak 1985: 401). In Africa, despite English being the official language in eight states and the semi-or co-official language in a further six, actual use and access to English is sometimes very restricted. While the official claim for Ghana is 30 per cent of the population, in Tanzania it is a tiny 5 per cent. In most countries of 'English-speaking Africa' it is estimated that the percentage of English-speakers is between 10 and 20 (Schmied 1991: 22–33). Bailey makes the point that, while many believe that English is expanding around the world, and that received wisdom often puts the number speaking English worldwide at over half the world's population, numbers of people making use of English, due to demographic trends in the developing world may actually be falling (Bailey 1991: vii).

This should not surprise us. Access to English parallels access to the fruits of society. The much-vaunted global economy has itself been a patchy affair leaving large swathes of the world untouched, or condemning them to stagnation or regression. For example, the percentage growth rates of the economies of developing countries fell during the last decade of globalization. Today Africa, with 10 per cent of the world's population, participates in less than 1 per cent of world trade and is increasingly sidelined, at great cost to its population.[3] In a similar fashion, the spread of English has been shaped and restricted by the constraints of late capitalism. This is especially the case in developing countries, but also within faster-growing economies. Crystal is correct to argue that the electronic revolution, which found English in the right place at the right time, has accelerated people's contact with English (Crystal 1997: 110). But when it is borne in mind that even in the heartland of computers, the USA, some estimates reckon that over a third of the population have never used a computer and that under a quarter have access to the Internet (Wilson 1997), it is not difficult to imagine just how removed new technology in the medium of English must seem in Tanzania or Thailand. Crystal himself points out the limited penetration of computers in other English-speaking countries, which he assesses at just 12 per cent, compared with 64 per cent within the USA (Crystal 1997: 106).[4] World English is thus cut down to size. Just like the global economy, while English seems to be everywhere, it does not seem that way to everyone.

The unequal spread of World English, while recognized by some Applied Linguists, is often shifted into purely linguistic terms. A plethora of acronyms have come to categorize the difference. The distinctions between English as Native Language (ENL) English as Second Language (ESL), English as an International Language (EIL), English as a Foreign Language (EFL), English as a Second Dialect (ESD), English as World Language (EWL) – as in for example Schmied (1991) and Gorlach (1988) – may possibly have some pedagogical relevance, but they also antiseptically efface social inequality. Angogo and Hancock's earlier distinction, which puts white and black native speakers of English into two (descending) categories, despite their defence of the legitimacy of 'African Vernacular English', is a questionable distinction (1980: 71). McArthur's emphasis on the 'tripartite model' of ENL, ESL and EFL in the European context raises similar difficulties. Not surprisingly, it is in the ESL – i.e. immigrant – category that McArthur identifies language as being 'a controversial (and politicized) issue' (McArthur 1996a: 12). While he uses this category to designate territories, and highlights the inadequacy of the 'birthright/ acquisition' distinction (1996a: 15), in the context of Europe and its immigration polices it is difficult to see how the ESL category is not shorthand for disadvantage and exclusion. Kachru, perhaps one of the first to highlight the stigmatization of the non-native speaker, attempted to draw attention to the social dynamic behind such labelling by his modified designation of the three circles of English. These he described as the *inner circle* of the traditional bases of English, the *outer circle* which involved the earlier phases of the spread of English and its institutionalization in non-native contexts, and the *expanding circle* in which English functions as an international language (Kachru 1985). His description has the merit of highlighting some of the social factors involved but it still fails to take adequate account of social factors and social differences *within* the circles. Rigid distinctions between would-be varieties of the language, a hard and fast categorization questionable even on linguistic grounds, is in itself an indirect expression of unequal access to English, either in everyday life or in education systems.[5]

Imperial Legacies

For many across the world, Kachru notes, English is not simply another language or an innocent term. The 'other tongue' is synonymous with subjugation, a ruthless instrument in the hands of the missionary, the colonizer, the commercial exploiter (Kachru 1982: 1). But equally these identifications, because they are historical products, are not unchanging, nor without their own contradictions, and while they are bearers of colonial baggage, they did not themselves usher in colonialism. The distinction between what constitutes social experience and what refracts and interprets it is a distinction which in itself has political ramifications in contemporary cultural debates. It resurfaces in past and present explanations of the spread of English.

The imperial legacy in matters of language policy has cast a long shadow – both in terms of who speaks what language today and through a recasting of imperial ideas by latter-day adherents. At the height of British imperialism, promoters of English were considerably more ideologically explicit. They made few attempts to disguise their new-found imperialist zeal and articulated it with breathtaking confidence. Macaulay was the author of the 1835 *Minute* which encapsulated Victorian educational thinking about India. Its stated aim was to make a class of persons 'Indian in blood and colour but English in tastes, in opinions, in morals and in intellect' who may be 'interpreters between us and the millions whom we govern' (Bureau of Education, India 1920: 116). Macaulay argued for cultural reconstitution of an elite only because he dismissed Indian and Arab culture as worthless:

> I have no knowledge of either Sanskrit or Arabic. But I have done what I could to form a correct estimate of their value. . . .I am quite ready to

take the oriental learning at the valuation of the orientalists themselves. I have never found one amongst them who could deny that a single shelf of a good European library was worth the whole native literature of India and Arabia. (1920: 109)

Macaulay considered that Indian languages were so 'poor and rude that until they are enriched from some other quarter, it will not be easy to translate any valuable work into them'. Trevelyan, part of the same group of British administrators who sought an Anglicist reorganization of education in India, also believed Indians to be 'utterly ignorant of the spirit of antiquity and all classical references' and in need of English as a source of value and culture and as a route to being 'imbued with the spirit of English literature' (Viswanathan 1989: 114).[6]

There may have been some disagreement about how to proceed with the imbuing of Englishness in the colonies, whether through the vernaculars or through English itself, through Orientalism or Anglicism. But there was general agreement that English would be acquired only by an elite. The aim of British Indian education, as Viswanathan shows, was conceived openly and unashamedly as to secure and consolidate power (1989: 167). Her account provides a valuable insight into the reasoning of the policy-makers. While they were in favour of the vernaculars being used in Indian schools, a classical English-literature-orientated education should be reserved for the few that Macaulay referred to. English was quite consciously parcelled out to the upper echelons of Indian society. This would leave a 'monument more imperishable than the pyramids of Egypt', as one academic journal of the time argued (Viswanathan 1989: 115). Effectively, one of the most lasting relics of British educational policy in India was the linguistic stratification of classes, whereby the upper classes of Hindus and Muslims, castes of learned men already set apart from the masses, were the only section intended to acquire English. Their English was to be uninfected by the trends of mass literacy prevalent in England. The British did not need mass education for a literate working class in India because it was raw materials, not production, that was of interest to the Empire. Furthermore, the early signs of the subversive potential of widespread literacy that had emerged among the working classes in Britain were to be avoided at all costs among the unquelled storms of India. The class of Indians that the British wanted to nurture, 'English in taste and opinions' were to speak 'the language of the *Spectator*', and carry its outlook as well as style (1989: 115–117). English and English-ness was to become the badge of the elite and those who wore it were loyal to Empire, under the Raj, at least.

Viswanathan's study also shows that promotion of English, and things English, is not reducible simply to an expression of cultural power. Rather, 'it served to confer power as well as to fortify British rule against real or imagined threats from a potentially rebellious subject population' and was 'a vital, active instrument of Western hegemony in concert with commercial expansionism and military action' (1989: 166–167). Indeed, the unclouded arrogance with which these early imperialists assert the civilizing benefits of English finds its origins in the sheer extent of British imperial power at this time. If Carlyle, Macaulay and Arnold speak of their project for English in such unshakeable certainties, it is because they speak from the centre of seemingly unassailable imperial expansion. For five decades from the 1830s to the 1880s, from the Chinese Opium Wars to the conquest of Egypt, the global reach of British economic and military power fed into an ideology of language and culture, articulated, almost without dissent, by the British ruling class.[7] Said, despite in earlier works sidelining this reality, makes clear, in *Culture and Imperialism*, the importance of the material underpinning to the promotion of British culture. He speaks of 'a convergence between the material reality of the vast scope of the Empire' and 'universalizing cultural discourses' which make the imperial metropolis 'for all the world, a source of light', in Ruskin's blithe terms (Said 1993: 125–128). Ahmad, who had found fault with Said's previous 'very textual account' of Empire, puts the economic foundation of language and culture in unambiguous terms:

What gave European forms of the prejudices their special force in history, with devastating consequences for the actual lives of countless millions and expressed ideologically in full-blown Eurocentric racisms was not . . . some gathering of unique force in domains of discourse . . . but quite specifically the power of colonial capitalism, which then gave rise to other sorts of powers. (Ahmad 1992: 184)

Colonial 'discursive practices', in other words, are not the same as the actual practice of colonialism, any more than it was imperial 'discourse' that ran the slave trade or destroyed India's cotton industry. Crude materialism drove the imperial project and in Victorian Britain this was universally taken for granted, by apologists and detractors alike. Today, when imperialism, with more market orientated and less visible manifestations of conquest, takes different forms, and seen through the intellectual haze of postmodern introspection, such fundamental questions of material primacy are not so readily accepted.[8]

The image of English as part of the civilizing mission was not just ideologically asserted. As the Age of Empire opened the way to new discoveries in science, these in turn influenced what was to become the dawn of a golden age of linguistics. New theories were brought to bear in imperialist directions. Some linguists interpreted Darwin's 'natural history of man' as a parallel to the 'natural history of languages' and arrived at an evolutionary theory of language that deemed European languages superior to all others. English and French linguists, writing from the faster-growing Empires, particularly excelled at this sociobiological slant. Racist overtones were scarcely camouflaged. Curtin recounts how Thomas Hodgkin, writing in 1835, believed that language was itself a racial trait and that people of one race were unable to pronounce correctly the sounds of another. The French linguist Guenebault developed this into the curious idea that those who could not pronounce the sound of the letter 'R' were cowardly (Curtin 1964: 394). Such pseudo-scientific notions were constructed in almost complete ignorance of the workings of African languages. Curtin makes the point that nineteenth-century studies of the Niger-Congo languages of Yoruba and Twi failed to see the semantic and grammatical significance of tone systems in these languages (Curtin 1964: 394). Yet ignorance did not stop linguists and others passing judgement, ironically in the name of civilization.[9]

Dismissiveness of African languages was part and parcel of colonial attitudes towards Africa. Behind the lofty phrases, the pragmatic interests of trade outweighed any commitment to formal education or instruction in English. 'Legitimate' trade, as opposed to the now illegal slave trade, would be the vehicle by which the civilizing mission was brought to Africa, a design based on the convenient belief that 'culture change and economic development went hand in hand' (Curtin 1964: 431). As a result, English instruction was largely ignored by government agencies and left to the missionaries. Even as late as 1920 British colonial policy operated on the basis that where trade did not touch, education was of no importance. Dismissing African languages as primitive only reinforced the distinction and underlined the crude commercial functionalism behind British attitudes. One education report of the time, after stressing the need for West Africans 'to know at least one of the languages of the civilized nations', stated:

> It is clear that there is comparatively little, if any advantage, in the continuation of a crude dialect with practically no powers of expression. It is also evident that the need for a common language is not essential to a large group of people speaking the same language and living under conditions that do not require much intercommunication. (Report of the Phelps-Stokes Fund 1924/25, quoted in Schmied 1991: 15)

The report then recommends that 'tribal languages' be used at the primary level, an African lingua franca at the secondary level, and 'the language of the European nation in control in the upper standards'. We see here not only the beginnings of a highly stratified, elitist strategy concerning English which has persisted to the present, but also the ideological content – the labelling of African languages as primitive and European as admirably modern – that is still to be found among some linguists today. In Africa, as in India, official English policy, with differing approaches, had the net result in both places of intensifying social division.

The idea that English equals progress was articulated widely, often by appeals to linguistic functionalism. In the nineteenth century the argument stressed progress through the identification of English with trade and, as a consequence, with civilizing qualities in general. A commentator in 1846, in a work devoted to the subject of language and commerce, captures the theme:

> Let the speech of Britain obtain access to the markets and the schools of those regions as the medium of mercantile correspondence and religious intercourse . . . let it be the ladder of power and door to office

and emolument; let the treasures of English literature be diffused amidst the people from Cape Comorin to the Himalyas, from the Indus to the Burranpooter, and British dominion will be consolidated, equal British rule will be cherished, British commerce will be paramount and the Christian religion and literature will diffuse their influences in the plains and among the mountains. (quoted in Bailey 1991: 116)

The text shows the degree to which the writer (writing, strangely, under the pseudonym, Eclectikwn) articulates the received wisdom about English in the Victorian era. Religious fervour and commercial enterprise are rolled into one, through English.

Even those who were not apologists for imperialism fell under the influence of these ideas. Conrad's *Heart of Darkness*, first published in 1899, is remarkable for its unequivocal denunciation of the brutality behind the colonial rhetoric. Yet Conrad still reflects something of the idea that European languages are superior. Africans are presented as howling mobs, 'making a violent babble of uncouth sounds' (Conrad 1990: 159), people who are denied speech or granted speech only to condemn themselves when they do speak. This is no doubt why Achebe has little time for Conrad, seeing him as one of those who dismiss Africa as a place of negations from which European culture had evolved (Achebe 1977). Certainly Conrad shows scant sympathy for African life, darkness being an abiding and unwelcome metaphor throughout the novel. However, Conrad also unveils the hypocrisy of imperial ideology. 'Heart of Darkness' stands as a harrowing and powerful indictment of the ravages of depraved and deranged colonial 'entrepreneurs', as represented by the brutal Kurz. Behind the rhetoric of the civilizing mission trade lurked the 'free trade *vulgaris*', noted earlier by Marx, with the so-called idyllic proceedings of Empire in fact ushering in the chief moments of primitive accumulation (Marx 1976: 280, 916–19). Conrad, too, was beginning to see what lay behind the scramble for Africa: his was one voice against the stream of Victorian imperialist fervour, and he refused to accept the equation of colonial expansion with benevolent civilization. Writing of the Belgian excesses in the Congo, Conrad noted reproachfully that the noble exploration he had dreamed of as a schoolboy was in fact 'the vilest scramble for loot that ever disfigured the history of human conscience' (Conrad 1926: 25).

Kipling's concept of the white man's burden was the supreme expression of how Africans and Indians were viewed – 'new-caught, sullen peoples, half devil and half child' – but also an unsavoury plea for imperialist paternalism to project progress, via supposedly the 'best bred', across the Empire.[10] Pratt points out, in describing later writings on Africa, that imperialists presented colonized lands as simply having no history. This assertion, made widely by Europeans about Africa, as Pratt notes, 'takes an extraordinary act of denial', given the African origins of European history (Pratt 1992: 219). What's more, far from colonialism representing a break with the 'primitive past', it continued some of the grimier aspects of African history while positively distorting others. African slave-holding, for example, was developed from local beginnings into a massive dehumanizing trade that dragged people to death or slavery across the ocean. Even African tribalism, far from being uprooted by colonialism, was reinvented to suit colonial rule. This latter observation, made by Ranger in his illuminating study, is of particular relevance to the use of English, because the argument repeatedly resurfaces that English in Africa is a neutral unifier against divisive, indigenous tribalism. Ranger shows how tribes were in fact far more fluid and overlapping collectivities than later colonial interpretations would lead us to believe. He presents evidence that tribes were not survivals from a pre-colonial past, but 'largely colonial creations by colonial officers and African intellectuals' who sought the support of local chiefs in the interests of social control (Ranger 1983: 247–252). Such things should be borne in mind when assertions such as 'English has always lain beyond the reproach of tribalism',[11] are sweepingly uttered in defence of the supposed political enlightenment of English.

English Better, or More Neutral?

The early imperialists' soothing descriptions of the qualities of English were, unfortunately, to resurface as English travelled further around the globe and are still surprisingly widespread today. These interpretations about English, from their own ideological standpoint, cover wider questions about the nature of language itself. One of the most widely accepted ideas is that English is a particularly well-endowed language, eminently suitable for its international role and that its intrinsic value partly explains its spread. Bill Bryson, in his popular book on the English language, *Mother Tongue*, reiterates this view when he asserts that the richness of the English language sets it apart from other languages and 'the wealth of available synonyms means that English speakers can often draw shades of distinction unavailable to non-English speakers' (Bryson 1990: 3).[12] It is not surprising that this belief in the virtues of English is so widespread, when writers of standard textbooks of language – dictionaries and grammars – themselves promote them. Robert Burchfield, former Chief Editor of the *Oxford English Dictionary*, speaks of the 'pedigree and credentials' of the English language, 'one of our greatest national heritages' (by which he means British) and then concludes that non-English-speakers are bereft:

> any literate, educated person on the face of the globe is in a very real sense deprived if he does not know English. Poverty, famine, and disease are instantly recognized as the cruellest and least excusable forms of deprivation. Linguistic deprivation is a less easily noticed condition, but one nevertheless, of great significance. (Burchfield 1985: 160–161)

This sleight of hand regarding the world's one thousand other languages is not only pulled off in more traditional quarters. Ahmad notes that anti-imperialists, for all their talk of post-colonial discourse, are also prone to disregard texts in languages other than English and seldom recognize the fact that their knowledge of 'Third World Literature' is based on Western languages (Ahmad 1992: 73–94). Another standard textbook, a widely used grammar of contemporary English, singles out the 'vehicular load' of English (a designation repeated elsewhere), meaning the extent to which it has become the medium for a science of literature or 'other highly regarded cultural manifestations' (Quirk et al. 1972: 2). Neither of these views asserts the wincing triumphalism of Jespersen's comment in the 1930s that 'it must be a source of gratification to mankind that the tongue spoken by two of the greatest powers of the world is so noble, so rich, so pliant, so expressive and so interesting' (Jespersen 1938: 284). Nevertheless, all claims made on the basis of the inherent superiority of English, whether in their weaker or their stronger version, make several assumptions about language spread that are flawed.

If intrinsic qualities of a language lead to its spread, then conversely, other languages must be less well-endowed. Most linguists concede that the notion that any language is inadequate, deficient in some way, hardly stands up to scrutiny. Some linguists would further hold that language differences, of lexical scope and ranges of syntactic structures, rather than reflecting any relative powers of expression, indicate differences in the social activities and organization in which they are used (Halliday 1978, Hymes 1981). In terms of powers of expression and the languages they used, Sapir has pointed out, Plato walks with the Macedonian swineherd (Sapir 1963: 219). What is different, however, is that the swineherd's language was needed for very different purposes and used in very different conditions to those of the urban, literate centres where Plato spoke Greek. As Beaken puts it, it is not languages that progress but societies that change, evolve and progress, and languages with them. '[H]uman languages are always good enough, if they carry out the tasks required by their speakers in their historical context. The human hand is the same whether it is making a stone tool or typing a computer program. But the tasks differ – and so in the long run the form of activity will differ' (Beaken 1996: 155). Language, in this respect, is no different to the human hand.

Second, and perhaps most obviously, belief is the inherent superiority of a language leaves history out. For all the confident claims in the eighteenth and nineteenth centuries that French was the language of rationality, of clarity, of abstract thought, of liberty even, the fortunes of French worldwide have declined. Flaitz has charted in substantial detail the fall of French as a lingua franca in the shadow of France's relative decline in power and influence. With the retreat of French imperialism, the vehicle of its message, the French language, declined in value and prestige accordingly (Flaitz 1988). Eco is similarly sceptical about conflating dominance of a language with its 'vehicular' properties, whether it be supposed easiness, economy or rationality. Such claims for English forget that its position is a 'historical contingency' arising from the extent of the British Empire and US economic dominance. '[Y]et had Hitler won World War II and had the USA been reduced to a confederation of banana republics, we would probably today use German as a universal vehicular language, and Japanese electronics firms would advertise their products in Hong Kong airport duty-free shops (*Zollfreie Waren*) in German' (Eco 1995: 331).

Third, the special quality ascribed to English, the notion that one language is superior to another, glosses over the fact that languages are themselves hybrid products whose supposedly unique characteristics derive from borrowings, fusions and linguistic heterogeneity. The making of English was a ragbag affair which underwent as many changes – wars, settlement, peace, raids, different systems of social organization – as its speakers encountered. The Germanic tribes of the Angles, Saxons and Jutes, early Christains with knowledge of Latin and Greek, the Danes and the French-speaking Normans all contributed freely to what, with a smattering of Celtic influence, became known as English, a point made so graphically in McCrum et al.'s *Story of English* (McCrum et al. 1986). Since all languages are cumulative and absorptive and forever in flux, they can hardly be said to have their own pure characteristics.

Another widely held view about English is that it is culturally and politically neutral. Perhaps the sociolinguist who has been most identified with this view is Joshua Fishman, whose founding influence in the sociology of language has ensured that his views on this subject have been quite widely accepted, and also contested (Mazrui 1975, Flaitz 1988, Cooper 1989, Phillipson 1992a, Pennycook 1994a). Because Fishman's view depoliticizes the question of language and language dominance, and because his linguistic approach and method have become the orthodoxy in this particular field, it is worth examining Fishman's case in some detail.

In one of the first studies on the spread of English, written in 1977, Fishman concluded that English was not 'ethnically and ideologically encumbered' (Fishman 1977: 118). This view was arrived at through the collection of data concerning people's attitudes to English in over 102 countries. There was found to be a positive correlation between English and former Anglophone colonies. Views about the status of English depended on religious factors, linguistic diversity and material benefits (taken to mean 'exports to English speaking countries'). Poorer countries were also found to depend more on English in education than richer countries (Fishman et al. 1977: 77–107). The instrumentalist framework of the study predetermined the results that would emerge: English was a relatively neutral, straightforward tool in social advancement. Again, from the way the study was set up, the question of the spread of English was seen primarily in individual, not social, terms. Fishman et al. were quite frank about. '[I]ndividuals, not countries, learn English as an additional language. An individual learns English moreover not because of abstractions such as linguistic diversity or international trade balances but because the knowledge of English helps him to communicate in contexts in which for economic or educational reasons he wants to communicate and because the opportunity to learn English is available to him' (1977: 106).

There is a certain circularity about this approach which, through the garnering of attitudes, tends to restate the status quo. Cameron holds that this is a general trend in what she terms 'quantititive sociolinguistics' (Cameron 1990). Seeing social developments as merely incremental individual ones underrates both the social constraints that curtail individual choice as well as the social factors which explain individual attitudes. In the case of the spread of English, this type of study may give some (quite predictable) answers to the question 'Why do people learn English?' but fails to reveal much about the role of English in the world and how it has arisen. As Phillipson notes, there is no attempt by Fishman to refer to or investigate global inequality and its structural determinants (Phillipson 1992a: 85). Even in the cherished terms of individual attitudes, this study, like many quantitative measures of attitudes, tends to channel responses into pre-set categories. In this process people are mainly viewed as conforming to a pre-existing state of affairs and individuals are seen as exercising their choice within those parameters. Perhaps this is why Williams has described Fishman's view of languages as simple instruments for carrying out social roles as deterministic functionalism reinforcing what is perceived as the norm. His labelling of the dominant language as a 'language of wider communication' depoliticizes language and English simply becomes 'the key to the door of the good life' (Williams 1992: 97–109).[13]

In an article in *English World-Wide*, Fishman attempts to clear up any misunderstandings that his formulation has caused (Fishman 1987). He restates the neutrality of English by stipulating that it is 'non-ethnoculturally (ie., non-Anglo-American) encumbered', and reiterates that

> neither British imperialism nor American capitalism nor the democratic ethos shared by both of these major English mother-tongue countries were major barriers or bridges with respect to the spread of English. Rather, English seemed to represent modern life, popular technology, consumer goods, youth culture and the promise of social mobility. (1987: 1)

To illustrate his point he focuses on the views of Nathan Birnbaum, a Jewish intellectual in nineteenth-century Eastern Europe. He notes that Birnbaum's attitudes to English, because his writings have been relatively influential and because he changed his political stance and views of English, have a 'broader currency'. They are a reliable measure of whether English is 'ethnoculturally encumbered'. Fishman gives an account of Birnbaum's attitudes to German, to Yiddish and to English. Birnbaum's view of English as being 'ideologically encumbered' stemmed from his own political stance at that time. It is clear from this account that Fishman understands ideology to be an individual, attitudinal affair and that 'ideological struggle' refers to individual tensions, not social ones. Fishman repeats Birnbaum's recognition that 'sociolinguistic attitudes, opinions, beliefs and overt behaviours are basically subjective' (1987: 8) and concludes that the only arena in which ideological reactions to English come to the fore is in 'encompassing culture change' in which 'elites are threatened by encroachment of their attitudes, behaviours, and values' (1987: 9). Fishman drains ideology of social content. Denuded thus of any reference to a set of ideas related to class interest, Fishman's view of ideology comes to reinforce an essentially subjective, individualist view of society and language.

Fishman's functionalism and belief in modernization finds a more recent exponent in Coulmas, co-editor of the *Journal of the Sociology of Language*. In *Language and Economy* (1992) Coulmas presents what is, essentially, a market-based model of English. His thesis is that languages not only develop, spread and die primarily according to the economic fortunes of their speakers but that language itself mirrors economic processes. Various strands of this thought are developed. 'Language is an asset' Coulmas takes to mean quite literally that multilingual societies have low incomes per capita and that rich countries are linguistically homogeneous (1992: 23–26). The economic profile of a language, which Coulmas admits is somewhat difficult to draw, nevertheless reveals how much 'language is not only a medium but also an element of economic processes' (1992: 88). This sliding from present economic orthodoxies to linguistic terms is a constant feature of Coulmas's conception. Free market economics, in terminology and in content, flow freely. His much-used metaphor of language as economics ('language as asset', 'at face value', 'economy in language') becomes an enthusiastic endorsement of free-market capitalism.

The likening of language to the economy is not just ideological: it also represents an impoverished view of language. For Coulmas, language is a means of exchange, signs for a purpose, and a system that follows all the principles of Just-in-Time efficiency. 'Economy principles permeate the linguistic system on every level,' he informs us, and these 'attest the pervasive influence on language of the Principle of Least Effort' which is 'grounded in the limits of human life which makes time a scarce resource' (1992: 258). Just how the principles of economy – by which he appears to mean time-saving – operate in relation to such forms of language use as repetition, euphemisms, over-lexicalization and ambiguity, not to mention poetry and novel writing, is not explained. The parameters thus set, we are led in fairly predictable directions: the death of minority languages is seen as inevitable, language spread arises from the power of trade, language adaptation – fulfilled most admirably by English – is the inevitable triumph of the workings of the market. This market fatalism makes an appearance well beyond Coulmas's more idiosyncratic work. In Spolsky's most recent standard introduction to sociolinguistics, for example, we encounter the same theme. As to whether English has been imposed or linked to imperialism, Spolsky's answer is that 'A closer look at the process by which English has developed into a global language suggests that in fact the demand has continually exceeded the supply' (Spolsky 1998: 76–77). Under the awesome influence of the demi-gods of supply and demand, the realities of unequal access to the products, of those who produce them and those who control them, of poverty and wealth, slide out of focus. The invisible hand of the market ensures that English is there, English is wanted, English shall be provided.

Coulmas's presentation of language is thus quite ideologically specific. It is striking how close some of the images used here are to those of the old-style imperialists, and involve, as before, dismissive views of the third world and the working class. Coulmas claims the West is the automatic procurer of modernization, 'which cannot be enacted without Westernization in the domain of language' (1992: 51). Multilingualism is seen as a stumbling block to progress. Coulmas sees the Hispanic community in the US as having by-passed the economic utility of English for 'sociopsychological reasons' (1992: 67). Where multilingualism does have its uses, he argues, it is where another language has what Coulmas calls a 'group specific utility value'. He uses the term advisedly, and, it turns out, with disparagement. The use of Hindi, Bengali and Punjabi in London's East End is one such example, since, we are told, 'in order to run a restaurant or a tailor's business it is not essential to have a command of a language which is also suitable for cognitive science or technology' (1992: 68). This narrow view of immigrants in Britian is the logical outcome of his extreme linguistic functionalism. Such views about people's proper place in the world and commercial enlightenment as the panacea, merely re-echo those of the Victorian Empire-builders – but in the economic tur-moil of the 1990s they rest on shakier economic foundations.

Linguistic Imperialism?

Coulmas's utilitarian approach to English is widely accepted. The appearance in 1989 of a major study commissioned by the *Economist*, significantly entitled *English: A World Commodity*, reflected the multibillion-dollar business that English had become, and the prevailing orthodoxy. 'English is divesting itself of its political and cultural connotations as it emerges as an international language', was its declared stance (McCallan 1989: 25) and this was the context within which the report presented the potential market size. The British Council has followed suit. In a leading British journal of English language teaching (which the British Council co-produces) an article entitled 'linguistic non-imperialism' adopts a no-nonsense approach to those who have worried about English's role in the world:

> English is fast becoming the only language for global communication. . . . For the foreseeable future that is the social reality, just as surely as water flows downhill and the sun rises in the East. So let us not, in discussing language policy, be too diverted by what our ELT [English Language Teaching] colleagues may or may not have said in the past. Let us rather concentrate on how best to cope with the reality of English today. (Seaton 1997: 381)

It was this type of cheery expediency, which Naysmith first described as the 'cosy, rather self-satisfied assumption', that English is a 'good' thing (Naysmith 1987), that prompted some to bring the politics of English out into the open. Phillipson's contribution in this respect was significant.

His book *Linguistic Imperialism* (1992a) raised themes hitherto unaired within English language teaching (ELT), and stressed the integral role of language in the functioning of the contemporary world order. His documentation of US and British English-language agencies – particularly the Ford Foundation and the British Council – is invaluable for revealing their actual role in bolstering cold war interests and the security of their countries' worldwide investments. What had been presented as impartial academic concerns were, as Phillipson shows, in fact driven by policies favoured by the British government. This was clearly the case under colonialism when a grammatical knowledge of the English language was, according to the Colonial Office in 1847, 'the most important agent of civilisation for the coloured people of the colonies' (Phillipson 1992a: 115). Equally, colonial administrators such as the Governor of Northern Rhodesia in the 1920s stressed that the direction of Native Education should 'not be in the same direction as European' (1992a: 120). It should be vocational rather than literary, 'the surest way to achieve the formation of a malleable and docile African worker', according to one missionary-educator (1992a: 119). After the second world war, in the changing world of emerging independent states, the

British government spoke plainly about the political potential of English. A British Cabinet report in 1956 recounted: 'within a generation English could be a world language: the tide is still running in its favour but it is important that its expansion should take place under Commonwealth and United States auspices'. Britain could not miss out on any opportunities and the report declares that Britain ought not to stand by while Libya is offered a German professor of English and Egypt exports its teachers to Kuwait (1992a: 148). Phillipson's conclusion concerning British government involvement in ELT is appropriate:

> It may prove something of a shock to members of the ELT profession who regard themselves as being concerned exclusively with cultural, intellectual liberal or non-political pursuits, to realize that the foundations of the academic professional world in which they operate were laid by a Conservative British Cabinet which was preoccupied with the Cold War and the security of worldwide British investments. (1992a: 151)

Phillipson also charts the involvement of United States agencies' programmes in the promotion of ELT. The Ford Foundation from the 1950s onwards had projects in thirty-eight countries. It funded Applied Linguistics research centres, and the Fulbright programme also contributed substantially to English teaching (1992a: 152–163). Phillipson's assessment of the role of English, whose foundations were relaid in the post-war economic boom, is accurately explained. State backing for ELT, driven by US interests primarily but also through Anglo-American cooperation, was motivated by political and economic interests that wanted to secure a linguistic backdrop 'which would favour the interests of capitalism in a changing world' (1992a: 152). Phillipson aptly quotes Chomsky, who pointed out that what was presented as a deep concern for human welfare was actually motivated by a desire to improve the climate for business (1992a: 155). Language policies reflected economic interests and consolidating English contributed, in a streamlined fashion to the shift.

The merit of Phillipson's work is to bring political questions centre-stage. His open anti-imperialist stance starkly uncovers English teaching agents' complacency about the divisive effects of their policies and the alienation that colonial attitudes have engendered. He also reveals how the ELT orthodoxy which favours English native speakers over local English teachers is part of the approach which is found in former colonial attitudes. He points out that '[T]he white man's burden has been metamorphosed into the British native speaker's burden' (1992a: 179, 1992b). Phillipson's placing of English teaching within the ambit of the interests of international capitalism was long overdue in Applied Linguistics. Even now, commentators in the field of English teaching shy away from references to social power, and certainly to imperialism. Crystal, for example, refers to the 'prestige' afforded to a language because of 'the different national histories which co-exist', hardly an accurate description of international and social inequalities. He then claims that the choice of the consumer is the most reliable antidote to linguistic domination (Crystal 1994: 114). But Phillipson's analysis, for all its welcome injection of politics into a previous insipidly depoliticized subject, does not provide the necessary theoretical tools to understand the modern world today.

Phillipson's theoretical framework is inadequate to explain how national states are themselves enmeshed in global capitalism. He sees the fundamental contradiction in the world system as that between the 'centre' and the 'periphery' – the rich first world and the poor developing nations. In the era of what he calls 'neo-colonialism', the crude stick of colonial rule has been replaced by a subtler 'cultural imperialism'. 'Linguistic imperialism' operates as a distinct type of imperialism within this sphere and is part of how the centre controls the periphery (1992a: 50–57).[14] Phillipson's reliance on the centre–periphery model ignores the material realities that simply cannot be explained in terms of that opposition. First the 'periphery' has not been stifled uniformly by the 'centre'. The East Asian 'Tiger' economies, for example, far from being crushed under increasing underdevelopment, as core–periphery theories argued, from the 1970s to the 1990s did achieve rapid industrial growth, even if they have run into crises more recently. Phillipson, in his remarks about Singapore, which he sees as an exceptional case, attributes its modernization to its 'pre-eminent' colonialism, the fact that it is a privileged partner of the West, and its adoption of the 'centre's norms' (1992a: 316). However, Phillipson's case is contradicted by growth that was experienced across the so-called Newly Industralizing Countries – South Korea, Taiwan, Hong Kong and Singapore, as well as Brazil, Argentina and Mexico – in the period he examines.

Second, it is local ruling classes that are the agents and beneficiaries of capitalist development, a fact that Phillipson's theory fails to explain. Overall Phillipson identifies modernization with Westernization *tout court* (1992a: 317) and sees 'indigenous groups' of most underdeveloped countries as 'dominated' (1992a: 318). His implied argument is that national states have an interest in breaking with the world economy. His view underplays the reality of class within developing countries, and in countries of the centre. Economic growth in Singapore or South Korea has developed alongside Western markets, fitting into existing niches to the huge benefit of local ruling classes. They are themselves competitors on the world capitalist market, which, more often than not, sees them alongside rather than opposing the bigger, imperialist players.

Phillipson's centre–periphery, north–south categorization, furthermore, locks him into an anti-imperialist strategy of nationalism and the promotion of national languages. Yet, nationalism does not necessarily mark a break with the imperialist order. Indeed, as a matter of historical record, it has been only too happy, under new leaders, to fit into the world order it once opposed. Post-colonial Africa is a testament not only to how modern world capitalism has bestowed nothing on most Africans but also to the stifling impoverishment that local wealthy elites have forced upon their populations, often in the name of nationalism. Bayart has charted this in Zaire, in Senegal and in Nigeria in a chilling indictment of these unequal states. Furthermore, he shows that, in the case of Nigeria, far from breaking with Western capitalism, its national ruling party received huge funds from a French civil engineering company that wanted Nigerian contracts (Bayart 1993: 79). Such things are the rule rather than the exception. In Ireland, the official promotion of Irish has sat happily alongside the enthusiastic embracing of high-tech capitalism and the toleration of widening social division.[15] Nationalism in one arena can mesh seamlessly with globalization in another, especially when it is a question of getting in on wealth on a global scale. Any number of recycled nationalists, in various parts of the post-colonial world has proved as much. The problem with Phillipson's model is that it fails to account for such links between local rulers and international capitalism or how economic exploitation arises from social relations within, as well as beyond, 'periphery' countries.

For it is local ruling classes who are responsible for educational and linguistic policies that suit their own interests, with or without the advice of specialists from the 'centre'. It is inadequate to describe this as 'cultural imperialism'. The Chinese state, as well as many African ones, have not needed prompting from the West for their various language programmes; they have sought them for their own ruling-class reasons. Western agencies are called in to implement policies that have already been decided (see, for example, Pennycook 1995, Jackson et al. 1997). Similarly, India's post-independence educational system and policy to promote English was implemented with little help from Britain or America.

But beyond educational policy, Phillipson's centre–periphery dichotomy fails to take adequate account of linguistic tensions *within* each camp. Not all speakers in the West dominate, nor are all speakers in the periphery discriminated against. The notion of class cuts across London as much as it does Lagos or Lahore. Hindi in India has been used as divisively as English, and Bahasa Malaysia has been seen as the badge of the Malaysian nationalist elite. In short, local ruling classes come to articulate ideologies that operate in their own interests, and are not just the ventriloquists' dummies of their Western masters.

Finally, the term 'linguistic imperialism' itself is misleading. It seems to highlight the glaring reality of linguistic oppression, but in reality it deflects attention from the source of the inequalities, as well as missing the contradictory character of language itself. Classical Marxist accounts of imperialism define imperialism as the domination of some states by others which springs from economic exploitation by the controllers of capital. Bukharin's description of imperialism, for example, showed how imperialism arose as intensification of competition on a world scale. Capitalists competed for labour power, raw materials, investment opportunities and for markets to realize surplus value. In this, capital became increasingly concentrated in fewer hands and ever more closely identified with national states, as 'state capitalist trusts' (Bukharin 1972: 144). It is here that ideology becomes so entwined with economics and states develop an ideology of imperialism to win hearts and minds to their project (1972: 109). Bukharin shows that politics intervenes because of the economic changes that have gone beforehand.[16] It is not the sum total of various aspects of imperialism – cultural, linguistic, ideological, political – all of which carry equal weight. The dominance of English makes no sense except viewed primarily in the broader perspective of the economic weight of the USA and the workings of international capitalism.

Linguistic imperialism also implies that language is somehow a decisive tool in the world order. The reality is more complex. A language operates within the overall process and not one-dimensionally nor in one direction. Phillipson concedes that language can be used to underpin the status quo as well as oppose it, to oppress people as well as to liberate them (1992a: 318). Yet the thrust of his argument does not allow him to take full account of this fact and forces him to conclude that the dominance of English can best be countered by its linguistic mirror-image – promotion of the local language. His laudable appeal for the recognition of linguistic rights for minorities – indispensable for the removal of linguistic oppression – becomes conflated with the promotion of indigenous languages, which is not the same thing. Often attempts to revive and impose a former national language can be a nationalist cloak under which new rulers' interests are hidden.

Furthermore, his claim that in the former Soviet Union linguistic oppression did not exist because there was 'functional bilingualism' sounds strangely out of keeping with everything that he has just said about English. Ukranian, Kazakh, Azerbaijani and Uzbek suffered oppression under 'Russification', as many of the speakers of these languages have openly declared since the fall of the old regime. Linguistic rights have to be about real choice, free of discrimination, particularly so in Eastern Europe where, ironically, English is almost exactly replacing the role played by Russian had accompanied by the same arguments and with a parallel sense of foreboding.

Phillipson's account of linguistic imperialism leads in nationalist directions. History has shown that nationalism neither breaks with the world order nor necessarily shows any greater respect for minority languages. His argument that linguistic imperialism in neo-colonial contexts operates in such a way as to legitimize unequal power leads him to focus on the promotion of local languages as a way of countering inequality. Yet where such strategies have occurred they have neither broken with the world order nor necessarily encouraged linguistic rights. Rather they have been used by local elites for their own purposes or else, as in parts of Africa and Eastern Europe, they can become an excuse to fuel divisions. Slovak was almost reinvented as a language for the nationalist purposes of the rulers of the new republic.[17] National languages do not necessarily lead in emancipatory directions; they can be as much part of oppression and division as English.

Postmodern 'Discursive Practices'

Others have also highlighted the political effects of the dominance of English. Pennycook (1990a, 1990b, 1991, 1994a, 1994b, 1995) starts from many of Phillipson's concerns. He is disturbed by the dominant role of English in a changing world where the power of international capitalism and 'free world' ideology parallels massive global inequalities (1995: 35). He too sees the 'predominant paradigm' as bland optimism resting on the acceptance that the world has opted for English and the world will get what it wants. He sees English as 'a gatekeeper to positions of prestige in society' and a major means by which social, political and economic inequalities are maintained within many countries. He also shares Phillipson's view that British and American governments have promoted English through their teaching agencies for their own interests. For Pennycook this raises profound questions about the practice of teaching English. His work in this respect is a welcome addition to the study of language in a political context.

Pennycook disagrees with Phillipson's reliance on Dependency Theory for explaining both these global inequalities and the role of English, but on different grounds to that I have argued above. Pennycook's main quarrel with Phillipson's view is that he sees what he terms 'neo-Marxist' frameworks as socio-economically determinist, reductionist and emanating from a 'positivist conception of knowledge' (1995: 46–47). Brushing aside Marxism as 'reductive', he sees culture and 'discursive practices' as having a key role in the construction of power. 'The world is in English rather than just English being in the world' (1995: 34–42). He is explicit about the influence of Foucault and views his work as part of the 'postmodern project'. Because these views have become widely accepted in post-colonial studies, it is worth examining in some detail what Pennycook's postmodernism offers for explanations of World English and what pathways it suggests.

Pennycook's writing affirms Foucault's frame of reference in a number of ways. An article entitled 'The diremptive/redemptive project: postmodern reflections on culture and knowledge in international academic relations' summarizes the main themes, although the argument is fairly densely made. First, he rejects what he terms 'totalizing discourses, such as liberal humanism or Marxism' (1990a: 62). For him, there is no rational body of knowledge and no overriding social causes to human activity, merely 'discursive practices' that are hegemonic. Concepts such as progress, development and modernization need to be demystified as so many modes of thought, traceable back to the European Enlightenment: today these concepts have become instrumental for delegitimizing third world cultures (1990a: 64). He also holds that the role of discourse in the process of domination is central. Power is constructed through culture and discourse; 'cultural practices are not constituted simply by social systems but are constitutive of those systems' (1990a: 62). Finally, against these systems of power (the 'diremptive project'), Pennycook appeals to the 'redemptive project' of the academic to produce and disseminate alternative knowledge, to avoid the death of local cultures, to help legitimize local cultures and knowledges and to decolonize the Western mind (1990a: 76).

In *Cultural Politics of English as an International Language* he applies these themes to English. He examines the degree to which a special 'discourse' has been constructed around English, how Applied Linguistics has been 'disciplined', in Foucault's term, to suit Western interests and how educationalists, policy-makers and various experts have created discourses which 'exert domination over people' (1994a: 61). Pennycook describes the colonial origins of the discourse of English 'not so much in terms of an expansionist drive as in terms of a will to describe' (1994a: 73).[18] He describes how English is used as a 'disciplining discourse' for colonial methods of control and evokes Foucault's image of the panopticon, the utilitarian Jeremy Bentham's design for a prison which allowed constant observation of the prisoners (Pennycook 1994a: 97–98). Pennycook returns to the panopticon metaphor elsewhere to show how

> the Third World is subjected to a form of surveillance – a 'normalizing gaze' . . . by the 'powerful and knowing' central tower, the Western intellectual and political institutions that construct discourses on the Third World and which lead the objects of that surveillance to become 'the principle of [their] own subjection'. (1995: 49)

He suggests that English today is the 'language of the global panopticon'. For Foucault too this exercise of discipline is power-giving in its own right and for Pennycook the panopticon symbol becomes power itself (1994a: 97–98). In condemnation of what he sees as the legacy of enlightenment, Pennycook adds that it is not coincidental that Bentham was also the originator of the word 'international' (1995: 49).[19]

Pennycook bundles together both 'liberal-humanism' and 'neo-Marxism' as being universalistic discourses, but the force of much of his attack is aimed at Marxism. What he sees as the economic reductionism of 'neo-Marxism' fails to take adequate account of culture and sees 'people as passive consumers of hegemonic cultural norms' (1995: 48). The source of this economic reductionism is not clear, for the only reference he makes to anyone claiming to be a Marxist is, very briefly, to Wallerstein (Pennycook 1990a: 56, 1994a: 56). Yet Wallerstein's world systems theory owes more to Dependency Theory than it does to Marxism. To claim that this cluster of 1960s radicals represent the final Marxist statement on imperialism seems strange. Wallerstein's centre-periphery model disregards relations of production and classes in the ordinary Marxist sense (Brewer 1980). But this aside, what of Marx, Lenin, Hilferding, Bukharin, Luxemburg? Surely any one of these might more reasonably be seen to represent the Marxist tradition on this subject. Furthermore, each one of these devoted quite a substantial amount of writings to analysing national and racial oppression, the brutalizing effects of colonialism on the colonized and what might today be called cultural nationalism. Marx wrote at great length about the treatment of the Irish in Britain, about British rule in India and the hypocrisy of colonial 'civilization-mongers', about colonialization in general as well as about the barbarous ravages of the British Empire and its effects on the people colonized (Marx and Engels 1959: 81–87). Regarding Ireland, Marx not only believed that people could be freed from dominant imperial ideas but actively campaigned to break anti-Irish racism in Britain and the US. He saw that the persistence of such attitudes in a British worker 'strengthened the domination over himself' (Marx and Engels 1959: 337). These are hardly the avenues of thought of economic reductionism.

Pennycook, like all idealist theorists, has a problem with causality: why exactly does one discourse become dominant? His own analysis is forced to partly concede the existence of the very overarching socio-economic categories that he theoretically rejects. His examination of the use of English in Malaysia recognizes the decisive character of social class. He shows that while Malay nationalists officially pursued pro-Malay language policies, wealthier Malays continued to have access to English for their own business purposes. Class was the determining factor, Pennycook's study admits, in access to English, even across ethnic groups of Malay, Tamil and Chinese (1994a: 198–199). Equally, despite his rejection of economic reductionism, his discussion of Anglicism and Orientalism, takes for granted that the spread of English was underpinned by the role of 'Britain as a pre-eminent industrialised nation of the globe' (1994a: 99). Similarly in his studies of Malaysia and Singapore, the colonial legacy forms the automatic backdrop to his description of English educational policies. For Pennycook, economic factors played their part at one time, but not today. History – material, economic, real history – was decisive but mysteriously is not in the modern world. He is struck by the link between international capitalism and the world in English (1995: 35) yet proceeds to talk only of discursive practices as the distributors of power. Such an approach involves freezing history and its social effects at a moment when, inexplicably, discourse comes centre-stage in power formation.

These difficulties emerge when the concept of objective reality and historical meaning is jettisoned and discourse becomes constitutive of reality. When the process of colonialism is the 'will to describe', when development and modernization are reduced to discursive practices, and 'international' becomes just someone's turn of phrase, then change, too, becomes locked in discourse. This is no doubt why Pennycook describes language as a 'site of struggle', and why what he calls the 'worldliness' of English is just discursive style, the way that language has of being open to an infinite number of interpretations. He recalls Mazrui's description of Mboya, on the eve of Kenya independence, reciting the poem 'If' by Rudyard Kipling, as an example of a struggle for meanings within discourse and the decolonizing of Kipling (Mazrui 1975). Pennycook sees this as language being a site of struggle in practice (1995: 51). Sadly he fails to see that the site of struggle in the Kenyan example was well beyond discourse. What had changed were events in the real world and the ousting of colonialism, which now made a different reading of Kipling possible. The end of colonial rule, in the Kenyan case, came about only through one of the bloodiest struggles in history in which the British, notwithstanding their copious discourse about the murderous rising of the Mau Mau, reverted to a brutality quite as extreme as the one they depicted. Those listening to Mboya that day would have fully grasped the materiality behind Kipling's poem (Lapping 1989: 469–522).

Here is the nub of the question of discourse. If meaning is constructed relative to particular discursive formations, where does that leave power relations outside discourse? The use of English as a world language is not just a discourse; English is also a historical and social product which can be used with different meanings by its speakers, themselves socially and historically rooted. Pennycook's notion of the 'worldliness' of English rests on 'the rejection of a unitary subject in favour of a notion of multiple subjectivities constituted by different discourses' (1990a: 69). This fissiparous view, forever fracturing into separate subjectivities, actually leaves the existing power structures intact. His 'insurrection of subjugated knowledges' seems more like changing your mind rather than changing society. For the postmodern, power becomes subsumed into discourse.

Pennycook has admitted the difficulties that reducing everything to a discursive interpretation raises (Pennycook 1991). Citing critically the US educationalist Giroux, he shows that by taking critical deconstruction only so far, postmodernists can use relativism for their own ends and, as in the case of Giroux, argue for critical pedagogy while still retaining their faith in the powers that be in the US. Against this, Pennycook argues for a 'principled postmodernism', which he sees as 'a way of moving forward from a deconstructive project to a reconstructive one responsive to political and ethical questions' (1991: 308). Regrettably, the theoretical tools of postmodernism and Foucault tie Pennycook's willing hands. The centring on language, in which meaning is specific to each discursive construction, engenders an extreme relativism which makes any principled reason for opposing power structures impossible. Geras is alluding to the same cul-de-sace when he says, in connection with postmodern anti-essentialism, that if there is no truth, there is no injustice (Geras 1995). Callinicos, locates the postmodern retreat into discourse in the climate of political disappointment felt by those radicalized in the 1960s generation. In the disturbing decade of the 1980s, as Callinicos puts it, they had nothing left to do except to fiddle while Rome burned (1989: 174). Postmodernism certainly knew how to fiddle.

These considerations perhaps explain why Pennycook's elephant gives birth to a mouse. For all the talk of the World in English and power strategies to match, Pennycook's 'redemptive' project sidesteps the question of social power and in the end falls into the traps that he accuses others of laying. He advocates 'critical pedagogy' in which academics, as 'as political actors' (1990a: 76), as well as teachers and as 'transformative intellectuals' (1994a: 299), bring social awareness to their students. Such strategies have perhaps their place in education, but with no reference to a larger social and political world (what Pennycook would, no doubt, term a 'totalizing discourse') they are forlorn attempts at any sort of change. What is more his solution has elitist overtones, with academics, and those in education urged to play the role of liberators.

Without any materialist analysis of the world, as Engels remarked about the Utopian Socialists, 'what was wanting was only the individual man of genius who has recognized the truth'.

Or, as Marx put it elsewhere, who educates the educator? (Marx and Engels 1970: 117, 1974: 121). Pennycook's transformative intellectual he claims is taken from Gramsci, but the use of the concept here does disservice to that fighter for social change, Gramsci would have baulked at the idea of politics being in the hands of professional intellectuals. Gramsci's organic intellectual was rooted in class struggle, not in the narrower margins of pedagogy (Gramsci 1971).

Ironically, Pennycook through his reliance on discourse as a master-category, ends up with the very conclusion that he accuses reductionist neo-Marxism of – assuming that people are 'passive consumers of cultural hegemony'. Indeed, he goes further.

> By considering the relationship between language and discourse, it is possible to go beyond an understanding of the structural concordance of English and forms of global inequality and to understand how people's subjectivities and identities are constituted and how people may comply with their own oppression. (1995: 54)

In this postmodern trope, linguistic determinism has come full circle. People are trapped within language and not only passively accept their fate but also comply with it. It is not surprising that in this scheme of things the entry of people on to the stage of history is written out and, by the same stroke, academics and teachers become the saviours. There is nothing very new about this particular version of enlightened educator: especially in North America, such a view has been the wellspring of just the liberalism that, ironically, so many postmodernists abhor as too complacent.

English, History and Dialectics

A historical approach to the politics of English has to encompass both historical determinants and ideological struggle and to explain how language is indeed made by its speakers, even if not in conditions of their choosing.

First, the social and historical roots of language spread explain why English is such a politically contentious issue across the world. '[T]he past is all that makes the present coherent, and further . . . the past will remain horrible for exactly as long as we refuse to assess it honestly'. James Baldwin's plea for the importance of history in his introduction to *Notes of a Native Son* (1995: 14) has particular relevance for coming to grips with the role of English in the world today. English has a heavy historical load for many peoples across the world and to ignore this fact by claiming that it is simply an 'additional language', a linguistic *tabula rasa*, is to deny the fact that for many English has been an *alien word*, brought at the point of a sword and synonymous with oppression. That is why the question of linguistic rights of all minority (and majority) languages is at the centre of the politics of English. The dichotomy in many African states where the home language seldom reaches the school is the result, not of linguistic functionalism, but of social inequality bolstered by the legacy of imperial oppression. Education in one's native tongue is a fundamental right and it is a shame that in discussions of English as an international language, it is seldom defended.[20] The fact that this demand is often advanced in the pursuance of nationalist ends should not obscure the fact that linguistic freedom and choice is the only basis on which to obtain any true internationalism. As Lenin wisely remarked on this subject, opposing those who argued against national rights in the name of unity, the right to divorce does not mean familial disintegration, but on the contrary the right to family ties on a democratic basis (Lenin 1947: 34). The same goes for linguistic rights. Very often, as many speakers of minority languages in the world have found, the simple demand for linguistic rights has been thwarted by the social inequalities that perpetuate oppression.

Yet many linguists write out history. When writing about pidgins and creoles – the languages that arose from merchant capitalism including slavery – some linguists fail to refer to the historical content of the making of these new languages. Coulmas barely mentions slavery in his reference to pidgins and creoles – which he anodynely describes as being 'found wherever European merchants established trade links with peoples on other continents; at the West African coast . . . in the Caribbean . . . at the Northeastern rim of South America' (Coulmas 1992: 157). Even Schmied in his study of African English makes little mention of slavery in his section on 'Early Trading Connections', concluding that 'only rudimentary knowledge of languages was necessary to ensure communication' (Schmied 1991: 6–12). In a surfeit of abstraction, and in their zeal to describe the linguistic phenomenon of the creation of new languages, linguists have effaced the people themselves. No doubt, it is omissions like these that make Ngugi wa Thiongo want to 'call a spade a spade' and show how imperialism continuously 'pressgang[ed] the African hand to the plough to turn the soil over and [put] blinkers on him to make him view the path ahead only as determined for him by master armed with bible and sword' (Ngugi 1985: 109).

Second, languages themselves, like their speakers, are the cumulative products of history. Of the many examples of the imposition of English, it is perhaps the slave trade from the coast of West Africa that epitomizes the brutal fusion of history and language. Britain was the foremost slave carrier for other nations and the chief promoter of 'triangular trade'. Its ships, laden with manufactured goods, sailed from Bristol and Liverpool for the west coast of Africa. This cargo was exchanged for black slaves, who were then taken on the notorious Middle Passage, to the Caribbean where they were sold to plantation owners to work as servants or in the fields. These ships then returned with sugar, rum, molasses, cotton and substantial profit for their merchant owners. As McCrum et al. put it: 'Every leg of the journey contributed to the making of a completely new kind of English . . . Black English itself was the product of one of the most infamous episodes in the history of our civilization, the slave trade' (McCrum et al. 1986: 210–11). Accounts written by former slaves bear witness to the human and linguistic trauma brought about by the enforced tearing of people from their own lands and from each other. Douglass, a former slave writing of his time on a slave plantation in the Southern States, tells how slaves never knew their exact age (Douglass 1995: 1); they were also robbed of their own language. Slave masters, fearful of rebellion, separated speakers of the same language. In his description of the passage to the West Indies, Olaudah Equiano, also writing from his own experience as a slave, in one of the most eloquent and damning accounts of European savagery, recounts how he was robbed of communication as well as of his freedom. In his autobiography (published in 1789) Equiano describes how finding someone who spoke the same language was one of the only sources of comfort on the slave ships (Equiano 1967: 27).[21] These accounts reveal the degree to which social relations, class struggle in the raw, literally suppressed, and then forged, language. Thus, the Middle Passage was no discursive exercise; language was all but submerged in the brutality of the experience. This was the pursuit of trade laid bare, 'a new refinement in cruelty', 'a scene of horror almost inconceivable' (Equiano 1967: 29), out of which Yorubas, Akans, Ibos, Angolans were forced to shape a new language – one that, would also be disparaged and stigmatized even after the abolition of slavery (Todd 1974: 87).

The slave trade was an extreme case, but the spread of English was often intertwined with conflict and oppression. In the last century, Irish schoolchildren were forbidden to speak Irish, and Irish emigrants met with hostility when they spoke Irish in the slums of Manchester or Liverpool.[22] In India English was a demarcation line between privilege and dispossession (Ahmad 1992: 212). In the Malay States under British rule, selective education in English for the few was based on racist stereotyping of most other Malays as 'lazy natives' (Pennycook 1994a: 89). These scars of oppression cannot be simply willed away. Volosinov describes the weight of this legacy: 'this role of the alien word led to its coalescence in the depth of historical consciousness of nations with the idea of authority, the idea of power, the idea of holiness, the idea of truth, and dictated that notions about the world be preeminently oriented toward the alien word' (1973: 75). If history intrudes deep into language it is also the case that languages have a history, moulded by specific social circumstances, and they too are fluid and in a constant process of change. This historical make-up of a language applies to English, and also to how it is perceived.

Perceptions of English are political and clash *because* they are rooted in historical experience and shaped by social classes. In India English is a matter of deep contention. Kachru explains how it is seen as an 'Aladdin's lamp' that lights the way to business, technology, science and travel and as the provider of power and travel (1986b: 1). Dua sees English as serving the vested interests of elites and bureaucrats, and its promotion as undermining Hindi (Dua 1994). For Ahmad, English is a badge of class in both colonial and post-colonial settings in India and in other states. New rulers have monopolized English through academic and state institutions (Ahmad 1992: 73). It is this embracing of English by post-colonial rulers that has led Ngugi, in the Kenyan context, to reject English as a bearer of colonial culture and alienation and to see writing in his native Gîkûyû as a political act (Ngugi 1993).

The ambivalence about English is well captured by Achebe in his novel *No Longer At Ease*. Obi, the main character and representative of the hopes and desires of Achebe's generation, is away from Nigeria in England on a scholarship. He expresses well the 'shame' that English evoked for him:

> Four years in England had filled Obi with a longing to be back in Umuofia. This feeling was sometimes so strong that he found himself feeling ashamed of studying English for his degree. He spoke Ibo whenever he had the least opportunity of doing so. Nothing gave him greater pleasure than to find another Ibo-speaking student in a London bus. But when he had to speak in English with a Nigerian students from another tribe he lowered his voice. It was humiliating to have to speak to one's countryman in a foreign language, especially in the presence of the proud owners of that language. They would naturally assume that one had no language of one's own. He wished they were here today to see. Let them come to Umuofia now and listen to the talk of men who made a great art of conversation. Let them come and see men and women and children who knew how to live, whose joy of life had not yet been killed by those who claimed to teach other nations how to live. (Achebe 1988: 214)

But also, Obi feels the impact of a new language:

> He said words in his mind that he could not say out aloud even when he was alone. Strangely enough, all the words were in his mother tongue. He could say any English word . . . but some Ibo words simply would not proceed from his mouth. It was no doubt his early training that operated this censorship, English words filtering through because they were learnt later in life. (Achebe 1988: 210)

Achebe highlights the slippery and highly political nature of language. It is the mixed feelings that Obi feels which show that English cannot simply be seen as uniformly oppressive. English cannot be equated with the language of the oppressor, which is why the concept of linguistic imperialism is inadequate. Sometimes historically it has been identified with those fighting back against imperialism. English in South Africa was linked with opposition to apartheid. In a population of 42 million only about 3.6 million speak English. Afrikaans was often enforced as a medium of instruction, and in 1976 the Soweto riots were sparked off by the apartheid regime imposing Afrikaans in black schools. English symbolized revolt and a link with opponents to the apartheid regime outside South Africa. It was a political issue – some even called it 'People's English' – which centred on access to education for the black majority (Pierce 1989). Another colonial language – French – was also not uniformly identified with oppression. At the time of the French revolution, the French language was no barrier to former slaves who rebelled in the Caribbean island of San Domingo; it was seen as the language of revolution. In Senegal, it was taken by some to be the language of freedom (Djite 1992). In other words, how a language is seen is not just as a mechanical identification with imperialism but is shaped by historical circumstance.

But beyond specific historical factors, divergent views of English rest on a deeper contradiction at the heart of imperialism itself. Marx in his writings on India reveals the degree to which the spread of colonialism involved two different but interwoven processes. It constituted primitive accumulation of capital which wrought destruction and oppression, what he called 'a bleeding process with a vengeance' (Marx and Engels 1959: 340). But it also represented social transformation arising from massive changes in production which spawned a social force which had the potential to overthrow imperial rule (Marx and Engels 1959: 85). Elements of this contradiction lie within language. The relationship between language and society is dialectical: it has been shaped by society but it can also act on society. Ahmad sums it up succinctly in a memorable passage, in which he recognizes the complexity of the debate surrounding English in India. He concludes:

One cannot eject English now, on the basis of its initially colonial insertion, any more than one can boycott the railways for that same reason. . . . History is not open to correction through a return passage to an imaginary point centuries ago, before colonial deformation set in, or before the insertion of Islam before that, or earlier still, before the invasions of what are generally called the Aryan tribes. Indian civiliza-tional ethos, if there is one, is in any case deeply marked by the processes of Indianization of idioms and instruments. . . . English is simply one of India's languages now and what is at issue is not the possibility of its ejection but the mode of its assimilation into our social fabric and the manner in which this language like any other substantial structure of linguistic difference is used in the process of class formation and social privilege in the here and now. (Ahmad 1992: 77)

Like railways, language can be used for many purposes, and not always those laid down by its British engineers. Ideology is not a given in language but contested even as it is spoken. Views of the spread of English that do not take this into account are caught in the historical dead-end of linguistic determinism.

The position of English in Ireland has always contained similar contradictions. A tool of oppression, it was also a useful instrument of revolt. In Ireland in the nineteenth and early twentieth centuries the death of Irish chimed with English dominance: 'to impose another language on [a] people is to send their history adrift among the accidents of translation – 'tis to tear their identity from all places', in the words of one early Irish nationalist (Davis 1974: 97–98). Yet even this was written in English, for the Irish nationalist movement, like that in India, spoke English. Very often those most resolute fighters against British rule were sceptical of the way nationalists used the Irish language as a cultural cloak under which the conservatism of their own project could be hidden. The Irish socialist, James Connolly, for example, debunked the mystical wanderings of some of the Gaelic revivalists. 'You cannot teach starving men Gaelic,' he wrote. 'The most priceless manuscript of ancient Celtic lore would hold but second place in their esteem beside a rasher of bacon' (quoted in Allen 1990: 22). Such an approach did not gloss over the fact that the suppression of the Irish language had been a part of British rule nor that the rise of cultural nationalism in the early 1900s was also part of a growing resistance to British rule, which culminated in 1916. But Connolly also saw, with foresight, that the linguistic equivalent of painting the pillarboxes green was an ideology with its own class interests and not one that socialists should accept uncritically (Allen 1990: 22–23).

In other words, promotion of the use of the indigenous tongue is not *per se* subversive of the existing order. Ruling classes have used the national language in twentieth-century history for their own class interests and to preserve the social order, not to upturn it. Formerly suppressed languages can become oppressive. The examples of these about-turns are many. Hindi has been used divisively in India, in the past and today by Hindu chauvinists seeking to oppress others. In Somalia, the promulgation of Somali has often intensified, not weakened, factional struggles. The promotion of Bahasa Malaysia in the Malaysia of the 1960s bred resentment among the Chinese and riots ensued (SarDesai 1997: 286). The use of Swahili in Tanzania turned out to be less about social inclusion than about continuing the colonial legacy: under German rule, Swahili was also promoted as the medium of instruction.[23] In Rwanda and Burundi where local languages have become official, they have also become the ticket to social promotion (Bayart 1993: 174–175). Throughout history, as Bayart insists, inequality has been given ideological expression through 'disglossy' – by the coexistence of a scholarly language, or one that is the conduit to positions of power, and a popular language. This is a political fact with linguistic trappings.

Even in Ireland, where the suppression of Irish by the British constitutes a sorry tale, new rulers came to give a particular slant to Irish in the Irish Free State, established in 1922, which was both self-serving and hypocritical. National identity and national languages are not timeless husks; their political significance is different this century to what it was in the revolutionary eighteenth. Even the promotion of Irish in the Gaelic League in an Ireland still ruled by the British linked it to radicalism in a way that it was not later, even if then it had its profoundly conservative advocates. Irish nationalists after 1922 came to appeal to the Irish language, for more subtle conservative reasons, seeking a wished-for unity in nation that the class divisions of Irish society belied. In the new state of Southern Ireland, with many nationalist dreams dashed on the rocks of partition, the Irish language became a route towards a government job and a badge of the new-style rulers. As Kiberd remarks, 'Whereas in the nineteenth century many had been caned for speaking Irish, many were now punished for not speaking it properly or for not speaking it all' (Kiberd 1996: 265). The story of Irish in Southern Ireland echoes many a similar tale in post-colonial countries where, as Harman points out, nationalist late-comers have sought to promote their own national language for their own class interests (Harman 1992). Far from it being a question of linguistic self-determination and choice, it has become another aspect of class society.

These realities make claims for language exclusion and revivalism appear often as a forlorn attempt to reinvent imagined communities and can end up as a mirror-image of the oppression it opposed. They miss, furthermore, the dialectical character of language. Language in history has to be taken not as language constructing history, but more dialectically, as 'practical con-sciousness' in Marx's terms. Caliban declares that if he has been taught language he has also been taught to curse. Achebe, too, in a memorable piece, picks up James Baldwin's observation that his quarrel with English was not with the language but with the fact that it reflected none of his experience. Achebe declares: '[F]or me there is no other choice. I have been given this language and I intend to use it' (Achebe 1977). Balwin and Achebe – from Harlem and Nigeria, respectively – are themselves representative of how the conditions that administered oppression can feed into revolt, of how English, once the language of the oppressor, can become the language of the oppressed. Speaking that revolt in English, what's more, may become the spectre that will come to haunt the world order which so confidently promotes World English today.

Notes

1 Crystal draws his data from a variety of sources and because there is little reliable direct research on actual numbers speaking English, he admits that he has had to make assumptions which are not fully reliable. For example where no official linguistic estimate is available, he was obliged to total figures from numbers assumed to have completed secondary or further education. In Africa, as Schmied (1991) points out, these figures are misleading since both attendance and actual English competence are nearly impossible to deduce from official figures of those attending school. Crystal is only too aware of these difficulties and his figures are much more modest than some estimates which have put the figure at 1 billion. The figures used in this paragraph are taken from the data mainly given in Chapter 4 of Crystal (1997).

2 Hume was a fervent promoter of English and all things English. He held that English in America would 'promise superior stability and duration' because in America 'we need dread the inundation of barbarians less', as Bailey notes (1991:

100). Hume's open racism is not often alluded to. *Of National Characters*, published in 1753, extols the virtues of the white race and suspects 'negroes to be naturally inferior to whites', particularly concerning their use of language (see Hiro 1992: 4). It is unfortunate that some linguists' opinion of Hume is not tempered by this fact (see for example Coulmas 1992).

3 Africa collectively has seen its share of world investment fall by half to 0.5 per cent since the early 1980s (World Bank, quoted in Oxfam 1995).

4 In Ireland, where many US computer companies are based, only a narrow band of relatively well-off homes have access to computers. The *average* household income of Net surfers is IR£35,000 and numbers accessing the Internet actually fell in 1997 (see *Irish Times*, 23 June 1998).

5 While EIL, ESL, etc., originally coined in the language learning context, are not normally referred to as varieties, in the growing literature on the spread of English these terms are more widely used in a descriptive sociolinguistic sense. Schmied in his typology of English in Africa is an example. It is indeed difficult to claim that EIL or EWL is a stable entity of English in any meaningful sense. ESL, certainly, due to the fact that it is often in a state of transition and incremental acquisition, hardly constitutes a constant or identifiable variety in the way that a pidgin or a dialect does.

6 This is the same Trevelyan that transferred from the Indian Civil Service to the British Treasury in 1838. During the Irish Famine he oversaw the export of food from Ireland and defended it in *The Irish Crisis* (1848). By this time, he had abandoned all linguistic and cultural aspirations for the natives and instead turned to more reliable *laissez-faire* methods – the market. These methods rid Ireland of 2 million of its native inhabitants, mainly by death, starvation, disease and emigration. This had a devastating impact on the linguistic map of Ireland, with numbers speaking Irish as a first language rapidly declining (see McCrum et al. 1986: 196, Hindley 1990, Eagleton 1995: 22–26).

7 Even more liberally minded people such as J.S. Mill saw themselves as 'Lords of Human Kind', in V.G. Kiernan's phrase. They sought to nurture a small elite group in India who would receive education in English. Mill believed that only the top layer of society should have an education geared towards training the mind since he believed that the acquisition of intelligence must be 'reserved for those who are not required to labour' (Viswanathan 1989: 150. See also 116, 149–150, 183 and Kiernan 1969).

8 Said's earlier works on the subject – particularly *Orientalism* – lay greater emphasis on discourse in its own right as a power construct. For a discussion of this, and a critique of Said's earlier position, see Ahmads 'Orientalism and after' in Ahmad (1992).

9 It was this type of ignorance and prejudice that fed later misunderstanding and disparagement of pidgins and creoles; even quite recently one writer on the subject held that Creole languages 'may constitute a handicap to the Creole speaker's personal intellectual development' (quoted in Todd 1974: 87).

10 Kipling's father was himself a teacher in British India. For an account of Kipling's pro-imperialist, nevertheless perceptive, view of imperialism, see Said's interpretation (Said 1993: 159–194).

11 Made by the Commonwealth African states in 1965 (quoted in Bailey 1991: 162).

12 He does qualify this by adding that other languages can say things that

English-speakers cannot. Yet his point is that English, with a larger vocabulary and greater richness, is invested with a special power.

13 Williams also sees Fishman's reading of *disglossia* (societal and institutionalized bilingualism) as mechanical. The social presence of more than one language is explained as language simply reflecting society. In this language/society reciprocity, according to Williams, Fishman presents a static view of society in which the way things are is inevitable and in which social conflict and change is absent (Williams 1992: 98).

14 In his analysis of imperialism, Phillipson takes much from Galtung. Galtung's view is a pacifist variant of Dependency Theory which sees imperialism in core–periphery terms. Its better-known proponents are André Gunder Frank, who characterized the third world as locked into poverty or the 'development of under development' as a result of transfer of wealth to the first world (see Frank 1978). Others include Amin and Baran, who argued that local ruling classes in third world countries were *comprador bourgeoisies* who were the puppets of Western regimes and pursued policies that locked their peoples further into poverty. For an account of these versions see Brewer (1980) and for a Marxist critique, see Callinicos (1987).

15 With 15.2 per cent of her people living in 'human poverty', Ireland has the highest proportion of people living in poverty in the industrialized world. These figures were given in the UN *Human Development Report* (1998); for a synopsis of its findings see the *Irish Times*, Wednesday, 9 September 1998.

16 See Haynes 1985 (Chapter 2) for an excellent account of Bukharin's account of imperialism.

17 Where under the former Czechoslovakia, there was no translation between Czech and Slovak, after the creation of the Slovak republic, Slovak subtitles conveniently appeared for TV programmes in Czech.

18 For a review of this book see Holborow (1996).

19 See Rainbow (1987: 206–212) for a shortened version of Foucault's account of Panopticism and its symbolism of the disciplinary methods that society uses for its will to power. Foucault accords these techniques power-giving properties and Pennycook, too, sees the panopticon as a symbol of colonialism's will to describe (1994a: 97–98).

20 Crystal, for example, defends multilingualism but then informs us that the suggestion for his book *English as a Global Language* came from the chairman of US English, the Official English campaign (1997: ix), which is not particularly reassuring for linguistic rights. (For the political implications of the Official English campaign see Ricento 1995.)

21 Although Equiano was first enslaved by Africans, the advent of the European slave trade brought new horrors of brutality, separation and estrangement. His account of the separation from his sister is unforgettable (1967: 21). Equiano, also known as Gustavus Vassa, was freed in 1766, and campaigned in England for the abolition of slavery. (See Edwards's introduction to his autobiography for an account of his life: Equiano 1967.)

22 Moody gives a vivid account of what it meant to be Irish in Little Ireland in the Manchester area in the 1850s (Moody 1982).

23 For an account of the use of Swahili in Tanzania see Kanyoro (1991).

4   Women, Language and the Limits of Feminism

'Brainwashing that deprecates Western learning'; 'The closing of the American mind'; 'A lumpen-feminist assault' (Bloom 1986, D'Souza 1992, Hughes 1993). No insult, it seems, is contemptible enough to describe those who advocate multiculturalism, sexual equality and the inclusion of black writers on degree courses on American campuses. The shrill attack on 'political correctness' in the US, where it originated in the late 1980s, has also found enthusiastic echoes this side of the Atlantic. Paul Johnson, for example, has excoriated this 'new form of totalitarianism' and 'the debased ideological caracoles' from these 'sex war puritans' (Johnson 1996). Political correctness (PC), an indeterminate label, more often invoked by those who oppose it than by its supporters, has become in the 1990s the catch-all *bête noire*, denounced in the media, and often the pretext to breathe life back into traditional notions of sexism and racism.

This is today's political context for any discussion of sexism and language. Language has figured large in the PC controversy, which one collection of essays on the subject describes as 'the War of the Words' (Dunant 1994). It has been hotly debated on campuses, with non-sexist guidelines being introduced in universities from Canberra to Cork, though few colleges outside the US have gone as far as adding disciplinary procedures. 'Politically correct' language is the aspect of the debate which has most impinged on popular consciousness. Expressions such as 'follicularly impaired' or 'vertically challenged' (rarely used by anyone, in earnest, at least) have been repeated in the media to drive the point home.

The controversy has divided supporters and detractors along unexpected lines. Berman remarks that 'liberals and old-school leftists joined the neo-conservatives' and this was a 'a new and significant aspect' (Berman 1992: 5). For example, Marxist historian of the American ante-bellum South, Eugene Genovese, is repelled by the 'campus totalitarians' and labels political correctness the new McCarthyism (Genovese 1991). Edward Said, one of the first to chart the political connections between culture and Empire, has unexpectedly accused PC supporters of glorified victimhood and casual reductiveness, seeing feminist interventions as 'negative, flat-minded thinking' (Said 1992: 176). Veteran radical campaigner Nat Hentoff of *Village Voice* condemns PCers as destructively anti-free speech and intimidatory (Hentoff 1992).

These charges, coming from such unlikely quarters, are serious, and seem to shift the political terrain. It is necessary therefore, before embarking on the main subject of this chapter, to look at origins of this debate and characterize the general political context. This background is essential to understanding the political signifi-cance of current approaches to language and sexism.

Despite what is claimed, political correctness campaigns, even at their most zealous, have little in common with old-style McCarthy-ism. As Molyneux reminds us, 'McCarthyism at its height had the power to arraign before Congress, fire, blacklist, deport, drive into exile and imprison thousands of supposed Communists and leftists from all walks of life including Hollywood, teaching and academia itself' (Molyneux 1994: 47). It is doubtful whether anyone has been forced into exile because of the power of feminists or multiculturalists. The social forces on the side of Senator Joe McCarthy in the 1940s, with all the power of state institutions on his side, were considerably weightier than the academics referred to today.

Contradicting certain accounts of the large numbers of 'tenured radicals', particularly those by Kimball (1990), D'Souza and Bloom, the composition of American universities remains overwhelmingly white and middle class and, in the majority, male. While 55 per cent of all college students in 1991 were women, women make up one-third of graduate students. In 1995, women represented 27–28 per cent of university faculties (Scott 1995). In other parts of the English-speaking world, women's participation in academic insti-tutions is far worse.[1] As many lecturers and students are aware, minorities and radicals are not in control in academic institutions.

The critics of political correctness also underestimate the extent of discrimination against women in society. Far from feminism being the dominant culture, and *despite* all the attention it receives, sexism is still widespread, in the US and elsewhere. Statistics reveal the international uniformity of women earning on average two-thirds of what men earn, remaining politically and economically discriminated against, and shouldering the main burden of parenthood (Callen and Wren 1994: 5, Nelson and Chowdhury 1994, Cockburn 1995, Utting 1995, McCashin 1996). This is the reality to be borne in mind when examining the political correctness issue. A challenge to sexist language, even an awkwardly formal one like advocating 'correct' usage, is a small counter-move against the overwhelming discrimination against women.

If such distortions exist, therefore, wider ideological questions would seem to be at issue. Gates has correctly characterized the anti-PC crusade as representing the nostalgic return to the US pre-Civil War days, when 'men were men and men were white, when scholar-critics were white men, and women and persons of color were voiceless, faceless servants and laborers, pouring tea and filling brandy snifters in the boardrooms of old boys' clubs' (Gates 1992: 17). Most commentators agree that the controversy revolves around the legacy of the radical 1960s (Berman 1992: 1–26, Williams 1995: 1–8). In the economic and political uncertainties of the 1990s in America, and elsewhere, conservative establishments have wanted to erase the memory of the 1960s which lingers so uncomfortably for them. Some former radicals have joined their project. Naomi Wolf, for example, under the misnomer of 'post-feminism', has condemned 1960s permissiveness and openly embraced the wonders of wealth and capitalism (Wolf 1994, 1997).

The steadfast defenders of radicalism, however, occupy a very different political terrain to that which they inhabited in the 1960s and it is this which makes the political correctness campaign vulnerable. Political awareness, according to their theories, takes crucial shape, not on the streets, nor indeed in society, but in the more lofty heights of academia and the prescriptive terrain of language. 'Political correctness' is a classic example of the attempt to reform by decree, and, like all such projects, is seen with suspicion by those who resent being told what is good for them. Guidelines, handbooks and anti-sexist committees are blunt political instruments. Instituted from above, they conduct the battle at one remove. The very concept of 'politically correct' language evokes a somewhat sterilized view of politics, removed from the cut and thrust of real political movements. Changes in language *happen* more than they are decreed. They occur as part of intense social upheaval, and certainly do not come about in any neat and tidy way that can be linguistically catalogued. Barbara Ehrenreich is right to highlight this abstraction and detachment from any real struggles and to point out that changing language is not the same as fighting for change in practice (Ehrenreich 1992).

This ultra-formalist approach springs from the social position that many of the fervent PCers occupy. Professors, members of faculty, some teachers and other professionals, are the same people who gained from the reforms and changes ushered in amid the 1960s' upheavals. Along with a few members of minority groups, some came to occupy established positions within a new middle class. Radicalism found itself stranded at the lecturer's podium, and marooned in the wake of the 1980s, one of the most right-wing decades. In these circumstances, academic interpretation came to replace political activity, as various strands of postmodernism arcanely sought to prove. Language became the battleground rather than the oppression itself. This was not a current restricted to the US. The political circumstances in Britain were somewhat different but the same emphasis emerged, particularly in academic circles. Feminist and linguist, Deborah Cameron betokens the trend when she claims: 'Radicals of my generation and succeeding generations do attach more importance to linguistic and other representation than their predecessors did, so that we regard words and images as useful material with which to work for social change' (Cameron 1994: 24). To what extent representation constitutes political activity or social change, and whether changing language is itself a political project, will be one of the subjects of this chapter.

These were some of the elements, then, of the overall political context of the PC controversy which determined the way the debate arose. They continue to infuse the discussion about women and language today. More generally, the question of sexism and language, how and why sexism manifests itself in language, goes to the heart of the relationship between language and society. English has been at the centre of the discussion about the sexist use of language, with sexism in language most debated in the US,

Britain and Australia. Non-sexist linguistic guidelines have been a mainly English phenomenon.[2] This chapter will examine critically the interpretations of the links between sex and language. First it questions the view that language is a sexist structure *per se*. In relation to this, it looks at the degree to which non-sexist language reform has influenced language and, more generally, the relationship of language change to social change. Second, it asks whether women can be said to speak in a special way or have certain speaking styles. Some feminist linguists have claimed that women are condemned linguistically to lose out, while others have argued that women have a more cooperative way of speaking which derives from their oppression. Third, women are said to be more status-conscious linguistically in so far as they tend to use more standard and prestigious forms. To what extent is this true? The chapter concludes on a question which others have begun to ask, namely whether the concept of gender is the best way to approach the question of women's oppression and language.

Is Language 'Man-made'?

'Males, as the dominant group, have produced language, thought and reality.' Ever since Dale Spender expressed this view in her book *Man-made Language* (Spender 1985: 143), there has been support for the idea that language does not merely reflect sexism in society but actually creates it. This view is most enthusiastically espoused by radical feminism (Daly and Caputi 1988, Penelope 1990). But other versions are more widely accepted, and standard textbooks on language and gender acknowledge Spender's influence (Thorne et al. 1983). In the US, Spender's singling out of language was given an intellectual boost by the influence of French post-structuralist feminism, which held that 'discourses were sexed' and that 'man seems to have wanted . . . to give the universe his own gender' (Irigaray 1993). Spender has reiterated her original standpoint more recently, underlining the causative role of language in sexism, this time in the context of cyberspace (Spender 1995). Spender's 1985 book marked the beginning of a particular feminist approach to sexism in language. Her plea for language reform was taken further with the appearance of non-sexist linguistic guidelines and speech codes (Miller and Swift 1989 being one of the better known). It is worth examining in some detail the suppositions behind the view that language creates women's oppression.

Spender's claim stems from the view that language itself determines the limits of our world. For Spender social experience *is* language. 'Language . . . is our means of ordering, classifying and manipulating the world. It is through language that we become members of a human community, that the world becomes comprehensible and meaningful, that we bring into existence the world in which we live' (Spender 1985: 3). This has much in common with what has come to be known as the Sapir–Whorf Hypothesis, and, more specifically, the writings of Benjamin Lee Whorf, as Spender acknowledges (1985: 163). Whorf's writings challenged dominant (and racist) views about 'primitive' peoples and languages, and showed how language, socially formed and socially specific, could not be taken uncritically as a neutral instrument of thought. His work on the language of native Americans, particularly the Hopi, led him to believe that language is itself a world view and that the 'phenomena of a language are, to its own speakers, largely of a background character and so are outside the critical consciousness and control of the speaker'. He argued that language is the pattern by which we 'cut nature up, organize it into concepts and ascribe significances': the way in which we order the world (Whorf 1956: 213). Whorf's conclusion that languages are non-equivalent and that linguistic categorization shapes thinking labelled him a linguistic relativist, and some of his more extreme formulations were linguistically deterministic. 'Mind in the grip of language' was how Bolger described Whorf's views (Bolger 1968: Chapter 13).[3]

Spender embraces many of the Whorfian themes, but takes his linguistic determinism further. She quotes extensively from Whorf and repeats his view that linguistic structures determine thought. Spender claims that there are two languages inhabiting two different worlds and experiences, one for women and one for men. The two are mutually untranslatable and do not mutually communicate, a kind of linguistic apartheid, as one Spender critic has described it (Beezer 1984).

Spender argues that language, and she refers explicitly to English, has been created by males and continues to be under their control. 'Historically it has been the structures, the categories and the meanings which have been invented by males . . . and they have then been validated by reference to other males. . . . There *is* sexism in the language, it *does* enhance the position of males and males *have* had control over the production of cultural forms. It therefore seems credible to assume males have encoded sexism into the language to consolidate their claims of male supremacy' (Spender 1985: 143–144). 'The position of woman as non-standard as other and in the wrong . . . was intentionally constructed in the English language' (Spender 1995: 18).

Spender argues that there is a number of ways that sexism structures English. The language systematically puts women down. In what she calls the 'semantic derogation of women' (after Schulz 1975), Spender charts the use of words which are marked for females and claims they have become 'pejorated'. Various examples are given: *Lord* still preserves its initial meaning but *Lady* has undergone 'a process of democratic levelling' and is no longer reserved for women of high rank. Other traditionally derogatory meanings exist for *Madam, Mistress,* and *Queen* unlike their male equivalents. This marks, according to Spender, the existence of 'a fundamental semantic "rule" in a society which constructs male supremacy' (Spender 1985: 17–18).

Spender sees the use of the generic *he/man* through this lens, which she categorizes variously as a male bias in language, androcentric, masculinist and patriarchal. This 'penalizing of women' (1985: 52) has proceeded through language prescription, the compilation of dictionaries and regulatory measures such as Acts of Parliament. For example, she recounts how John Kirkby, in 1746, formulated his Eighty Eight Grammatical Rules, which insisted that men were entitled to be more important because they were 'more comprehensive' (1985: 148). She states, 'Apart from the fact that he was male – and that he had inflated ideas about his own importance – Richard Kirkby doesn't appear to have had any other qualifications for making his new rule; the only basis for *man* becoming the standard seems to be that he – and a few other like-minded men – felt that their sex had a greater claim to humanity.' She quotes the 1850 Act of Parliament in Britain which decreed that man should be the standard form and that by law it would encompass woman (Spender 1995: 19).

Finally, Spender declares that women's meanings have been 'muted' and women themselves silenced by the dominance of 'male language'. Women need to reclaim their own language, write their own dictionaries and invent new words. 'The politics of naming', following the model of women's consciousness-raising groups, can create the world anew and give voice to oppression, the 'experience without a name'. 'We need a language which constructs the reality of women's autonomy, women's strength, women's power' (Spender 1985: 190). The inventing of 'women's words' is, according to Spender, the way out. 'Words make a difference'; *herstory* and *malestream* are examples she gives as being 'very meaningful terms for women' which 'name things which happen to women every day as they are confronted with male versions of events and find themselves dismissed outside the male-mainstream' (1995: 28).

Spender's assessment of the role of language is, as Cameron rightly points out, highly determinist (Cameron 1992: 146–148). Whorf at least made some concessions to social and cultural influences in the construction of language systems by comparing two languages in two differently organized societies. Spender posits a uniform, male, linguistic 'encoding' within one society, irrespective of a social experience shared by both sexes. Where Whorf's determinism was social, Spender's is biological. Whorf's linguistic determinism contained the obvious flaw that if language categories are causally linked to cognition, it followed that meanings were inaccessible across languages. However, translation does tell us something of the original meaning. Whorf himself *does* manage to express in English very detailed insights about the Hopi world despite the language constraints that he acknowledges. Spender is caught in the same contradiction. Linguistic codes and symbols are all we have, she tells us: we may never know the 'real'. 'Once [human beings] have a language, they can only see arbitrary things' (Spender 1985: 138). 'The trap that we have made is so pervasive that we cannot envisage a world constructed on any other lines' (1985: 142). This begs the obvious question about how Spender has managed to escape from the linguistic weight of male words, and see the light.

Furthermore, no explanation of the origins of this awesome power that men have is ever given. Spender simply posits the existence of male power and builds a theory upon this assumption, the important theoretical question as to why sexism in society exists is not explored. We are told that 'patriarchal society is based on the belief that the male is the superior sex and many of the social institutions and much social practice is then organized to reflect this belief', and that the characteristic of 'patriarchy . . . is the means by which one half of the human population is able to insist that the other half sees things its way' (1985: 1–2). We gather that 'patriarchy' is a social structure, but why or how society or societies should be organized around patriarchy or why it should assert itself at a particular time is given no historical or social foundation. It simply *is*. Why men should so conspire, how social institutions have come to be at their disposal, we are not told. Spender's understanding of society, as Beezer points out, is one which falls back on the tautology that males are powerful because they are males (Beezer 1984: 18). This is not an uncommon assumption in writings about sex and language, as we shall see.

The view that male domination is overriding is inadequate as a social theory but it is also, Beezer notes, damaging to the very people it hopes to address – women. For the other side of the inevitability of male power is the inevitability of women in thrall. Language, for Spender, is the root of the dichotomy. But, if language is 'man-made', with expression and meaning being determined by the male of the species, where does that leave women's use of the language? Why would women acquiesce in the speaking of a language that is not 'theirs'? Spender's only way out of this conundrum is to introduce the concept of a 'women's language', the encoding of women's meanings, 'the naming from their own perspective' (Spender 1985: 61). This path involves some sweeping statements about what women linguistically do, which are uncorroborated and strangely redolent of stereotypical views of women. Spender declares, for example, that women do not use slang (1995: 28), despite the fact that research has shown otherwise.[4] Spender posits not one language that humans speak but two; one defined as being 'authoritative', 'serious', 'direct', the other, presumably, none of these things, or their opposite. Linguistic determinism spills over into biological determinism. It

locks women into a fated oppression which now becomes their
defining condition, including the language they use. Women as
agents in history, the possibility of emancipation, in terms of
women being equal participants in human society, simply does not
figure in this determinist construction.[5]

Spender's determinism springs from extrapolating a theory of
male domination from an intuition about how women speak.
Ironically, this approach, far from challenging dominant sexist
ideas, starts from the same instilled beliefs. She sees language and
society in ahistorical terms; semantics and syntax are presented as
if suspended timelessly, like the sword of Damocles, above us all.
Her description of the 'fundamental male semantic rule' is an
example. She claims that words which are marked for females,
through the 'fundamental male semantic rule', have become
'pejorated', but fails to explain *how* and *when* they came to be so,
and why, at one time, they were not. She notes changes between
courtesan and *madam* today compared with their more neutral
meanings in the past, but fails to explain what moved males to
intervene to bring about this change. Her list is highly selective and
seems to ignore the many different meaning and emphases to any
given word. Nor is it the case that even *woman* and *lady* have the
wholly negative and demeaning connotations that Spender claims
for them.[6] What Spender leaves out is any dynamic to language,
that meanings are *unstable* because they spring from interaction
between listener and hearer, and in a specific historical context.
They are, in Volosinov's words, multiaccentual, bridges thrown
between speaker and hearer in specific historical and social
territory (Volosinov 1973: 86).[7] Yet Spender's view of language is
static and imposed.

Language is not a changeless given, and does not blindly follow a
semantic rule. Even with the use of the generic *he/man*, things are not
so one-dimensional, nor so all-encompassingly 'man-made'. It is
true that across-the-board use of *he* for unmarked nouns and *man* for
humans or humanity does not take account of women and is thereby
sexist. This is not to say, however, that, down through history, its
use ensured that women were unambiguously demeaned or that
every time it was used it was a blow struck against women. Life
was rather more complicated. Despite Spender's claim, Kirkby's
Grammatical Rules which proposed the male generic, for example,

were not simply an example of the creation of ideology by fiat. Rather, they were a reflection of a social set-up already in existence where women were relegated to second place. Kirkby was part of an increasingly dominant social class that was consciously developing its own world view, in which language prescriptivism, and sexism, played their part. It was the articulation of an ideology which was historically functional for the ruling orders, not a sudden biological impulse on the part of men.

Furthermore, explaining the linguistic use of the generic *he/man* as part of an overall male stratagem is unsatisfactory. Spender is in no doubt that men conspired to introduce these conventions with the express purpose of putting women down, and that they were spectacularly successful. Yet, even the generic *he/man* has been riddled with ambiguities and historical contingencies. Such expressions while linguistically demeaning women do not have the same social force or predictable uniformity as oppression in real life. Far from there being an undifferentiated male imposition of the generic *he/man*, from the eighteenth century to today, its meanings and uses have been ambiguous. Spender's claim that 'man' has always stood for men alone is misleading (1995: 20). After all, it was a linguistic convention that was supposed to stand for men *and* women, and language-users took it as such. To say that women were cut out altogether, as Spender and others suggest, is to make language-users into duped speakers and women inexplicably accomplices in their own denigration and effacement. *Mankind* and *man* are sexist generics because they did cover women, whether in anthropology or in evolution.[8] The example that Spender gives taken from Miller and Swift (1976: 26) – 'man being a mammal breastfeeds his young' – which they claim is taken as a joke (1976: 21) may well be, but it also stands as a dramatic example of ambiguity and brings the contradiction of the convention to the fore. Even those concerned with linguistic discrimination against women do not see women written out of the generic *he*. Robin Lakoff, as late as 1975, when she first published her book on women's language, quite unthinkingly uses the generic 'he' (for example Lakoff 1975: 18–19), but one could fairly assume that she is including women. The problem was that these terms bore and still bear the ideological contradictions of their societies. To present ideology as an undifferentiated steamroller against women is to misunderstand the way in which women's social position has been subject to change, how oppression itself has been perceived and experienced differently, and how language is replete with all the contradictions of its users, men and women. Language is not amenable to total oppressive manipulation, because human beings actually use language rather than merely spouting it.

Language and Social Change

Spender's work provided something of an impetus to language reform and the introduction of non-sexist speech codes. In many institutions – universities, professional associations, trade unions – it is now quite common to have guides for the use of non-discriminatory language. Miller and Swift's *Handbook of Non-Sexist Writing*, first published in 1981 and reprinted in both the US and Britain, was one of the first in a general trend of such publications. The University of Western Australia, for example, issued such a guide in 1993. It explains that 'the use of gender-marked terms perpetuates and reinforces the outdated attitude that women are to be considered first as female and second as persons of skill and talent' (University of Western Australia 1993). The University of Strathclyde's *Guidelines for Staff and Students* advocates 'gender-free language' with reference to similar examples, adding a section gender-marked for 'Equal Speaking Rights' calling for men not to interrupt women and urging chairs of meetings to 'be aware of gender-related patterns in who speaks and who is silent' (University of Strathclyde 1994). It is such guidelines that have triggered some of the controversy described at the beginning of this chapter. Leaving aside the motivations of those who have objected to these guidelines, the question about the political role the guidelines play remains. How much can language reform do towards eradicating sexism in language?

Let us start by recognizing that what words people use is a highly political issue. Very often it is precisely those words that describe people which are most strongly infused with the particular character of the social relations. In microcosm they mark the divisions within society. And they can be used with great effect, seeming to legitimize divisions as well as recording them. It is no coincidence that the word 'race', for instance, entered the European languages just when the slave trade developed. It is a term with little scientific basis and meaningless except in ideological terms. As one American anthropologist has argued, it represents a word that has exercised evil tyranny over human minds and as one of 'the most tragic errors of our time' should be permanently removed from the vocabulary (Fryer 1993: 61). Such words have become distilled ideology and their use a political statement. The meaning of words as social phenomena constructed within social relations was described by Volosinov as a bridge between one socially organized person and another. This intensely ideological aspect to language was well summed up by Bakhtin, who explains why language is such a political issue:

> language for the individual consciousness, lies on the borderline between oneself and the other. The world in language is half someone else's. It becomes 'one's own' only when the speaker populates it with their own intention, their own accent. . . . Prior to this moment of appropriation, the word does not exist in a neutral and impersonal language . . . but rather it exists in other people's mouths, in other people's contexts, serving other people's intentions: it is from there that one must take the word and make it one's own. . . . Language . . . is populated – over-populated – with the intentions of others. (Bakhtin 1981: 293–294)

Bakhtin calls this struggle for meaning, this coming together of the general and the individual, *social evaluation*. This process is an integral part of the construction of meaning in language, and linked to both the overall dominant ideology and the 'historical actuality' of the individual utterance. Words can become a cross-roads for different ideological meanings.[9]

At times of social upheaval this process is abrupt and generalized. When the ruling order is challenged, the conventional language associated with that order is also contested. In the 1790s in Ireland the United Irishmen appropriated the word *citizen* to identify with the revolution in France. Early socialists and Owenites in Britain during the cataclysmic social changes of the 1840s challenged the use of coarse and obscene language at the expense of women (Taylor 1983: 227). In the May events in France in 1968, *vous* as a mark of respect was hotly contested and people in authority – from professors to managers – were forced, for a short while, to get used to being called *tu*. Some of the flexibility remained even afterwards. In the wake of the 1960s and 1970s, the words *black* and *woman* became generally accepted and widely used in the wake of struggles for racial and sexual equality. The Russian revolutionary, Trotsky once wrote that during social revolutions, 'practical linguistics holds its historical supreme court' (Trotsky 1971: 28). It would seem that 'practical linguistics' has ruled on the introduction of *she/he, s/ he, they, people, humanity* etc and, thankfully, begun to consign sexist and racist terms to the margins. Even more traditional institutions, such as *The Times*, have conceded these changes. Simon Jenkins notes in *The Times* style book that journalists should avoid causing needless offence to women, even though he denounces the 'new authoritarianism' of political correctness (Jenkins 1992). Recogition of the need to change linguistic usage from these more hidebound quarters indicates the degree to which these changes have become a general social phenomenon, and not just the preserve of the politically committed. This change, in evidence across all levels of society, cannot be seen apart from the wider changes effecting women in society, particularly their historically unprecedented entry into the workforce over the past two decades.

It would seem important, therefore, while defending the concept of removing divisive and demeaning uses of words about women (and other oppressed groups), to see language reform in its rounded social context. Old, oppressive usages are not just a matter of words. They are charged and weighted in favour of dominant ideas in society, buttressed by a whole array of educational, cultural and state institutions, which have the effect of making the traditional expressions seems natural and normal. Those advocating speech codes can lose sight of wider society and are too quick to take linguistic change for social change. Mey, for example, speaks of 'emancipatory linguistics' and 'the linguistic war against sexism'. In his enthusiasm for change in the way society speaks and writes about women, he omits to make reference to actual social changes in the area of women's lives, or, indeed, to the discrimination that women still suffer. 'A change in language is a way of telling the world that it has to change as well' is his claim (Mey 1997: 313–314), but, regrettably, the world does not always listen.

Nevertheless, the invention of new words and meanings as the way to free women has a certain following. The corrective to 'man-made' language, it has been suggested, is the creation of women's words and the writing of feminist dictionaries (Spender 1995: 27). Yet usage of expressions, somewhat artificially coined, in this context, such as *wimmin*, or indeed *herstory* or *malestream*, has remained marginal. *Wimmin* and *herstory*, perhaps because they are contrived, are used by only a few. Some academics speak as though such terms are generally established. *Malestream* is a case in point. For example, Abbott and Wallace explain in their introduction to a feminist sociology text, 'We write this book as two feminists who argue that malestream research has ignored, distorted and marginalized women and that feminists are concerned to reconceptualize the production of knowledge' (Abbott and Wallace 1997: xii). Their assumptions show the degree to which academic feminism has carved out a furrow for itself, even if its terms are not much heard beyond academic corridors. Non-use of these more esoteric terms stands in stark contrast to far wider acceptance of *she, woman, person,* etc. Linguistic voluntarism, linguistic labels pronounced in the hope that they will catch on, dismisses the ongoing input from speakers in wider society. Ironically it appeals to just the elitist prescriptivism which those who decry the sexist nature of language have condemned, and ignores the barriers of social inequality. 'Man-made' language forgot about those men not in positions of power. Those who enthuse about women creating their own language have urged women to join the 'citizenship in the electronic world', to 'natter' on the Internet. Such exhortations forget that even e-mail takes place in a wider social world and gloss over social inequality.[10]

Cheris Kramarae, co-author with Paula A. Treichler, of *A Feminist Dictionary* (1985), is in agreement with Spender. She places dictionaries very much at the centre of language production and regulation:

> dictionaries have systematically excluded any notion of women as speakers, as linguistic innovators, or as definers of words. Women in their pages have been rendered invisible, reduced to stereotypes, ridiculed, trivialized or demeaned. Whatever their intentions, then,

> dictionaries have functioned as linguistic legislators which perpetrate
> the stereotypes and prejudices of their writers, who are almost
> exclusively male. (1985: 8)

Yet the degree to which dictionaries actually do 'legislate' for
languages, as many have pointed out, is debatable. Certainly they
are invested with unquestioned authority and have often resisted
change. As Green notes, the out-and-out partiality of a Samuel
Johnson or a Noah Webster leaves us in no doubt as to the degree
to which dictionaries are immersed in ideological matters (Green
1996: 373). Preserving the language *with* all its social markers has
clearly been the concern of some lexicographers and their
publishing houses.[11] But it is conservatism in general that seems
to have carried more weight in dictionaries than male bias *per se*.
Vernacular language in general use by most people, male and
female, is relegated to the non-standard, regional, slang, colloquial
or simply not included. However, even if the aim of dictionaries is
to prescribe, it is striking just how unsuccessful in this project they
are. People speak without deferring to dictionaries; they continue
to invent and flout dictionary definitions. Dictionaries are only a
measure of ideological bias in language, not the cause of it. They
are forced to recognize change even if it is not without comment
and often much later.[12] To focus, therefore, on the reinvention of
dictionaries as part of women 'breaking out of their silence'
(Houston and Kramarae 1991) overestimates the role that dictionaries actually have in the making of sexism in language. Writing
dictionaries is, also, a highly specialized enterprise, not exactly
open to everyone, and touching on dictionary reform more than
social change. Such projects end up addressing only that narrow
layer concerned with such matters (Green 1996: 378).[13]

   With non-sexist guidelines, too, there is a danger of missing the
broader social dimension. It is true that those who raise objections
to sexist guidelines are often doing so in order to preserve the
sexist status quo and their claims about the linguistic inelegance or
inaccuracy of the new expressions are often disingenuous. Nevertheless when speech code enthusiasts conflate linguistic guidelines
with social change they are misrepresenting, as well as simpli-
fying, the role of language in political change. For example,
Cameron's struggle for 'gender-free' language, the demand for

apologies when sexist formulations are used (Cameron 1995a: 138), the promotion of campaigns which she names (somewhat ominously) 'verbal hygiene', illustrate a disproportionate attachment to language reform. She counters this by claiming that the focus on language does not mean leaving out struggles over real issues. Unfortunately, the example she gives reveals how easily the overall social context can slip away. She rightly shows how a statement from George Bush, made in justification of the invasion of Panama – 'we cannot tolerate attacks on the wife of an American citizen' – assumes that the citizen is male. Bush simply did not think about women in connection with the category 'American citizens'. She invokes us to ask him to be more explicit and not 'leave his particular brand of androcentrism untouched' (Cameron 1995a: 136). Her example is unfortunate. The effects of the invasion itself, deaths and injuries of men and women, are not even mentioned. Sticks and stones, alas, *are* of a different order to words. Concentration on speech codes misfocuses and misfires; it eclipses more severe social realities, as this example illustrates. Gates makes the very valid point, in connection with the PC debate, that writers, teachers or intellectuals like to claim greater political efficiency for their labours than they are entitled to, and that they take literary criticism as 'war by other means'. Surely here Cameron is in danger of seeing words as war by other means, of forgetting, to paraphrase Gates, the distance from speech codes to the streets (Gates: 1992: 19).

Sex-speak and 'How Things Are'

The idea that men and women talk differently has a long history and it is still being updated. Desmond Morris's particular slant is the claim that such differences are rooted in sociobiological necessity, dating back to primitive times:

> Women are interested in people, men in things. . . . [F]rom primeval times . . . men [have been] more interested in technology, women in social skills. . . . In addition to being more fluent, primitive females would also have been more cautious . . . because they were too

important to the reproductive success of the tribe. . . . In a nutshell, the women had to be fine-tuned as careful communicators and organizers, capable of doing several things at once without becoming confused. If men had to improve their single-minded concentration, their visual skills and their sometimes rash bravery, women had to become better at multi-directional thinking, verbal skills and common-sense caution. (Morris 1997: 32–33)

Morris's quaint justification of the 'facts' about women's and men's abilities and behaviour is so familiar that it seems common sense. More than any other social difference, those pertaining to the sexes are naturalized, presented as springing somehow automatically from innate biological differences, and apparently so obvious as to be beyond question. As Rose et al. note, 'biological laws brook no appeal' (Rose et al. 1984: 135). By making it seem that sexual differences have emerged from biology rather than from society, sexual inequality is made to appear inevitable and, conveniently for the status quo, 'how society works'.

Accounts of men and women's language follow the same pattern. Earlier, linguists took for granted verbal differences arising from sex. Jespersen was one of the early linguists most prone to wild generalizations. He devoted a chapter to women's supposed conversational quirks, one of which was their unfortunate compulsion to speak before they think (Jespersen 1922). Others introduced social perceptions into their schemas but accepted language differences along sex lines. Furfey examined divergences in the language usage of men and women in early societies. He concluded that many of these differences were on the basis either of the sex of the speaker or of the sex of the person being addressed. He found that the distinction indicated dominant social roles for men (Furfey 1944). Taboo was a reason given by others as to why earlier societies had certain differences between men's and women's speech, but as Trudgill points out these distinctions rest more on kinship systems and this does not explain why they need be value-laden (Trudgill 1974: 61–67). A generation ago, preconceptions about the psychology of sex differences were, as summarized by one writer, that females were simply 'seen as more receptive within the tactile and auditory domain' and that they were weak on spatial relations. 'Cerebrally they live with language in the left hemisphere' whereas males, 'fearless and independent', were 'parasympathetic and right hemispheric' (Rose et al. 1984: 139). More sophisticated versions of this biological determinism are now to be found. With the development of cognitive linguistics, and greater emphasis on genetic aspects of language, theories that rely on sex differentiation, rather than on the social formation of sex roles, seem to have resurfaced. Chambers, for example, maintains that sex-based variability shows that women are able to verbally outperform men in a number of sociolinguistic situations. Chambers holds that sex-based brain asymmetry may provide the basis for the females' advantage in linguistic wellbeing and in verbal skills (Chambers 1995: 128–137). The burgeoning field of neurolinguistics may well revive, yet again, mechanical biological explanations of verbal behaviour.

Strangely, even those who may reject biological determinism for women are often quick to accept uncritically the underlying principle of women speaking differently. This can have significant political implications. Deborah Tannen is one who has raised the theme of the mismatch of men and women's speaking styles before (Tannen 1990). In her book, *Talking Nine to Five*, subtitled *How Men's and Women's Conversational Styles Affect Who Gets Heard, Who Gets Credit and What Gets Done at Work*, she is quick to point out that her charting of characteristic male and female styles does not have an inherent, biological basis (1995: 31). The patterns she describes, she claims, are merely characteristic of women and men in a particular time and a particular place, in this case within companies:

> Amy was a manager with a problem: She had just read a report written by Donald and she felt it was woefully inadequate. . . . She made sure to soften the blow by beginning with praise . . . then she went on to explain what was lacking and what needed to be done. . . . Donald seemed to understand what was needed. But when the final report appeared on her desk. . . . Donald had made only minor changes and none of the necessary ones. . . . 'You told me before it was fine,' he protested. (Tannen 1995: 22)

Tannen tells us that this is one of innumerable misunderstandings caused by the inevitable differences in men's and women's styles. Conversation rituals that men employ involve using opposition such as banter, joking, teasing and strategies that avoid 'the one-down position'. Conversational rituals common among women involve maintaining an appearance of equality, being sensitive to the other person, downplaying themselves to 'get the job done without flexing their muscles' (1995: 23). She claims women would be wiser to recognize the limits of their own styles and learn how to adjust them (1995: 316).

Tannen is making two assumptions, neither of which is ideologically neutral. One is that women have these distinctive and identifiable speaking patterns; the other is about the way power works in society.

Women whose conversational styles she is recording are quite a distinct social layer – 'middle-class Americans of European background', as she concedes (Tannen 1995: 14). We are not told the degree to which other social factors influence ways of speaking. Women seem to behave somewhat differently depending on who they are talking to. Tannen quotes many examples of women who do not match the aggressiveness expected of them in managerial positions yet also quotes research that points to social hierarchy being more determining of conversational style than sex.[14] Although she admits that many women do not have the styles she claims they have, she nevertheless concludes overall that 'speaking patterns by gender'. While the method of selection of her samples of conversations is not fully revealed, we are led to believe that around 70 per cent of the women she recorded did conform to the conversational styles she describes (1995: 315). She then proceeds to make the categories even more watertight by declaring that 'obviously women and men can talk like the other gender if they want to' (1995: 316).

This method of social commentary has a certain circularity. What are *believed* to be women's and men's speaking styles are her starting point, these aspects of speech are selected and then recycled as frequently occurring examples of these styles. The problem is exacerbated by her qualitative research methods, in which data are selected rather than given. Such accounts become something of a self-fulfilling prophecy. We can see this specific reasoning at work in any number of passages in Tannen's text, which brims with generalizations, but this piece, entitled 'The Image of Authority', is a particularly salient example:

Part of the reason images of women in positions of authority are marked by their gender is that the very notion of authority is associated with maleness. This can result simply from appearance. Anyone who is taller, more heftily built, with a lower pitched more sonorous voice, begins with culturally recognisable markers of authority whereas anyone who is shorter, slighter with a higher-pitched voice begins with a disadvantage in this respect. (1995: 167)

This is a well-trodden social commentary path. It is so self-evident that it appears true. Males equal authority. Males are tall and have deep voices. Tallness and deep voices equal authority. The syllogism is complete. Tannen makes a similar claim to patent truth about the relationship between conversation styles and power.

But the methodological flaw runs throughout. Women are recorded speaking. A number of other things about women are observed – that they are not in higher positions, in spite of being qualified to be in higher positions. Then a causal line is drawn between the first observation and the second, irrespective of the presence of other possible social variables. The way they speak now becomes what prevents them being in higher positions. This circular explanation is only a step away from making the solution changing how people speak. We learn that Tannen's motivation for doing this study was the suggestion made to her that she should investigate the problem of the 'glass ceiling' – why aren't women advancing as quickly as the men who were hired at the same time (1995: 16)? Her findings lead her to confirm the hunch that she had at the beginning. It is the speaking styles of women which have become the stumbling block to positions of power. Social inequality is about how people speak, and a social problem is converted into an individual one.

The political solution becomes self-evident. Women should work within the rules, wake up to how they are selling themselves short and adjust to the male norm. As Cameron has accurately observed about Tannen's approach, readjusting conversation styles becomes part of 'the peculiar self-help ethos in which anyone can change the world by a private act of will' (1995a: 195). The presence in wider society of social discrimination against women becomes blotted out. No doubt this is why Tannen's *You Just Don't Understand* (1990) drew such angry criticism and why Tannen, who claims to be a feminist, was so indignant at the criticism (Tannen 1991). Troemel-Ploetz accused Tannen of blaming women for their own disadvantage, of not recognizing in verbal interaction the reproduction of the social hierarchy between men and women and of appeasing the male chauvinist backlash (Troemel-Ploetz 1991). Tannen fails to draw the links between the way women are viewed in companies as corresponding to the way in which women are discriminated against in society at large. Her preoccupation with speaking styles reduces women's experience of discrimination into how women 'present' and having the 'wrong' attitude. What jars about Tannen is the way the capitalist ethos runs through her self-improvement approach. The verbal style she advocates amounts to super-management-speak at its worst, both in its ideological assumptions and its bland acceptance of a prevailing business ethic.

Indeed the book is highly ideological. US society, she tells us, is 'egalitarian', prizes the democratic ideology that 'all men are created equal' and judges hierarchy, apparently, negatively (1995: 213–215). In such conditions women had better learn to talk in ways that bolster rather than undermine their influence, for 'how you talk creates power' (1995: 317). This is not just advocacy of assertiveness training; it also encapsulates the thinking of normative functionalism. Power, it seems, springs from effective social interaction at the level of the individual or in Tannen's words the 'ability to influence others, to be listened to, get your way rather than having to do what others want'. Tannen is categorical that successful communication techniques equal success, and in the business world this is 'simply a matter of human nature'. '[I]nfluence flows along lines of affiliation and contact' (1995: 136). Capitalism is not about social relations but about super-efficiency and super-communication and it is about time women got in on the speaking act. Speaking styles, for Tannen, are not just about men and women, but what makes the world go round, the way work gets done, what entrepreneurial capitalism is all about. This is not an unfamiliar hymn, but perhaps we are unaccustomed to it being sung under the aegis of either feminism or linguistics. It is part of a growing amount of literature in business feminism, and the success of Tannen's work reflects the number of women now in managerial positions in the US, but also elsewhere.[15]

Do Women Have 'a Language'?

Much of the literature on language and sex takes as its starting point that men and women as categories do speak differently. The difference is asserted, rather than demonstrably proven. Indeed, it has been pointed out that much of the sex differences uncovered in language, as in other behaviour, may be the result of an artifact of the sampling more than difference *per se* (Crawford 1995: 5). Sex difference in language is often somewhat loosely extrapolated from the existence of women's oppression in society. Graddol and Swann express a common assumption in the field when they say: 'Since gender is such an important social division in all cultures, it would be remarkable if it were not part of the social identity which people demonstrate through their use of language' (Graddol and Swann 1989: 66). A recent work on gender and discourse, while recognizing the need for more research in the area, nevertheless expresses the same conjecture in its introduction: '[g]ender is a major organizing principle in all societies that are known to us, so we can expect it to account for many aspects of the way that we use language' (Cheshire and Trudgill 1998: 1).

In other words, sexual inequality in society *should* be reflected in the language that women and men use. Women's language should bear the imprint of the oppressed and men's language, conversely (though given less attention until recently) should contain features of the oppressor. Women's language should display various manifestations of women's subordination. Certain language usages and forms seemed particularly susceptible to this type of classification because they seemed to perfectly symbolize aspects of power. Zimmerman and West (1975) found that women speakers exhibited most silence in cross-sex conversations whereas in same-sex interactions the distribution of silence was nearly equal. Women have been found to talk less in public contexts than men and more in less formal contexts (Holmes 1992a). Women ask more questions and more often indicate approval, whereas men interrupt and dispute statements (Maltz and Borker 1982). Men tend to control the outcomes of conversations whereas women 'attempt to manage affiliative goals within the domains of inter-action that are prescribed by men' (Smith 1985: 167). Women are more conscientious conversationalists: they do 'the spadework' and keep the conversations going (Fishman 1983).

These studies in different ways and with different interpretations share the view that language identically enacts what are perceived to be the dominant power relations in society. In these versions, language is not just a verbal expression of some other reality but is the power relation itself. For example, Fishman perceives conversational interaction quite literally as 'the work women do'. Her study found that women failed to get their topic going because males did not respond to them, whereas topics men initiated succeeded because women responded positively. She concludes that 'there is an unequal distribution of work in conversation'.

> As with work in its usual sense, there appears to be a division of labor in conversation. The people who do the routine maintenance work, the women, are not the same people who either control or benefit from the process. Women are the 'shitworkers' of routine interaction and the 'goods' being made are not only interactions but, through them, realities. (Fishman 1983: 99)

Zimmerman and West similarly see turn-taking in conversations 'as an economy in which the turn is distributed in much the same way as a commodity' and that differences between men and women in speaking parallel the difference between them in society at large, conversation being seen as a system of distribution of resources (Zimmerman and West 1975: 124) Graddol and Swann also pursue this theme and refer to conversation as 'the sexual division of labour (Graddol and Swann 1989: Chapter 4). They offer a more circumspect version than Fishman's, pointing out that 'it may seem odd to view conversation as work' (1989: 69), but nevertheless claim that the 'sexual division of labour appears more directly in conversational activity' (1989: 94).

The identification, one-for-one, of social relations with language interaction, even if its effect is intended to be rhetorical rather than literal, is inaccurate, not to say absurd. It is ironic that Marxist terminology is invoked. Turning language into a thing, into a system of division of labour, requires a substantial leap of the imagination. Metaphors are misread as reality. Marx derided idealists for letting their own creations run away with them, for forgetting that, after all, they were only pining under the yoke of 'phrases', and reminded them that the *idea* of gravity never drowned anyone (Marx and Engels 1974: 37–41). In these reified versions of language, it is worth remembering this material fact.

Besides language and society being of a different order of things, it is important to distinguish between individual interactive processes and the prevailing social relations in which they occur. Language-in-use is the coming together of the general and the particular, in a fusion that is neither one nor the other. It cannot be simply overlaid with social relations in a mechanical fashion, and certainly not identified symmetrically with them. Linguistic exchanges, and this can sometimes be the very reason that they happen, do not run along predictable power lines.

Language is not just an extended repertoire of speaking styles or registers that speakers pick and choose from. This would amount to an extreme reading of linguistic pragmatics. Some pursue this theme when they take literally the idea that conversation itself is the means by which members of a society produce a sense of order (Schiffrin 1994: 232). Conversation strategies, according to this view, are directly related to social power, indeed, are a decisive factor in it. Fairclough has rightly pointed out that the free-for-all assumption that pragmatics tends to make about individuals achieving goals through their own strategic initiatives leaves social constraints out of the picture (Fairclough 1989: 9). But for Fishman the strategies are not just power brokers but also seem to have been handed out in advance – the effective ones to men and the dreary 'maintenance work' to women. Invoking a stock of pragmatic skills fails to explain why some have them and others don't, or why some fail to use them and some don't. If language resources determine who has power, how have males come to have more resources? Why do women acquiesce in the use of these belittling conversation strategies? Making language into a thing in itself invests conversation pragmatics with social power. Yet, social power is not produced at source in linguistic exchanges, nor even reproduced in identical fashion. The flexibility that exists in verbal exchanges can flourish, even between socially unequal speakers, precisely because speakers are aware that social power resides beyond conversation.

Reifying language is a common thread to many who analyse women's language. Certainly this was the case for one of the pioneers in language and sex studies. 'Language uses us as much as we use language' was Lakoff's opening statement in *Language and Women's Place* (Lakoff 1975: 3). Lakoff's influence is undisputed (Crawford 1995: 23). So much has Lakoff's work set the tone for subsequent developments in sex and language studies that it is worth listing the features that she claims constitute 'women's language':

- words related to women's special interests;
- 'empty' adjectives such a *divine, charming, cute;*
- question intonation and rising intonation;
- the use of hedges ('words that convey uncertainty', saying things indirectly);
- intensive use of 'so';
- hypercorrect grammar ('women are not supposed to talk rough');
- super-polite forms ('women don't use off-colour or indelicate expressions');
- avoidance of jokes ('moreover women don't 'get' jokes');
- speaking in italics (women express 'uncertainty with their own self-expression'). (after Lakoff 1975: 53–57)

The list has a certain predictability: many might come up with similar items if asked to pick out how they thought women (or children) talked. They encapsulate what society expects women to be. Indeed, as we shall see, it was these very features that cropped up again and again in research into sex and language. The exercise itself, although purporting to be a linguistic one, involves referring to a general social view of women and draws on dominant ideas in society. This process constitutes the reaffirming of a sort of 'common sense', so sensitively highlighted by Gramsci, by which a set of assumptions and beliefs become generally held, an intuitive view of the world which is fossilized, often anachronistic, and bundled together under the name of folklore (Gramsci 1971: 323–325). This is what Lakoff has done here. Indeed she explains the process of her methodology with a rare, and honest, insight into the ideological content of her research:

> The data on which I am basing my claims have been gathered mainly by introspection. I have examined my own speech and that of my

acquaintances and have used my own intuitions in analysing it. I have also made use of the media; in some ways, the speech heard, for example, in commercials or situation comedies on television mirrors the speech of the television-watching community. . . . The sociologist, anthropologist or ethno-methodologist familiar with what seem to him more error-proof data-gathering techniques such as the recording of random conversation may object that these introspective methods may produce dubious results. But first, it should be noted that *any* procedure is at some point introspective: the gatherer must analyze his data, after all. (Lakoff 1975: 4–5)

This intuitive approach, however, even if it starts from the positive desire to challenge sexism and 'male chauvinist ways and assumptions' (1975: 2), results in reinforcing those received ideas about women, the very ideas that uphold sexism. Lakoff stereotypes women further, as was pointed out in one early angry response to her work (Crouch and Dubois 1975). She defines women's behaviour in the terms of the dominant ideology and 'women's language' becomes the next obvious step, a truism.

Lakoff's linguistic analysis tended to be equally unthinking. She was selective about the meanings of certain language forms, and failed to see that polysemy (the various meanings attached to a word) and 'multiaccentuality' in which speakers themselves construct different meanings in different contexts, was an integral part of the dynamic of language (Volosinov 1973: 81). Her claim that question tags mainly express hesitancy, 'mid-way between an outright statement and a yes–no question' (Lakoff 1975: 15), is patently false. Question tags can express many other things – like a request, a forceful assertion intended to forestall opposition, and other things besides (Crouch and Dubois 1975). Crawford gives a conclusive illustration of the vigorous use to which a question tag can be put. It is from Mandy Rice-Davies, a witness during the Profumo scandal of 1963, in Britain:

Counsel: Are you aware that Lord Astor denies any impropriety in his relationship with you?
Rice-Davies: Well, he would, wouldn't he? (quoted in Crawford 1995: 45)

The question tag here has nothing to do with hesitancy. The example shows how, in quite unfavourable circumstances and notwithstanding social pressures and expectations, Lakoff's categorical labelling of the question tag as a weak form used by women simply does not fit.

Lakoff's notion of women's language was criticized for reinforcing stereotypes. O'Barr and Atkins, in their study of courtroom language, suggested that women's language was in fact 'powerless language' since it was associated with persons having low social status and often with little experience in daunting official settings. Powerlessness was a condition that could apply to men as well as to women. 'Women's language' features were simply not patterned along sex lines and the features did not constitute a style or register since there was not a perfect correlation (O'Barr and Atkins 1980).

While this study had the merit of drawing attention to social class as a factor of verbal confidence, it tended simply to draw more people into the powerless language net, rather than seeing language as a dynamic entity the same speakers use to different effects in different situations. Its conclusion was that powerless language reinforces inferior status (1980: 110). It made language, in the last resort, a determinant of social position and failed to grasp that powerlessness in society does not necessarily translate into 'powerless language'.

Women's Accents – More Prestige Conscious?

The idea that women tend to speak 'nicely' and more correctly than men, that they shouldn't use, or sometimes hear, 'bad' language is widely held. It fits with stereotypical ideas about women being 'gentler', in language as well as behaviour. Quantitative, sociolinguistic studies seemed to support such views, although closer scrutiny of their findings show that they are premised on assumptions about women's supposed innate propensities. Here as in other areas of sex and language it is difficult to separate the myths from reality.

A number of sociolinguistic studies of phonological variation show that women use fewer non-standard forms and more prestige forms than men (Martin 1954, Macaulay 1978). The most famous was Labov's New York City findings which suggested that lower middle-class women were instrumental in the diffusion of a certain pronunciation, the postvocalic /r/.[16] Labov argued that lower middle-class women, in careful speech (when they were aware of being listened to) used fewer stigmatized forms than men and were more sensitive than men to standard forms. They were particularly conscious of the prestige value of this pronunciation and used it as a method of social assimilation (Labov 1972a). Labov has elaborated his views on sex and language. Starting from the findings that women used more prestigious forms and that they are linguistic innovators in diffusing new forms, he has examined the interaction of sex and social class. He found that women in intermediate social classes adopt prestige forms more rapidly than men and react more sharply against the use of stigmatized forms. Labov suggests that the forces behind this principle are associated with upward social mobility (Labov 1998).

Labov's work was very influential and has in many ways set the theoretical parameters for subsequent studies on how women relate to standard forms. Trudgill confirmed some of what Labov had found (Trudgill 1974). In his Norwich study, Trudgill found that women believed themselves to be using more prestigious variants than they actually were, whereas men tended to under-report their use of standard variants. Trudgill concluded that women thus rate the prestige pronunciation far more favourably than men (1974: 97). Conversely, men seem more concerned with identifying with non-standard, low-status speech forms. Trudgill claims men are thus signalling the presence of some sort of *covert prestige*, a loyalty to working-class speech features which is more influential than the aim of social status. '*Covert prestige* exerts a more powerful influence on men and "normal" prestige on women' (1974: 98). Trudgill makes this case even more strongly when he refers to other findings which indicate that men are linguistic innovators only where changes are taking place in the direction of the spreading of non-standard forms, whereas women continue to show preference for adoption of the standard forms (1974: 100).

Feminist critics highlighted the difficulties of taking women as a social group and questioned how women had been socially defined in these studies. Women were ascribed to social classes on the basis of their father's occupation if single, and to their husband's if married or widowed.[17] Their criticism was that this constituted both an inherent male bias and a methodological error. Women were wrongly ascribed and therefore wrong conclusions were drawn about their greater use of prestige forms. It was claimed that women may not share parity of status with men within families and that women's social ambitions may be different as well. These critics also claimed that women may actually be higher up the social scale than the menfolk around them (Cameron and Coates 1985).

The weakness of Labov's and Trudgill's conclusions about men's and women's speech have, I think, less to do with social categorization than with their view of social norms. First, there is the way in which the studies take standard and non-standard as given, agreed-upon categories. Yet 'standard' and 'non-standard' forms on a phonological basis, even more than grammatical categories, are not self-evident, nor unproblematic categories. Rather than two distinct varieties of language, non-standard and standard form a continuum and are viewed in different and contradictory ways by speakers. Second, differentiation is itself evaluative and something which defers implicitly to dominant ideas in society. Labov was so influential because he made working-class language a subject of study in its own right. His concept of linguistic change from below also placed social factors at the heart of language. However, the fact that he stressed upward social mobility, instituted through speakers' willingness to adopt prestige forms, led him to accept uncritically the notion of a standard. Its presence he saw as spontaneous evidence of social hierarchy. The 'exterior standard of correctness' was so much taken as a baseline that speakers' deviation from it was described as 'linguistic insecurity' (Labov 1972b: 186–188). He saw that greater attention to speech, as opposed to spontaneous speech, always involved shifts towards the standard, or 'hypercorrection' (1972b: 191–195). His identification of style-shifting from the 'subordinate' to the 'superordinate' form indicated the awareness of social judgement. But he left the ideological aspects of this buried under a social stratification approach which took all hierarchy as natural.[18]

The categorization of standard and non-standard phonetic pronunciations is an ideological question. Thus, use or non-use of such forms is not just convergence on or deviance from accepted norms but an expression of social class, about who someone is speaking to, about how one wishes to be seen socially, where someone places themselves *vis-à-vis* the status quo in society, whether someone is skilful at adopting different accents, and other things. Therefore, quantitative measurement of distances from these norms tells us only about conformity to these norms not about people's underlying attitudes to society, to the status quo or to people from other social classes. For example, Trudgill assumes that if women say they have an RP (received pronunciation) accent, then they would like to have an RP accent:

> The women, we can say, report themselves in very many cases, as using higher-class variants than they actually do – presumably because they wish they did use them or they think they ought to and perhaps therefore actually believe that they do. Speakers, that is, report themselves as using the form at which they are aiming and which has favourable connotations for them rather than the norm that they actually use. (No conscious deceit is involved, it seems.) (Trudgill 1974: 97)

The only unfathomable aspect that is considered is deceit. More contradictory attitudes are simply ruled out. Trudgill assumes that the women surveyed view RP as favourable. Yet of course attitudes are not only discrepant but also changing. They depend on who is forming the attitude, with whom and when. What may be true in one situation does not mean that it holds as a general social fact. Women with standard accents can be perceived negatively. In one British study, for example, Northern-accented females were perceived as less aggressive and egoistic and more likeable and sincere than RP speakers (Elyan et al 1978). The over-reporting and under-reporting of prestige forms, attributed by Trudgill to women being more status conscious, may in fact reveal more about the person they are reporting to (or to who they think they are reporting) and how they see their relationship with that person, than it does about the one fixed attitude that women are supposed to have. Bell's account of language use and use of different styles according to who is being spoken to, language style as audience design, underscores the relevance of this aspect of standard forms (Bell 1984). Such interactive dynamics are not fully taken into account in Trudgill's survey.

The social stratification approach, adopted by both Labov and Trudgill, is a social-group framework which posits a non-conflictual social structure, and which holds together because its members recognize its validity. Society is construed as operating on a consensual basis and there is little recognition of social divisions and tensions, either between classes or within sexes, in this model. Acceptance of norms becomes the operative factor; so much so that pressure to conform with norms overrides everything else.

Covert prestige, a concept adopted by both Labov and Trudgill, reflects this norm-focused approach. Covert prestige is defined in terms of its opposite – socially accepted prestige – and in terms of norms about masculinity. 'Attitudes of this type,' Trudgill claims, referring to Labov's definition, ' are not usually overtly expressed, and depart markedly from the mainstream societal values (of schools and other institutions) of which everyone is consciously aware' (Trudgill 1974: 96). In answer to why this counter-prestige should prevail, and hold sway against other social pressures, Trudgill replies that it is associated with masculinity, 'which leads men to be more favourably disposed to non-standard linguistic forms than women' (1974: 94–95). Women conform to one norm, we are told, because ' [O]ther things being equal, these pressures will be stronger . . . because of their greater status consciousness' (1974: 95).

This reliance on conforming to prestige-giving norms lead in some puzzling directions. Social power becomes thus simply the operation of competing influences. Existing power relationships in society become inexplicable or non-existent. If covert prestige really operates why are its forms socially stigmatized? From another point of view, if women apparently adapt better to socially prestigious overt norms, why do they not have more power in society than they actually do? The possibility that adherence to non-standard speech forms may have something to do with class identity is simply glossed over. Attitudes and actions that arise from people's class in society, socio-economic factors like how much they earn, where they live, where they go to school and if they go to college, all these things which influence ways of speaking in different circumstances, become explained by people's attitudes. Society falls out of the equation and individual self-perception becomes socially defining.

Many of the attitudes that are identified as typical of men or women very often coincide with prevailing ideas about men and women. Working-class speech, we are told, inexplicably, is associated with toughness, which 'is quite widely considered to be a desirable masculine characteristic' (1974: 95). Trudgill summarizes this reasoning in a seemingly irrefutable view of the way things are. 'Men and women are socially different in that society lays down different social roles for them and expects different behaviour patterns from them. Language simply reflects this social fact' (1995: 73). Women, in terms of attitude or speech, are entirely left out of this picture. Any contribution that they may make in either speech or attitude becomes strangely classless because, according to Trudgill, they are just waiting to become upwardly mobile.

Labov's view of society is also one constructed on the basis of social attitude and reflects a similar functionalist view of society. First, his social categories are occupational, often containing within them rather large social overlap in class terms. The five social categories that he uses (taken from those used by US censuses) – Unskilled, Skilled Labor, Clerical, Managerial, Professional (and owners) – fail to take account of different weighting of social power within each group. Second, upward social mobility is taken as a social fact which occurs when successful adapting to prescribed norms takes place. The adoption of 'better' or more correct speech comes into this category. Labov tells us that in disadvantaged communities, sensitivity to exterior standards of correctness is 'associated with upward social mobility'. In black communities female students who show greater sensitivity to 'exterior standards of correctness' also show greater success than males in school and experience greater employability. This is taken as a 'symptom of an overall readiness and opportunity to take advantage of prevailing community norms' (Labov 1998: 15). Further, Labov sees females' more acute awareness of social mobility as the force behind greater sexual differentials in higher social categories (1998: 43).

The same functionalist approach can be detected in Labov's explanations of language change. Besides women being more ready to adopt prestigious language forms, they have been found to initiate a number of significant linguistic changes. Labov suggests, as an explanation, the fact that childcare-givers are most often female. As he puts it, because the first steps in language learning are dominated by women, language is, in more senses than one, *la langue maternelle*.

> The differentiation logically begins in the acquisition of the first forms of the language by the language learner from the primary caregiver. . . . In all societies studied so far, that caregiver is most often female – a mother, grandmother, aunt, female babysitter, or daycare worker. . . . The simple logic of the situation will inevitably accelerate the advance of female-dominated forms. (1998: 42)

This, too, is stated rather than explored. Mention of socially provided childcare as opposed to individual family provision should surely be made here, particularly as possible social class differentiation of the two would expose the child to different speech. Comparison of the speech of children in both types of childcare would have to be explored before broad assumptions about speech influence in childcare can be made. Similarly, the presence of other children in socially provided childcare would constitute strong speech models, apart from the carer. Admittedly Labov's suggestion as to the influence of child carers is only tentative. Nevertheless it is noteworthy that it follows the same reaffirmation of role allocation that Labov accepted as regards social stratification. In commenting on Labov's work, Coupland and Jaworski point out that social stratification was presumed in advance and confirmed in the studies (Coupland and Jaworski 1997: 164). The same would appear to be the case in relation to females' roles.

Despite Labov's claims that sex and class intersect as regards women's linguistic behaviour, perhaps the most unsatisfactory aspect of Trudgill's and Labov's work is their tendency to see women as a homogeneous group who all seek to conform to linguistic norms, a view that reinforces dominant views of women in society. Nichols, in her study of a rural black population in coastal South Carolina challenged the assumption that women behave as a kind of universal speech group. She found that women's willingness to adopt standard variants depended, not on their sex but on the life experiences of the speakers. Women on the mainland in the lower socio-economic groups did show less tendency to switch from Gullah – the creole language spoken locally – to English because their work as labourers and domestics, in a confined physical area, did not require them to. Women who were on one of the offshore islands, and who in the course of their work were in touch with the standard variants, exhibited more innovative linguistic behaviour. The men's jobs – construction and blue collar work – did not require them to use standard English and so they retained the creole variety of their childhood. In other words, differences in language use derived from livelihoods and language contact. Women will exhibit both conservative and innovative behaviour. 'Whatever the particular pattern, language used by women must be dealt with in terms of the social roles available to them, rather than dismissed as one of the great mysteries of the universe' (Nichols 1978: 111). Interestingly, Labov's interpretation of Nichols' study, while conceding that women's access to standard norms influences whether they use them, still accepts that the 'conservative' tendency in women is paramount. 'It stands to reason that the conservative tendency of women applies only when the opportunity for it to apply is present', is his claim (Labov 1998: 14). His reasoning supposes *a priori* that women tend towards the standard. The value of Nichols's study is its rootedness in the actual lives of the speakers. Indeed, Nichols's study may be of wider significance since it reveals the degree to which women's greater use of standard forms coincides with the types of jobs that they do rather than any innate attitude.

Inventing 'Difference'

Some have taken the female/male dichotomy further than attitude or role allocation. Jennifer Coates's now fairly standard introduction to the subject, *Women, Men and Language*, interprets the relationship of gender to language as being characterized by two interacting strands – *difference* and *dominance*. These are the pivotal concepts in the defining of men's and women's language and involve, again, the direct identification of social power with language. 'Power relations are reproduced through talk', was how Coates put it (Coates 1993: 194). Where in Fishman's accounts the social division of labour was rudimentarily transposed into the linguistic domain, here, too, we see a similar procedure. Language becomes a metaphor – crucial and weightily symbolic – for power relations in society. How Coates refers to men's and women's language is instructive and reveals the degree to which the metaphor is acted out.

'Women tend to organise their talk *co-operatively* while men tend to organise their talk *competitively*.' We are told that women 'respect each others' turn-taking', they use 'strategies that signal involvement', make frequent, well placed responses, offer 'reassurance and support', avoid verbal aggressiveness, value listening and make sure that everyone participates. Men, on the other hand, 'compete for dominance', establish hierarchy, make 'abrupt topic shifts', often 'lecture other speakers', frequently use verbal aggressiveness and 'infringe women's rights to speak' (Coates 1993: Chapter 9). In this model, ways of speaking are simply overlaid with the predictable and assumed virtues and vices of the sexes. It is not surprising, therefore, that male–female miscommunication is said to occur as a result of this divergence, and that all-women talk epitomizes the supposed cooperative principle that women purportedly prioritize (Coates 1998).

Coates repeats here an emphasis that began with Lakoff and was further pursued by Tannen. Her interpretation, however, leads her in a different direction to Tannen's call for self-assertiveness. Coates stresses the *positive* in women's language, how some features of women's talk, especially emotional expressiveness, could be usefully adopted by men (Coates 1993: 195). She has argued elsewhere that female collaborative styles are appreciated as 'enabling' by men and that the 'interactive patterns into which women are socialized offer substantial benefits to academic and professional teams' (Coates 1995: 29). But, in somewhat of a contradictory turn, she also points to *women's linguistic disadvantage* and how this parallels the disadvantage that minority groups in society experience (Coates 1993: 195–202).

Coates's assumption is that women form a social group (1993: 7–9). She admits that they are an unusual social group, because of their social interconnectedness with members of the other assumed social group, men, and because class cuts across women and men. Notwithstanding, she claims that, as regards how women see themselves, women do indeed constitute a social group because they have 'a poor self-image'; thus her definition of social group is constituted around self-perception. She also stresses that there is an in-group solidarity among women which is particularly detectable in same-sex conversation. She investigates these themes through the study of a group of women friends who met at each other's houses at social gatherings and her findings are that women's talk is cooperative, that women 'all other things being equal . . . interact with other women as equals while when they interact with men they are relating to superiors,' and that this style and language reveal the presence of a 'female subculture' and that women form a speech community (Coates 1998: 148–150). She specifies that her group was white, middle class and concerned with the establishing of a career, but while these social specifications are given they are not seen as particularly relevant for language outcomes. Coates stresses the communality of all women, refers to a speech community of women, and makes no further mention of social factors. Sex becomes the organizing principle.

Yet 'women's talk' is characterized less by their sex or gender than by their social situation, both broadly and specifically, and it is difficult to see how women with different social experience and backgrounds can be said to share a female linguistic style. This had already been recognized even by those who had formerly embraced the concept of women's language. Thorne, Kramarae and Henley, for example, came to reject the term 'genderlect' (a dialect according to gender) as overemphasizing both the similarities among women and the speaking differences between the sexes (1983: 14).

In more detail, Penelope Eckert's study forcefully brought out that sex categories were different to other social groups, and that women could not be grouped together on the basis of shared 'language' or ways of speaking (Eckert 1989). She examined two class cultures within a public high school in Detroit: 'Jocks' who identified with the school ethos and represent middle-class culture, and the working-class 'Burnouts' who tended to rebel against school authority and whose social experience was on the streets rather than in sporting events surrounding the school. Her focus was to counter some of Labov's assumptions that women's linguistic behaviour could be based on the biological category of sex. She found that being a member of the Jocks or the Burnouts was more significant in terms of what pronunciations were used than whether you were a boy or a girl. Within that overall social group identity, girls were asserting their category membership through language more than boys. This did not spring from any innate femaleness, but from women having less power in society and, as she saw it, their use of the social symbols of language to compensate. Her findings about how the girls used language refute the idea of women's language as a recognisable entity. She argued that there is not necessarily any simple, constant relation between gender and variation and that seeing language differences simply in terms of the men/women binary opposition failed to take adequate account of social factors. The latter resulted in differentiation *within* rather than between sex groups: girls defined themselves linguistically with respect to other girls (1989: 259).

Eckert's study was also important for what she noted about women's oppression compared to other oppressions. She shows that language and sex do not intersect in the way that language and social class or ethnicity do. Her claims are an important antidote to the now common assertion that different forms of oppression are essentially equivalent. Gender is not a category comprised of two divergent, antagonistic parts. Nor do women form a social group in the way Coates describes. Eckert explains that gender and gender roles are in fact 'normatively reciprocal' (Eckert 1989: 253). While the social positions of men and women may be unequal, the day to day context in which these power relations are played out differ sharply from those of class or ethnic group. As she explains, 'it is not a cultural norm for each working class individual to be paired up for life with a member of the middle class or for every black person to be so paired up with a white person' (1989: 254). It is to be expected, therefore, that sex markers in language will be quite different to markers for class and ethnicity. Here Eckert touches on something missed by any simplistic identification of women's oppression with class, or with other oppression such as racism or discrimination against other minorities. Dominant ideas which promote the heterosexual couple as the norm, that advocate both sexes living together in the one house, including with children of different sexes, are of a different order than those dominant ideas which discriminate through the promotion of social distance, of the 'other', the 'unnatural', the 'unknown' and other racist formulations. For these divisive ideologies to prevail, a certain degree of *de facto* social segregation is required. By contrast, women and men, boys and girls, live cheek by jowl. This fact itself further undermines the claims for separate languages for men and women.

Nevertheless, Coates pursues the class and ethnic analogy further. She suggests that women, like other minority groups and the working class, suffer *disadvantage*, and that the language used by girls and boys is connected to this disadvantage (Coates 1993: 195–202). She examines studies of classroom talk and refers to research which has shown that boys receive more favourable attention from their teachers.

Coates concludes that this discriminatory behaviour amounts to educational disadvantage.

Some studies have not seen girls as verbally disadvantaged at all. Maccoby and Nagy have gone so far as to claim that that superior female competence in verbal tasks is one of the more solidly established generalizations in the field of sex differences (Maccoby and Nagy 1974: 75–85). Coates admits that the relationship between girls or women as a group, the language they use and disadvantage is a complex one (Coates 1993: 201), but she draws conclusions that barely fit educational trends. Her claim that girls lag behind in participation in higher education is not borne out by the facts internationally. Girls score consistently as well or better at end of school exams. In Britain in 1996, girls were more likely than boys to gain five or more GCSE qualifications, and at higher grades, and the differential is widening. They have also overtaken boys in GCSE A Level success. There are slightly more females in full-time higher education than males (CSO 1996). In Ireland 53 per cent of students attending third-level institutions are female (Department of Equality and Law Reform, 1997). What is striking, indeed, is the degree to which social class remains a very much more accurate predictor of educational attainment than sex (HEA 1997).[19] The discrimination that women experience in employment, referred to by Coates, clearly does not result from poorer educational achievement, but from social pressures, particularly those relating to childcare. It is not that women's language, or other skills, are not recognized by society but rather that women's achievements and potential are thwarted by what society expects women to do. At issue here is discrimination not disadvantage as such, social relations not 'power relations through talk'. This is not an idle distinction. It is the social set-up that triggers discrimination, not some inherent female way of being or talking. Coates's mistaken conclusion that women are educationally disadvantaged may be a logical conclusion to stating women's linguistic differences, but it does not fit the facts.

Marjorie Goodwin, too, has challenged the idea that women are powerless speakers and denies that gender asymmetry in speech exists in the way that has been claimed. Her study of the black children of Maple Street in Philadelphia gives a valuable insight into the vernacular used by these boys and girls. Her comprehensive collection of data provides a rounded view of language in its social setting. Because it involves the collection of extended conversations over a long period of time, it allows interactive strategies and features of the language used to emerge with more force than would be possible from the quantitative recording of selected features. She is able to define a number of features that the children use. A particular type of gossip dispute used exclusively in the girls' peer group – what the children call 'he-said-she-said' – is particularly revealing. It consists of one girl accusing another of having talked about her behind her back but the accusation is made through a third party:

> *Annette*: And *Arthur* said that *you* said that *I* was showing off just because I had that *blouse* on. (Goodwin 1990: 195)

It is a highly intricate verbal strategy and one which may result in high drama and extended disputes, with a girl perhaps being ostracized from the group for months. Goodwin's findings are that the 'he-said-she-said' disputes involves issues of 'justice and rights' rather than a supposed female ethic of 'care and responsibility', that competition and cooperation are not mutually exclusive to men and women but often coexist within the same speech activities, and that women's talk is often directed at the public arena. Far from girls deferring to boys, her study shows that they hold their own (1990: 264).[20]

> Dichotomies such as domestic and public . . . or nature and culture . . . are of relatively little use in explicating how boys and girls on Maple Street come to process experience in different ways. . . . The diversity of activities children on Maple Street engage in across age/gender groups is remarkable. . . . [The] girls and boys have in common not only a similar social space but also procedures for carrying out numerous conversational events. (1990: 265)

Goodwin concludes that studies, often those of middle-class white children, tend to stress gender differences in social interaction and ignore the features that they have in common.

Goodwin's study reveals the role language plays in the social interaction of the children – themselves treated as actors actively engaged in the their social worlds rather than as passive objects who are the recipients of cultural stereotypes. She notes that the neighbourhood differs from school, where teachers sort the children on the basis of gender. Goodwin's understanding of the social dynamic of interaction and the role of language as a practical processor of social organization owes much to Vygotskian tradition. Her definition of talk as social action and the linking of linguistic patterns to social and task activities of the children build upon Vygotsky's themes (see Chapter 2). As regards language and sex, Goodwin's study bears out the degree to which language is about social activity and cooperation, including cooperation across the sexes. In the sense of language as practical consciousness – language as a microcosm of human consciousness, in Vygotsky's phrase – it makes very little sense to talk of women's and men's language. Indeed, the difference view that stresses different arenas of men's and women's language tends to completely underplay the role of women as social actors through language. Goodwin's study redresses the balance and places girls as equal social actors in their community. Not surprisingly perhaps, Goodwin also rejects the deficiency theory for black-working class children. She demonstrates that black working-class speech, much like that of the girls she has examined, constitutes a powerful manifestation not only of linguistic competence but of social and cultural competence as well (1990: 287).

The Limitations of Gender

Much of the analysis of women possessing their own language, of having certain speaking styles, springs from the assumption that gender is a category that can explain women's oppression. Indeed gender has been adopted widely in various academic fields, often quite uncritically. In this last section I question this assumption and argue that many of the determinist assumptions as regards sex and language use spring from the theoretically unsatisfactory aspects of this classificatory term.

Some have begun to question the wisdom of stressing 'difference' as part of gender (Oakley 1972, Showalter 1989, Gordon 1991, Modleski 1991, Cameron 1995b). These doubts have come about in response to the fracturing of feminism as well as the development of an aggressive right-wing current which has applauded the status quo, and the *naturalness* of the division between men and women. While the backlash and the splintering of feminism into left and right may have occasioned many feminists' misgivings, gender as a concept is fraught with inconsistencies which have contributed to the divisions within feminism.

The distinction is made between gender and sex, with writers at pains to point out that gender is socially constructed rather than biologically made (Graddol and Swann 1989, Cameron 1992, Coates 1993, Holmes 1995: 290). Nevertheless, in its early days, gender was often used as simply another term for women. Partly this was because it arose specifically in the wake of struggles for women's rights and therefore anything to do with 'gender' became shorthand for, in whatever way, challenging sexism. Partly also the adoption of the concept of gender accompanied what might be termed the academic making of feminism. Oakley claims that academic feminists gained respectability by naming what they do as being about 'gender' rather than being about 'women' (Oakley 1997: 30). The flowering of women's studies courses in many English-speaking countries indicates that gender has gained widespread institutional acceptance.

Now in the late 1990s, gender has come logically to embrace its other half, men. Where the focus hitherto, in relation to language and gender, has been 'women's language', there is now a burgeoning of interest in men's culture, masculinity, male identity and male language. One collection of articles on 'language and masculinity' started from a certain unease about the focus on women and women's language and one contributor wondered whether gender did not only refer to women but also defined women as being in greater need of problematization (Johnson 1997). More often than not, though, the exploring of men's identity follows the same trope that Coates charted: women equals cooperation; men equals competition; women powerlessness, men, power. But 'doing gender' (Coates 1997) has been taken further than merely men imposing aggressive and dominant styles on conversational exchanges. Some have even claimed that racism and imperialism have been constructed on male gender identities (Brittan 1989, Rutherford 1997) and that imperialism is about gender power which, over class or race, was fundamental to securing the imperial enterprise (McClintock 1995: 6–7). Gender has become the driving force behind all manner of social events, it seems.

Gender was never just about describing inequality between the sexes. Its theoretical assumption, more often invoked than explained, was that the causes of women's oppression, in some way, lay with men – men's behaviour, men's attitudes, men's social conditioning, men's language. The term 'patriarchy' grew out of this male focus. Patriarchy, although an amorphous, loosely used term, attributed the existence of women's oppression, mediated or not, to men. It was 'a system of discrimination that works in the interests of males at the expense of females', as one recent book on discourse has described it (Mills 1997: 93). This view was intuitive rather than explanatory, static rather than historical, and seldom subjected to rigorous theoretical clarification. Even proponents of the patriarchy view claim there are ambiguities in the central features of patriarchy and how it is perpetuated (see Lovenduski and Rendall 1993: 8). Walby identifies six 'patriarchal' structures – mode of production, paid work, the state, male violence, sexuality and cultural institutions (Walby 1990: 20). She believes that patriarchy has moved from the private to the public but her categories and claims are more descriptive of various aspects of power in modern society than specifically characteristic of male power. Her 'patriarchal' structures seem less convincing because in some of them women managers now have a significant presence. It has been pointed out that, although widely invoked, patriarchy is a loose theoretical construct that falls back on the male/female dichotomy. Gender is a complementary aspect of the patriarchy theory and because it posits rather than explains the male/female framework, it fails to move beyond stating the existence of oppression (German 1981).

This survey of views of women and language has argued that the insistence on gender and the differences between men and women freezes aspects of women's oppression and appears to fix it for all time. A gender focus comes to mirror in a distorted way the oppression it seeks to describe. As Crawford notes, '[e]ssentialism conceptualizes gender as a fundamental, essential part of the individual . . . as a set of properties residing in one's personality, self-concept or traits. Gender is something women and men *have* or *are*. [It] portrays women's speech as relatively uniform across situations and determined by early socialization: women speak in particular ways because they are women' (Crawford 1995: 8). Thus we have women's language which is polite, hesitant, careful, respectful, full of apologies and punctuated with so many literal manifestations of women's subordination. The language of women becomes fixed into a supposed female identity. It becomes essentialized in a deterministic twist far harsher than old-fashioned sexist biological determinism.

This determinist bind seems to spring naturally from the category of gender. Some have sensed the difficulty of the *difference* emphasis that gender implies and they have attempted to refocus on the social. They stress that gender is *socially constructed* and therefore neither unchanging nor inevitable. Cameron, for instance, rejects the way in which gender difference has been reified in the difference model. She berates what she calls a kind of 'social essentialism' in which difference become an inescapable fact of life. She speaks ruefully of the feminist 'regime of truth' produced by feminist linguistics which is an interpretation of what it means to be a gendered speaker and serves to re-emphasize women's exclusion (1995b: 40–44). Crawford, too, makes an impassioned and convincing plea for rejection of the essentialist sex-difference approach and points out, correctly, how 'gender can be perceived as a self-fulfilling prophecy – a set of processes by which gender difference is created, the observed differences conflated with sex and belief in sex differences is confirmed'. Against this, she argues for a 'social constructionist approach, which views languages as sets of strategies for negotiating social landscapes' and for a critical re-examination of how people come to have these beliefs about sex differences (1995: 14–18).

Yet the difficulty with even these critics of gender essentialism lies in their failure to find any social or historical roots for women's oppression in society. Beliefs about gender norms are described but it is never explained how they came to be the dominant ones. We are led to believe that they reside in social conditions and institutions but are never given any reason why social organization should be thus arranged. Crawford tells us that sexism is socially constructed, but not *why* it is. Women's oppression in society is vaguely defined as springing from a 'gendered social order' (Crawford 1995: 180) or the ongoing production of 'gendered subjects and the conditions and male behaviour that keep women as outsiders' (Cameron 1995b: 43). With no discussion of the historical and social roots of women's oppression there is no way out. There is a vacuum at the heart of gender, a vacuum into which pours individualism. Empowerment becomes empowerment on an individual level, with language playing a major part. Cameron explains: 'there is no such thing as being a woman outside the various practices that define womanhood for my culture – practices ranging from the sort of work I do to my sexual preferences, to the clothes I wear to the way I interact verbally' (Cameron 1995b: 43). Practices become not political practice but personal or attitudinal ones. This is a common theme amongst those who write about a feminist approach to language. The 'discursive framework of femininity' is about clothes, bodily stances, and how women think of themselves. It may determine 'the type of clothes she chooses to wear, the types of bodily stance she adopts and ways of thinking about herself in relation to power' (Mills 1997: 18). Crawford's view is also about the options open to individuals because she sees language as *the basis* of social organization (1995: 18). Communicative transactions, in effect, become *the* social relations. This attention to language practices, from the critical perspectives of feminism, can change 'the gendered social order' (Crawford 1995: 180). Release from oppression becomes in all these versions condensed into personal style or ways of presenting oneself.

Descriptions of 'gendered subjects' and a 'gendered social order' set up a binary opposition between men and women's behaviour which, even if claimed not to be on the basis of sex alone, does not actually provide any theoretical underpinning other than the category of sex. Radical feminists such as Spender or Penelope endorse this polarity since they see things in separatist terms. Tannen's concerns are, as we have seen, more towards adjusting women's styles, thereby implicitly accepting what she supposes to be men's more effective styles. But this slippage from gender to sex also happens in those studies which are more committed to a social dimension. Gender, when referring to users of language, becomes in practice men and women speakers on the basis of sex. Coates's study of the organization of men's talk finds that men use a one-at-a-time model, where they tend to hold the floor as an expert (Coates 1997: 126). Despite claiming that gender is a socially constructed category, she asserts that 'all-male groups typically choose this style whereas all-female groups organize talk using a collaborative floor' (1997: 126). Effectively the gender distinction is collapsed into a sex one. The distinction between socially constructed male speakers and male speakers *tout court* is never explained. Studies end up taking women speakers as women and men speakers as men. In other words, despite gender theorists' claim to social intervention, their work tends to abide by, not qualify, the binary biological sexual opposition.

Much of this difficulty arises from the quandary of distinguishing on what basis gender can be measured when dealing with men and women speakers. Does a man speaking with a supposed women's style have a female gender? Or is he the exception which proves the rule? Cameron claims that *gender identity is performed* by people presenting themselves in certain ways through language. Gender thus becomes a floating identity, and speakers pick and choose from aspects of masculinity and femininity almost as they please. 'When can men do so-called feminine talk without threatening their constitution as men?' Cameron asks (1997: 60). The answer she gives is when their masculinity is under threat. Again *why* they should cling to certain stereotypes is not explained.[21]

The difficulty is that women's oppression is not just a speaking style or a way of being. In practice, much of the gender focus comes down to getting men, and some women, to change their attitudes. Gordon puts it quite succinctly: 'Speaking of "gender" got some men to do housework' (1991: 92). Holmes argues that changing men must be part of the way of effecting change, although she doubts whether even well-intentioned men will succeed in sharing valued talking time without some assistance (or even insistence) from women (Holmes 1995: 223). Consciousness-raising becomes a key element (Holmes 1995: 218–220, Cameron 1995a: 179). Consciousness-raising in the academy comes to be seen as particularly important. The focus on attitudes and on academicism overlap; both are strategies aimed at the individual and, it has to be said, only available to relatively privileged individuals. Yet the gap between the academy and social reality is wide. As Gordon notes, the institutionalization of women's studies courses occurred just when conservative reaction set in and in the US, during one of the worst periods of immiseration for the urban poor. It is ironic that at a time when gender gained ground in the academy, actual women's rights in the real world, particularly among working-class and black women, were quite seriously eroded (Gordon 1991). Women's studies courses are a welcome addition given that women have been so hidden in academic accounts and institutions. But they are no accurate barometer to the winning of rights for women as a whole. The inverse proportion of the rise of women's studies in academia to the winning of women's rights across society and the world sadly proves that the changing of individual attitudes remains a relatively select affair and not one to fundamentally challenge power in society.

Our study of the question of language and sex stresses that a truly historical approach needs to address both the social origins of women's oppression and the nature of language itself. Women's oppression arises from social relations; sexual relations do not emerge in a predictable way but are shaped by the wider parameters of society. Studies of pre-class societies have found that women's social position varied according to women's role in the productive process (Engels 1972, Oakley 1972, Leacock 1981, Sanday 1981, Coontz and Henderson 1986). Women's oppression is a historical product, which arose in a systematic form with class society, and has therefore changed within different societies. In capitalism, the privatization of childcare, the burden of domestic care of the old and the young borne mainly by women, these are the material roots of the inequality that women experience. Far from women's oppression springing from individual attitudes, still less from individual men, its cause is social. The same class relations that exploit in the name of profit, neglect investment in childcare for the same reason. This is the material basis of women's oppression upon which sexist ideology in many various and contradictory forms is built. It is not ideas that create oppression – oppressive as such ideas may be – but rather how a society is organized, and in whose interests it is run. In its material origins, women's oppression is no different to other oppressions: racism cannot be explained without reference to the slave trade, sectarianism and ethnic division without reference to colonialism, and women's oppression without reference to the mode of production that forces women, in the main, to take care of children.

Women's oppression is also experienced very differently across social classes, something that the concept of gender fails to take adequately into account. Far from there being a communality, linguistic or otherwise, of women, there are sharp social lines that divide. Class separates women as much today as it has down through history (Cliff 1984). Quite apart from stark wealth differences in absolute terms, the class gap seems to be widening. A recent study in Ireland shows that female senior executives earn 86 per cent of their male equivalents salaries while earnings for women as a whole stand at 61 per cent of male average earnings.[22] As Johnetta Cole has argued, an exclusive emphasis on gender can mask or deny class relations (Cole 1986). Behind gender, what is being avoided is reference to the social relations among women. The myth of the empowered executive *à la* Tannen or Wolf, neglects to say who she is in charge of – probably some other women: a secretary, a home-help, a nanny. African-American poet Audre Lorde put it with characteristic frankness:

> If white American feminist theory need not deal with the differences between us, and the resulting difference in our oppressions then how do you deal with the fact that women who clean your houses and tend your children while you attend conferences on feminist theory are, for the most part, poor women and women of color? (Lorde 1996: 160)

The class difference that Lorde refers to here is not just *another* difference, another instance of the plurality inherent in the analytic category of gender, another relationship of power, as Scott maintains (Scott 1996). It is one that actually influences the intensity of oppression. What constitutes oppression diverges across social classes, and methods of challenging it vary accordingly. It is worth recalling what was written at the beginning of the century in pre-revolutionary Russia:

> For the majority of women . . . equal rights with men would mean only an equal share in inequality, but for the chosen few it would indeed open the doors to new and unprecedented rights and privileges that until now have been enjoyed by men of the bourgeois class alone. (Kollontai 1977: 61)

Kollontai's observation strikes home as much today and perhaps it is this class difference that determines the setting in which gender occurs. Gender as we have seen is weak from a theoretical perspective. In masking class divisions, it remains merely a reformulation of a dichotomy that the ruling class has little difficulty living with. Some go further and see, with some justification, the exclusive insistence on gender as positive block to change. Audre Lorde writes: 'as a tool of social control, women have been encouraged to recognize only one area of human difference as legitimate, those differences which exist between men and women' (Lorde 1996: 169).

It is the male/female emphasis of gender that, despite social constructionist claims, fails to explain or elucidate language use as well. The gender approach shares with those who deny women's oppression an important common strand: a generalization about men and women that, without specific causes, becomes timeless. This prevents the social dynamic of language being grasped. It blocks the understanding that language is socially cooperative, including between men and women. Feminist accounts which set women's language apart from men's, or make male linguistics strategies competing with women's, or who speak of miscommunication between the sexes, underplay the relationship between language and history and also women's role in history. Linguistic *exchange* between men and women, some have argued, was a crucial element in the evolution of the earliest human societies (Leacock 1981: 229). Yet accounts which place male power at the centre of human society, yesterday or today, disregard the degree to which men and women must cooperate for social purposes. By the same stroke, they make women victims of male-dominated linguistic communication rather than active agents in language production and innovation.

Much of the work on sex and language surveyed in this chapter starts from an essentialist male/female divide that the conceptualization of gender encourages. I have argued that sexism in language is not inherent to the structure of language *per se*, nor to supposed innate speaking styles of men and women. Neither is it the case that sexism in society can be alleviated somehow by changing speaking styles, which themselves are based on received ideas about men and women. Language reform, when not linked to social change, is inevitably limited. Where these changes occur on a generalized basis they refer much more widely to general social changes that have impinged on individual consciousness rather than being the result of any voluntaristic attempt to impose new meanings on language. Language, in other words, is as much historically and socially situated as women's oppression. It is this historical and social dimension that gender misses and that fails to account adequately for the social nature of language. Language and verbal interaction, far from being determined or accounted for on the basis of sex, spring from all the complexity of social factors and situations in which language-makers, men and women, find themselves and intervene. Marjorie Goodwin's study, *He-Said-She-Said*, quoting from Vygotsky, asserts: 'The true direction of the development of thinking is not from the individual to the social but from the social to the individual' (Goodwin 1990: 13). The relationship between sex and language, as her study so vibrantly proves, is best seen in this light. The concept of gender, by contrast, would seem to start, and finish, with the individual.

Notes

1 In Ireland, for example, women constitute 1 per cent of all Professors, 6 per cent of Assistant Professors and 7 per cent of Senior Lecturers. While over 50 per cent of undergraduates are female, only 17 per cent of academic staff are female (HEA 1977; see also Andy Pollak in the *Irish Times* Saturday 27 June 1998 for an

account of recent research into female participation rates in Irish academic institutions).

2 French feminist linguistics is more structuralist, with a psychological emphasis on the way language is 'sexed' (Irigaray 1993). See Appignanesi (1994) for the relative downplaying of political correctness in French.

3 Whorf's ideas, along with Sapir and following Boas, influenced a whole generation of American anthropologists, psychologists and linguists. Margaret Mead was very influenced by these ideas, for example. In the 1960s, however, with a renewed emphasis on cognitive and structuralist linguistics, and particularly Chomsky's emphasis on mental processes, the pendulum swung away from Whorf's ideas. There was an eclipsing of the social and cultural in language. The current interest in identity – cultural and other – has revived the idea that culture and language are deeply interlocked (Gumperz and Levinson, 1996 is one such example).

4 Other research in different social settings has found that young women are just as likely to use slang as young men (Eckert 1989, Goodwin 1990).

5 Spender claims that her view does not necessarily resort to biological determinism 'but neither does it exclude a biological dimension' (1985: 77). However, she is in no doubt that 'in patriarchal order' women and men inhabit different worlds (1985: 78). Other radical feminists go further, arguing that women collude in the male project. Penelope claims that in the 'Patriarchal Universe of Discourse' 'women's minds do the work of patriarchy' and calls for the recreation of a women's world, through redefining the structure of English (for the near-mysticism of this view see Penelope 1990: introduction, and particularly xxxvi).

6 Longman's *Dictionary of the English Language* (1991), for example, still gives the first meaning of *lady* as 'having authority or rights of property especially as a feudal superior' and the two subsequent meanings given refer explicitly to social position. For *woman*, the first two meanings emphasize age and occupational contexts, with the sexist use of 'mistress' being listed afterwards (Longman 1991). Dictionaries are a little more circumspect in their sexism than some would make out.

7 For a full account of Volosinov's dynamic view of language see Chapter 2.

8 That Darwin's *The Ascent of Man* referred to humanity is fairly obvious from his reference to both sexes. Women's decisive role in evolution is convincingly addressed by Tanner (1981).

9 Volosinov's term was 'evaluative accent' (see Chapter 2 and Volosinov 1973: 80–81). Volosinov describes the process in strikingly similar terms – a word being 'a two-sided act'. As he explains, 'I give myself verbal shape from another's point of view, ultimately from the point of view of the community to which I belong' (Volosinov 1973: 86). See also Chapter 2. See Dentith (1995: 146–190) for a succinct account of both Volosinov's and this aspect of Bakhtin's work.

10 Negroponte, whose book *Being Digital* (1995) Spender so uncritically quotes, is at one with Spender's unbounded optimism for computers. 'If the [present] rate of growth were to continue (quite impossibly) the total number of Internet users would exceed the population of the world by 2003', we are told on page 3. Spender herself describes the new technologies as ' reprogramming the human condition', no less. See Chapter 3, pp. 58–59. for figures about relatively restricted access to computers.

11 Green recounts how Burchfield, when editor of the *Oxford English Dictionary*

Supplements, defended the use of *Jew*, despite complaints that the entry was abusive, insulting and reflected a deplorable attitude (Green 1996: 375).

12 Green (1996) quotes one example: *cherish* in 1968 was explained as 'A mother cherishes her baby.' By 1983 this had become 'Parents cherish their children' (Green 1996: 378). A minor adjustment but one which indicates that dictionaries are forced to recognize some social realities in order not to become completely aloof and irrelevant.

13 Kramarae and Treichler explain that their dictionary is one of 'feminist thinking and word-making'. Other dictionaries can be quite abstruse, such as Daly and Caputi's *Webster's First Intergalactic Wickedry of the English Language.* Another example would be Kramarae and Treichler 1985.

14 Tannen recounts research which showed that in the case of talk in an all-female office, female office managers showed some assertive 'male' linguistic characteristics to their secretaries (1995: 223)

15 The number of women managers in the US increased from 16 per cent in 1970 to over 40 per cent in the mid-1990s. See O'Leary and Ryan (1994) for an account of the growth in US women managers and these attitudes. See O'Connor (1996) for women's supposedly super-capitalistic management techniques.

16 The postvocalic /r/, also known as the non prevocalic /r/, is when 'r' is pronounced after a vowel. In, for example, *barking* or *mother* the 'r' would be heard.

17 Cameron and Coates refer to this in Trudgill's study although in Labov's later Philadephia study women who were working were classified according to their own occupations (Labov 1998).

18 Labov was more concerned with the methodological difficulties about findings skewed towards production of the standard than he was about the substantive ideological issue of whether standard/non-standard was perceived in the same way for everyone.

19 In Ireland in 1997 only 18 per cent of all full-time students belonged to the skilled, semi-skilled and unskilled workers group, whereas 58 per cent belonged to the managers, professionals and farmers group (HEA 1997)

20 Coates misinterprets the thrust of Goodwin's conclusions and continues to maintain that boys are uniformly more adversarial and competitive (Coates 1993). She omits to say, for example that the girls' *he-said-she-said* strategy is a *dispute*. She claims it is an example of typical indirect 'female' speech. She misses Goodwin's point that face-saving in this case is not a feature of cooperation but of more effective accusation.

21 Cameron's study analyses the content of what the selected men are saying, in this case a particularly sexist and anti-gay conversation, as she points out. 'Performing gender identity' would seem to be a singularly anodyne term for this.

22 See *Business and Finance*, 23–29 April 1998.

5   The Politics of Standard English

The Italian socialist, Antonio Gramsci, in one of his many writings on linguistics, maintained that language controversies always arose alongside other social problems as part of the ruling class's attempt to reassert its ideological sway. The 'language question' in Italy was, as the Sardinian Gramsci knew well, an aspect of political struggle, and the imposition of one language, a political act (Gramsci 1985: 182–187). Today the controversies surrounding Standard English, from whatever part of the English-speaking world they surface, betoken the ideological unease in periods of political upheaval observed so accurately by Gramsci.

In Britain the debate over Standard English has arisen in a specific political and educational context. The attempt to foist conservative views about language in teaching fitted with the Thatcherite and traditional Conservative view of education, language and social class. The project was ideologically motivated and ideologically driven, with the Conservative Centre for Policy Studies leading the fray.[1] While some of that debate has subsided in Britain, the issues continue to resurface (Honey 1997). Some might say that, looked at from an international perspective amid a sea of other Englishes worldwide, the Standard English debate as it has occurred in Britain seems narrowly parochial. Yet the debate has been bitter and shrill. 'Theories based on worthless pieces of scientific reasoning', emanating from 'the guru Foucault' and 'various Marxist or neo-Marxist irrational belief systems', is how one vocal traditionalist brands the 'enemies of Standard English' (Honey 1983, 1997). Another, Marenbon, is more apocalyptic: a 'new Orthodoxy has gained control of the educational establishment and is sweeping away many of the traditional landmarks.' There is no question that Standard English is superior to 'unrefined' dialects (1987: 24). 'May God grant [politicians and Committees] . . . firmness of resolve for in the future of its language there lies the future of a nation!' he declares (1987: 40). Others, from a different viewpoint, confirm how political the issue is. According to one, for and against Standard English positions range

> from a view that standard English is correct English and must be uniformly enforced in all context of use (with dialects extirpated) and that children not drilled in the rules of standard grammar are both deviant and disempowered (strong right wing position) to a view that Standard English is a badge of upper class power and that to require children to learn it is a form of social enslavement (strong left-wing position I) to a view that Standard English must be taught to working class children so that they can wrest linguistic power from those more privileged than themselves (strong left-wing position II). (Carter 1997: 8)[2]

Political labelling has become the norm in what has been written on Standard English. 'Authoritarian', 'libertarian', 'egalitarian (people with socialist and anarchist views)', the 'uncertain' and the 'eclectic' are descriptions of the various political positions in the debate (McArthur 1998). Those perceived as 'against' Standard English are seen as subversive. So much so that McCrum, Cran and MacNeil felt duty bound to proffer the following disturbing rider in the Preface to their revised edition of *The Story of English*:

> We are glad to take this opportunity to emphasize the importance of Standard English, American and British, throughout the world. . . . It is the English of the Oxford English Dictionary and the Random House Dictionary and, as its name implies, is the 'standard' from which all the other varieties of the language depart. In the world of language, Standard English is like the air we breathe, comparatively so colourless that it passes almost unnoticed. Yet it remains the cornerstone of the language and the guarantee of its future as an international phenomenon. (McCrum et al. 1992)

This effusiveness about one Standard English, from those who write so convincingly about a language and its many varieties and had considered entitling their work *The English Languages*, jars strangely. *The Story of English*, in its book and TV form, represented something of a watershed in its popular presentation of English as heterogenous and variable. Perhaps it is a measure of the social weight of their critics and an indication of where the real orthodoxies in society lie that they should issue this incongruous statement. Gramsci stressed that no language was ever 'just a piece of clothing that could fit indifferently as form over any content'; languages represent an integral conception of the world (Gramsci 1985: 226). Standard English, it seems, would appear to be no different.

In this chapter I examine first some widely held ideas about Standard English and attempt to show that they are based on ideologically laden views of language itself. I look at the historical roots and social basis of the emergence of a standard and how in Britain in the seventeenth and eighteenth centuries it came to mean different things to different social classes. I look at how Standard English, from the Victorian era onwards, came to be promoted by the ruling class for hegemonic purposes and how its linguistic assumptions fitted with the Saussurean view of language. I consider how the concept of Standard English, including what is meant by grammar, sits ill with the realities of the flux of spoken speech. Finally I examine what is meant by non-standard varieties and to what extent they can be regarded as separate linguistic entities.

Myths about Standard English

In a very real sense, language is something about which everyone has an opinion because every speaker knows something about it. We have a deep sense of attachment to how people speak, to ways of speaking that we know or identify with. As Raymond Williams wrote: 'the making and hearing of certain sounds [is] a large part of our social sense' (Williams 1961: 214). This profoundly social aspect of language means that ideas held about language are interlaced with wider views about society. Many of these ideas, often expressed intuitively about language, constitute part of what Gramsci called 'common sense'. By this, he meant the largely unconscious way of perceiving and understanding the world, a taken-for-granted world view, which has been inherited from the past. Though appearing natural and self-evident, it is in fact, as Gramsci makes clear, the articulation of an ideology of a specific social class in its own interests, at a specific time (Gramsci 1985:

323–333). Gramsci's notion of common sense is particularly apposite for the assumptions made about Standard English. I shall first look at some of the myths surrounding Standard English – myths which seem to fit superficially with social experience but myths which are not ideologically innocent.

Without it English will collapse. Society needs a language standard otherwise no one will be able to understand anyone else and communication will break down. The integrity of Standard English becomes a symbol for the integrity of society as a whole. People see bad grammar as a social symptom. Frequent letters on this subject to national newspapers and periodic public statements align falling English standards with social decay and collapse, often in tones of moral panic (Cameron 1995a: 82–85).

For conservatives, there is a simple equation between Standard English and social stability. Respect for Standard English equals respect for discipline (Honey 1997: 137). English must be 'safeguarded', mainly from a disrespectful populace and brazen linguists who fail to show a veneration for certain forms of language (1997: 138). Honey intones a foreboding quotation from Milton: '[w]hen the language in common use in any country becomes irregular and depraved, it is followed by their ruin and their degradation' (1997: 149). He sees this as a creeping affair from the bottom of society upwards and singles out a number of 'losses to the English language' and 'the invasion of RP by features of popular London speech'.[3]

Honey's claims are not new. Pronouncements about the terminal decline of English have peppered the history of the language. In the sixteenth century, Philip Sidney lamented Latin intrusions into the language. *Contaminate, geometrical, segregated* and *integated,* for instance, were supposedly too Latin-sounding to be included in English. His plea failed to stem their adoption (Greenbaum 1988: 4). Jonathan Swift saw linguistic innovation as a sign of degeneracy. He declared in 1712 that 'our Language is extremely imperfect; that its daily improvements are by no means in proportion to its daily Corruptions' and that it was full of abuses and absurdities (Crowley 1991: 31). He even argued, unsuccessfully, for an academy to regularize the 'Manglings and Abbreviations' that were polluting the language and to restore 'the quiet of the Nation' (Kelly 1988: 89–103). Daniel Jones, a phonetics specialist writing in the 1930s, was utterly persuaded of the connection between standards of speech and social conduct: 'You cannot produce a uniform high standard of social life in a community without producing a uniform high standard of speech' (Bailey 1991: 7). More recently, after the second world war, English was declared by some to be suffering from degeneration caused by American-isms, while many others in the US also saw their English in decline mainly due to the changes of the 1960s (Newman 1974: 9).

Nostalgia for a supposed better language of former times becomes a comforting rallying call for those wanting to resist change. In reality, the presence of a standard makes very little difference, either to society or to language. During the times when there was no standard, English suffered little in its written or spoken forms. In America, before Webster's interventions in the name of standardization, there was a high degree of uniformity in the English spoken. One observer described this as quite aston-ishing, given the linguistic and dialectal variety of the settlers (Baugh and Cable 1993: 351). In England, likewise, during the three centuries before Standard English was used with its modern sense – for the first time in 1844 according to Harris – English did not disintegrate (Harris 1988: 17–20). A standard language is an afterthought, not an integral part of actual language development, which takes place with or without a standard say-so.

All change is bad for the language. The assumption is that language is timeless. 'If English was good enough for Jesus, it is good enough for you', an Arkansas town school superintendent, unthinkingly, once said.[4] His assumption chimes with those who hark back to a golden age in which every sentence was a correct sentence and every speaker deferred, if not to God, at least to great literature. Standard English is seen as arising from centuries of civilization and culture. The fact that Chaucer and Shakespeare wrote in different varieties of English is beside the point. Standard English becomes an ideal of usage so that it is invested, as Leith notes, with 'an aura of transcendence, so that like the nation, the law and the market it supposedly operates at a level above the merely human' (Leith 1997: 32).

These time-free notions about language echo equally detached ideals of nationhood. Standard English is presented as being the repository of all that is British, British *par excellence*. Not everyone, of course, is included in this esteemed heritage. Murray, the diligent Victorian lexicographer, dictionary maker, and something of reformer in other fields, made it plain that Standard English was about 'the race of English words which is to form the dominant speech of the world' as opposed to any other English spoken throughout the globe (quoted in Harris: 1988: 18). Much later, Enoch Powell repeated the same point in support of white, racist claims to English: 'Others may speak and read English – more or less – but it is our language not theirs. It was made in England by the English and it remains our distinctive property, however widely it is learnt or used' (quoted in Greenbaum 1990: 15).

Yet one pure, timeless English does not stand up. Language change is part and parcel of the general flux of human society. The very fact that there are other recognized Englishes elsewhere in the world – US English, Australian English, Nigerian English, Canadian English – in itself somewhat detracts from the monolithic, authoritative entity that is claimed for British English. Swift may have started to find ways to fix the language for ever, but even he came to see the futility of the task and gave up on his proposals for a language academy. Standard English cannot regulate, or even 'manage', change as Honey would like, because a language cannot be put in a time capsule away from society or other ways of speaking. After a century and a half of standardization, not only is the standard ever more elusive but regional and other dialects, local ways of speaking and varieties of English have not faded away. The wider presence of mass media has not led to greater linguistic uniformity, as it was first believed it would. As Trudgill has pointed out, just hearing Standard English on TV or the radio does not appear to influence people's production of speech (Trudgill 1990: 11). Indeed those most in favour of standardization cannot escape the fact that the would-be standardizer *par excellence* – the media – have singularly failed to engender speech uniformity.[5] Standard English may be held up as the model but language-users pay little heed and Standard English is left forever trying to catch up.

Written English is *the* standard. Standard English is often taken to mean the opposite of colloquial English, slang or dialect. 'By standard English I mean the language in which this book is written, which is essentially the same form of English used in books and newspapers all over the world', Honey tells us, disingenuously, at the outset of his book (Honey 1997: 1). He sets Standard English against dialect, Black Vernacular English, and the 'broadest forms of regional accents'. The grammatical forms he selects, usually to berate their misuse, are in fact assessed as correct on the basis of whether they should be written (1997: 149–160). In *The Language Trap* he tells us that a whole generation of theorists has succumbed to the idea that one language is as good as another. The following, we are told, is set to become the norm in schools:

> [I]f a London schoolchild for example writes 'Me and my mate never don nufink like what them geezers said we done', his teacher should applaud rather than correct it. (Honey 1983: iii)

The example reveals the crass stereotyping of working-class speech that lies behind many pleas for a standard. It also glosses over the distinction between written and spoken speech, for it is unlikely that such a sentence would ever be written. This confusion encourages the stigmatizing of certain speech forms, on the basis that they do not conform to written conventions. Yet all spoken forms diverge from written ones. Spoken speech and dialects have grammars which follow different principles, and deferring to one paradigmatic Standard English fails to take cognizance of this fact, a point to which I return. Written language is just one type of language use with its own conventions. If everyone actually applied these conventions to spoken speech all the time, verbal interaction would be long-winded, unwieldy, and often foolish.

Standard English is an indispensable tool for social advancement. Honey, more populist in his presentation than Marenbon, rests his case on a subtle appeal to class in British society. Working-class students in schools, he tells us, will be missing out if they are not taught Standard English. Standard English is the 'Gateway to Liberty' (1997: 90). Honey subscribes to the social ladder view of society. 'There is vastly more equality now than there was fifty years ago', he cavalierly assumes (1997: 65). Regrettably, the facts disprove his case. There is ample statistical evidence that, over recent years, in education as elsewhere, class segregation has increased, not decreased, and that the British school system constitutes one of the most glaring examples of a new social apartheid (Adonis and Pollard 1997: 34–63).[6] As regards continuing social inequality, modern-day capitalism, perhaps, more than access to Standard English, seems to be the cause.[7]

Social betterment touches on another opinion held about Standard English. It evokes imprecisely, but unmistakably, a certain kind of accent. 'King's English' and 'Queen's English', 'Oxford English' and 'BBC English' are referred to in some definitions of Standard English. 'Received Pronunciation' – a conveniently agentless term – is probably only spoken by about 12–15 per cent of the population (Trudgill 1990: 2). It is this association with accent and its social underpinning that gives the debate about Standard English in Britain its particular twist. 'RP' is often claimed to be 'above' dialects, and to mean speaking 'without an accent'. So ingrained is this idea that Trudgill has to remind us that '[a]ll of us speak with an accent and all of us speak a dialect' (1990: 2). Australians, Americans, New Zealanders, South Africans, Kenyans and Irish would simply take this for granted. Certainly Italians and French recognize their standard languages as dialects. Such perversities in the British context stem from Britain's history and its specific class ideologies, some of which I examine in the next section.

But the belief that there is a Standard English and accent is not just held in popular consciousness. It has been promoted by some linguists. Early this century, Henry Wyld, a historical linguist otherwise open-minded to sound change and different accents, rated RP very highly. He informed us that that the Lancashire 'r' is 'peculiar' and has 'to southern ears' a 'very harsh ugly sound' (Wyld 1907: 51). Later Daniel Jones, whose publications on English pronunciation became extraordinarily popular, while formally recognizing all types of accent, left the reader in little doubt that the public school ('in the English sense not in the American sense,' Jones hastens to point out) is where the desired RP is learnt and is the best (Jones 1964: 12). Honey is even more categorical. Regional accents are for the most part judged by him to be 'incorrect' because of their associations with 'the uneducated, the unsophisticated, the ignorant', whereas RP is associated with the educated and should naturally be admired (Honey 1997: 104). 'Educated' here is a euphemism for class. Leith sums up the connection between class, accent and Standard English: '[T]he association between Standard English is not altogether surprising. Socially, pronunciation is the most pervasive aspect of speech and carries with it a host of associations. In the case of RP these include power and influence – the very qualities also projected onto the notion of standard English' (Leith 1997: 34). Nevertheless whilst the RP accent rests on social class, it is presented as a natural order of things, miraculously 'received', and the best way to speak. So pervasive is this idea that the overwhelming majority of speakers who do not happen to speak in this particular way are 'branded on the tongue', in Orwell's phrase.

Social Class and the Emergence of a Standard Written Language

It is important not to read the ideological positions of the present debate about standard language mechanically back into history. The call for Standard English from conservative sources today does not mean that it has always been a reactionary rallying call. Views about language are deeply embedded in history and any appraisal of these ideological questions necessarily involves a full 'consciousness of their historicity', in Gramsci's phrase. By seeing the present in terms of the past the traditionalist comes to resemble what Gramsci aptly termed 'a walking anachronism, a fossil not living in the modern world' (1971: 324). However, from another perspective, to characterize standardization as always having been a conservative project imposed from above would be to suffer from an equal disregard of the forces of history.

Standard English evolved from a number of different impetuses: from the development of trade and industry and the consolidation of the nation state and later from mass industrialization and education. In the period from 1600 to the 1830s the drive for a standard English represented the social changes of the times. As part of its increasing economic and social wealth, the ruling class wanted to devise a standard language out of many spoken idioms, which then became downgraded to dialects. Those who spoke dialects wanted access to the standardized written form as a means of gaining new knowledge. With the momentous changes of the industrial revolution, Standard English came to be identified far more closely with a specific ideological project of the ruling class. It is to these developments that I now turn.

Developments in England, due to the relatively early consolidation of the national state, gave the forging of standard language a distinctive character. Leith, in his now classic social history of the language, identifies the emergence of a standard variety of English with four crucial and interrelated factors: the selection of a dialect, the adoption of this variety by the ruling class, the elaboration of functions afforded by the use of this variety by the powerful, and the codification of a written standard (Leith 1997: Chapter 2). The East Midland dialect, spoken in a triangle between London, Oxford and Cambridge, became the lingua franca of an increasingly powerful, self-conscious merchant class. A growing array of linguistic functions became identified with this new dominant dialect. Church and state, religion and law provided significant input to the expansion and spread of the new dialect, with an authorized English version of the Bible appearing in 1611. The controversies that emerged about the role of Latin and French and their influence on the English language reflected the spread of a more secular education and greater political and economic independence from France. Codification of the written word sought to order language in a rapidly changing world. Johnson's *Dictionary*, which appeared in 1755, along with other attempts to officially stamp certain grammatical usages as 'correct', represents the latter stages of the codification of a written standard.

It is worth stressing the importance of the role of the rising dominant class in the process in which a standard came to be recognized and accepted. The standard was centred on the English spoken in London, where the merchant class was particularly strong, and the southern side of a triangle that included the centres of learning of Oxford and Cambridge and not, as in the Elizabethan era, on the language of the court. 'It was the polite language of gentlemen' with all the social connotations that this implied (Blake 1996: 239). It was a dialect spoken and written by an influential commercial class which was using its wealth to buy land, and to gain prestige and political representation.[8] Williams, in his seminal essay, insists on this point: the emergence of the East Midland dialect was less the rise of one regional accent than the emergence of a class dialect. 'The class structure of England was now decisively changing, at the beginning of a period which can be summed up as the effort of the rising middle class to establish its own common speech' (Williams 1961: 220). The emerging standard language reflected the economic and political concerns of a certain class, its priorities and its growing interest in science and learning. It has been claimed that the privileged position of this dialect was a historical and geographical accident (Milroy and Milroy 1985: 33, Carter 1997: 57). In one sense, of course, this is true: it could easily have been any other dialect in England at the time that could have come to play such a decisive role. There was nothing inherently superior about the East Midland dialect that specially prepared it for its future role. Dialects are equal; it is their histories that are different. But from another point of view, the growing ascendancy of the East Midland dialect was not a historical accident. It was not chance that London came to have such a decisive role, nor accidental that populations from the surrounding counties poured into that city and that Oxford and Cambridge became vital. It was a development that can only be understood with reference to the growing trading class based in London and well placed to begin investing in the industries that would so revolutionize production. It was these expanding economic activities, overseas as well as at home, that allowed the East Midland dialect to gain dominance. Class relations in this sense were decisive in the selection of that particular dialect.

Social class also shaped attitudes towards a new standard written language. In the second half of the eighteenth century, which ended with the American and French revolutions, a stark political map was being drawn. Class and political divergence meant that a 'common speech' meant vastly different things to different people. It meant one thing to those frequenting the urbane coffee houses and trading places of London, and quite another to the lower orders of these cities whose speech differed from the new standard. Burke and Paine, in their clash over the significance of the French revolution, represented the two poles of this social division. Smith has convincingly shown that their political differences made themselves felt also in matters of language. They wrote in markedly different styles, with Burke drawing on the classical and Paine on the vernacular. The terms used for language – the 'vulgar and the refined', the 'corrupt and the pure', the 'barbaric and the civilized' – stood for divisions in society (Smith 1986: 3). Similarly, Walker's *Pronouncing Dictionary* of 1791 confirmed that the model pronunciation was London, and that 'people of correct taste' should be contemptuous of the language of the lower orders (Leith and Graddol 1996: 159–161). In this changing social world in which starker social divisions were emerging, attitudes to language, like everything else, had reactionary or revolutionary undertones. Two figures identified with language and politics in this era epitomized this polarity. Dr Johnson held up the model of a 'refined' language for the rising middle class. William Cobbett, writing half a century later, proposed a radically different model. The contrast between Johnson's and Cobbett's views of English merits examination for their opinions on language stand at opposite ends of the social and political spectrum.

Johnson and Cobbett: Different Standards

Samuel Johnson (1709–84) in background, career and social standing was typical of a new class that was growing in confidence. Born in Lichfield, the son of a bookseller, he had attended Oxford before becoming a schoolmaster. In 1738 he began writing for the *Gentleman's Magazine*, and eventually became its Parliamentary correspondent. Edward Cave, editor of the magazine and a close friend of Johnson's, had dabbled in some of the industrial inventions that were to take off in the next decades.[9] Johnson was part of a new social layer of learned people who were familiar with the new discoveries in medicine and science and new theories in economics. Johnson's *Dictionary* reflected this zeal for learning. It was compiled by one who, born outside the landed class, was making his claim to be part of cultivated eighteenth-century society.

A clearly defined social world for his class was emerging. Englishness was becoming defined in opposition to England's commercial rival, France. The pupil and friend of Samuel Johnson, David Garrick, heralded the publication of the *Dictionary* (1755) as a blow against the French because it had been produced without an academy (McCrum et al. 1992: 139). Johnson was the model of what good talk was in an age when conversation was prized, yet, unlike France, social and moral discipline, not aristocratic patronage, was what was respected. Johnson was intensely patriotic, believing that liberty was an English trait and that the 'genius' of English lay in the English way of life. English grammar reflected all that was good and to flout its rules was to flout God (Leith and Graddol 1996: 161). McCrum et al. summarize how the project of the *Dictionary* brings all these things together:

> Beyond the practical need to make order out of chaos . . . keen to ape their betters and anxious to define and circumscribe the various worlds to conquer – lexical as well as social and commercial – it is highly appropriate that Dr Samuel Johnson, the very model of an eighteenth-century literary man . . . should have published his *Dictionary* at the very beginning of the heyday of the middle class . . . Johnson . . . raised common sense to the heights of genius. (McCrum et al. 1992: 137)

In his well-known definition of the lexicographer, Johnson described himself as 'a harmless drudge' and writers of dictionaries as 'unhappy mortals' (Johnson 1768), touches of ironic modesty that capture something of the disposition of this burgeoning nation of shopkeepers. The compilation of the *Dictionary* itself presaged the modern. This was not a project sponsored by the leisured gentry; Johnson's 'dictionary workshop' had salaried employees, paid copy clerks and accountants, and was fitted up, appropriately enough, like a counting house (Green 1996: 220).

Green describes Johnson as occupying a pivotal moment (Green 1996). His look backwards at the golden age of Shakespeare is intended to offer a reassuring model for his own era. Social stability must be upheld as the bulwark against change. Johnson makes a last-ditch stand: 'Tongues like governments have a natural tendency to degenerate: we have long preserved our constitution: let us make some struggle for our languages' (quoted in Crowley 1991: 42). Not surprisingly, it is literary language that is the model. Words in English with a Latin, or supposed Latin, origin were admired and Latin grammar was considered a rule-giver to emulate. 'Grammar school' in Johnson's dictionary is defined as 'a school for teaching the learned languages'. The spoken language was considered vulgar and lacking in refinement, particularly the language of the 'laborious and mercantile part of the people' (1768). Johnson was extraordinarily dismissive of ordinary people's speech. He put it thus: 'Of the laborious and mercantile part of the people, the diction is in a great measure casual and mutable. . . . This fugitive cant, which is always in a state of increase or decay, cannot be regarded as any part of the durable materials of a language and therefore must be suffered to perish with other things unworthy of preservation' (Johnson 1768).[10] Dialect words, Johnson also completely rejected. Having himself received a classical education, outside the ranks of the landowning class, Johnson wanted to uphold a model of language which was also a means of class distinction. A sharp demarcation between the classes, between the mercantile middle class and the labouring poor, was the basis of social order, which a standard language should reflect. His *Dictionary* has been described as supplying

> a pretext for reinforcing the political status quo, religious authority and cultural authoritarianism. Its technical criteria are designed to exclude insubordination, dissent and subversion – everything that offers to destabilize verbal meanings and social values. (Mengham 1993: 114)

The *Dictionary* reflects in tone, religious zeal, and Johnson's many personal interjections, a deep-seated resistance to change. His entry for 'Freethinker' is 'a contemner of religion' and for 'Tory' – 'one who adheres to the ancient constitution of the state'. Johnson wrote in an essay in the *Rambler*: 'I have laboured to refine our language to grammatical purity and to clear it from colloquial barbarisms, licentious idioms and irregular combinations' (quoted in Baugh and Cable 1993: 267). In this moralizing tone, he spoke of how he saw the need to protect not only language, but society, from subversion.

William Cobbett (1763–1835), on the other hand, had a somewhat different starting point for his *Grammar of the English Language*, first published in 1818 in New York. Where Johnson represented the new urban middle class, pre-French revolution, Cobbett was the spokesman of the rural poor, the small producers, the artisans who as a class stood midway between 'the people' and the industrial working class of the nineteenth century. Born in

Surrey, destined to become a farm labourer, he joined the army as a private soldier. After a period in revolutionary France and disillusioned with what he saw, he went to America and worked as a political journalist, returning to Britain with what he called 'an acrid patriotism'. This belief was not to last long. He founded the *Political Register* in 1802 but quickly discovered the limits of British freedom of speech when he was imprisoned for two years for printing an article against the flogging of British soldiers who had refused to obey orders (Green 1983: 345). He returned to America, where he published his *Grammar*. It was also published in Britain where he returned to continue his tireless indictment of poverty alongside wealth, and the 'oppressive commercial system'.

Perhaps nowhere do politics and language intertwine so clearly as in Cobbett's early *Grammar*. Its subtitle stated that it was 'especially for the use of Soldiers, Sailors, Apprentices and Ploughboys'. To it was appended six lessons 'intended to prevent Statesmen from using false grammar and from writing in an awkward manner' (Cobbett 1984). Everything about this *Grammar* of English was unconventional. The work is presented in the form of a series of letters addressed to his fourteen-year-old son, James, who beyond the informal reading that he had picked up would now need 'to acquire knowledge connected with books' (1984: 3). Cobbett regarded questions of language, including which language was to be the model, as an integral part of the British class system and the act of learning grammar on the part of 'the great body of my ill-treated and unjustly condemned countrymen' as an act of defiance (Green 1983: 418).

Writing was a weapon against tyranny, the study of grammar no idle pursuit. Knowledge of grammar was needed in 'struggles in the cause of freedom' (Cobbett 1984: 4). It was also needed to dethrone those men of letters such as Dr Johnson who extol classical learning in order to create a distance between themselves and those they castigate as 'unlearned'. Cobbett challenges the idea that classical languages are the model and that learned English necessarily the best. Learning 'is in the mind and not on the tongue' and he castigates the hypocrisy of the aristocracy for branding everyone else as unlearned (1984: 118). He makes use of non-standard dialects elsewhere in his writing, with great effect. He writes of 'shoy-hoys' and 'mawkses', local dialects for scarecrows, and compares them to politicians who renege on their promises. Cobbett uses language in a way that is, in the words of Thompson, 'solid and related not to a literary culture but to commonly available experience' (Thompson 1980: 823–824). The fact that his *Grammar* sold 100,000 copies, and that 'people were talking and arguing like Cobbett all over the land', indicates that his approach had a strong resonance. Like Paine before him, Cobbett uses a language that radically challenges the existing order, not least because it speaks directly to a new audience in their own language about their political concerns.

Present day advocates of Standard English have chosen to see Cobbett as a prescriptivist, because he appealed to grammar. Honey claims Cobbett for support of own argument, saying that Cobbett saw the acquisition of the grammatical forms of Standard English as a gateway to social acceptance (Honey 1997: 91–92). The analogy is misplaced. Cobbett's view of the proponents of the Standard English of his day was that their authority should be challenged and their dogmatic conservatism revealed as class privilege. Cobbett described them as 'dependants of the Aristo-cracy' and 'living on the sweat of other people's brows' (Cobbett 1984: 55). This is hardly the respect for the pillars of society that Honey espouses. It is true that Cobbett's stand towards tradition was ambiguous and certainly he was no revolutionary. The *Gram-mar* was dedicated to 'her Most Gracious Majesty Queen Caroline' and implored her to stand with the people against 'the Nobles and the Hierarchy'. Nevertheless he spoke, with an instinctive sense of their predicament, on behalf of those from country and town who had been pushed into being 'abject dependants' of the new industries. He was representative of the bottom of society, the artisans, the field labourers, the labouring poor, not yet fully industrialized, and his viewpoint contained a mixture of back-ward-looking and progressive ideas. These contradictions made Cobbett first a conservative but then, as reaction set in, increasingly radical. Cobbett came to give shape to a collective consciousness which, as he argued in defence of his *Grammar*, would ensure that 'the whole body of the people might become so completely capable of detecting and exposing the tricks and contrivances of their oppressors that the power of doing mischief will die a natural death in the hands of those oppressors' (Mengham 1983: 131). This rebellion in society and in language that Cobbett represented the very reason why his popularity soared, is entirely overlooked in Honey's account.

Cobbett's plea for grammar was an act of defiance since what it highlighted was in fact inequality of education. In an era before widespread access to written language, to demand it for the labouring classes was less advocacy of a standard than advocacy of justice. Cobbett, on more general matters of language, also stands in a different tradition to Johnson. He refutes the existence of a hierarchy of languages going back to Latin and Greek. In connection with languages that would have been branded 'primitive' by the orthodoxy of the day, Cobbett explains that the dichotomy 'unlearned/learned' in relation to languages is false. All languages are equally expressive and the labelling of some as 'learned' is intended to refer to the person who possesses their knowledge rather than the languages themselves (Cobbett 1984: 118). Cobbett's progressive views on language, finally, are part of a democratic view of language in which it is the people who use language, not the 'learned', who are important. Cobbett wanted to see a People's English, the English of the ordinary people, drawing on their experience and giving voice to their concerns. His political writings, as does his *Grammar*, reflects this priority.

Thus, in the eighteenth and early nineteenth centuries, language, like society itself, was in a state of flux. Johnson's *Dictionary* was a precursor of Standard English but in conditions of limited literacy amongst the overall population which lessened its impact.[11] Popular radicalism, as represented by Cobbett, challenged traditionalist views of language and sought to claim for the people access to the written language.

Standard English: a Class Dialect

Victorian Britain was a period of extraordinary social change. Production was revolutionized, cities mushroomed and upturned rural life, railways hurtled goods and people between towns and ports. As coal, iron and steel, shipyards, factories and slums brought new industrial landscapes, all aspects of social life were transformed. It was the age of capital expansion and one in which social class came starkly to be the defining feature of people's lives.

It is no coincidence that it was in this period that the term Standard English was first officially used,[12] it too, a mark of class. Increased political representation and mass education took shape under the aegis of a new and more confident bourgeoisie. Macaulay, who so often encapsulated the thinking of the ruling orders, made no apology for how they should see their role:

> The higher and the middling orders are the natural representatives of the human race. Their interest may be opposed, in some things, to that of their proper contemporaries, but it is identical with that of the innumerable generations which are to follow. (quoted in Thompson 1980: 905)

They defined themselves in opposition to the 'lower orders', were more self-conscious of their role as a governing class and wanted their values to leave their mark. This was the backcloth against which Victorian lexicographers and grammarians consolidated their work. Previously a unified language, particularly in its written form, had arisen organically, emerging from the needs of a society whose developing trade and industry made it an imperative. Now, as class divisions hardened, the new ruling class sought to put a clearer ideological stamp on the process. Standard English thus shifts from a functional convenience of a metropolitan class to a badge of social distinction (Williams 1961: 220).

Harris (1988), in an important piece on Standard English, argues that James Murray (1837–1915), lexicographer and editor of the first *Oxford English Dictionary* (*OED*), and the Cambridge philosopher G.E. Moore (1873–1958) shared a view of language that was to come to characterize thinking on Standard English. Harris shows how linguistic thought in the late nineteenth and early twentieth centuries separated language and philosophy into two separate spheres. This separation led to the description of language in self-referential terms, in which acceptability was defined according to linguistic correctness and meanings of words were given in terms of other words. At the heart of this, Harris maintains, is a flawed conception, because it ignores the fundamental character of language. Users of language do not assess correct usage in this way, for in real life evaluations are always connected to the context. Nevertheless Murray and Moore in different ways concentrated on a 'fixed code' concept of language and 'Standard English', being the representation of 'correct usage', merely became an extension of this idea (Harris 1988: 10). It is a procedure that rests upon the artificial distinction between a language in general and actual language use.[13]

This distinction, of course, was the one that Saussure made familiar as *langue* and *parole*. Saussure is often seen as something of a linguistic loner, his theory presented as removed from any social context and as a necessary step to linguistics becoming a science. Harris argues that the language standardization question in Britain and Saussure's view can be seen as part of the same intellectual and ideological current. Saussure's prioritization of the general system of language over actual instances of speech may thus be seen as simply another approach to standardization (Harris 1988: 23). In both versions, an abstract view of language came to be the focus of study and a realm over which, it appeared, nobody had any control. Harris maintains that 'this was standardization at a level never before seen'. It ushered in a 'grammarian's paradise', in which language became a detached object of study, removed from social realities (Harris 1987: 110–113).

Harris thus places Saussure's work in a political context. His insights, paralleled by Fairclough (1989: 22), complement what Volosinov had already observed, that the separating of language from its social roots is not ideologically innocent.[14] Harris shows that Saussure's view shares the same disdain for the vernacular as the Victorians', for it brushes aside dialects and ordinary speech as irrelevant. It thus becomes an idealized view of one nation, one language, embodied in the concept of a standard language (Harris 1987: 112).

Standard English became a linguistic imperative, an exemplary speech form and a cloak for elitism, all rolled into one. Consensus about the most desirable variety of English took shape within a narrow social stratum and according to the value-judgements of those within it. Standard speech came to be defined as the variety of speech which 'by reason of its cultural status and currency is held to represent the best form of that speech' (Harris 1988: 18–19). Items were selected and then sealed: '[a]s soon as a standard language has been formed . . . the lexicographer is bound to deal with that alone' (quoted in Crowley 1989: 117). The publication of the *OED* thus 'set a historic seal of approval on that choice'. Thus, Murray's compilation of the dictionary becomes both the discovery of the standard language and the creation of it. As Harris notes: 'There can hardly be a more remarkable example in intellectual history of quoting one's own evidence in order to establish the validity of what was claimed.' Standard English was simultaneously discovered and created. It was indeed a self-fulfilling prophecy (Harris 1988: 17).

The invention of this particular brand of Standard English fitted well with the ideology of the dominant social class of Victorian times. It provided a convenient model for mass education which set Standard English aside as the language of the educated and also implied that the speech that working-class children brought to school needed to be improved. By the end of the century, this divide between Standard English and people's spoken language had become an established fact. This description in Hardy's *Tess of the D'Urbervilles* (1891) captures something of the degree to which this division had become 'common sense':

> Mrs Durbeyfield habitually spoke the dialect; her daughter, who had passed the Sixth Standard in the National School under a London-trained mistress, spoke two languages: the dialect at home, more or less; ordinary English abroad and to persons of quality. (Hardy 1992: 28)

Standard English had thus become what 'persons of quality' spoke, a badge of education and class. It was during this period that further distinctions were made for 'correct' pronunciation. Where previously the lengthening of the vowel in such words as *path* and *past* denoted regional speech they now became a mode of class speech. Crucial in this process was the new cult of uniformity in the public schools (Williams: 1961: 224). The public school was to become the principal agency for an elite homogeneously acquiring a remarkably uniform (compared to other countries) standard language, which made it singularly cohesive as a symbol of social power. By 1908 phonetician Henry Sweet could write: 'Standard English . . . is now a class dialect more than a local dialect; it is the language of the educated all over great Britain' (Sweet 1908: 7). Sweet became immortalized as Professor Higgins in Bernard Shaw's *Pygmalion*, itself a somewhat ambiguous interpretation of the class pretensions surrounding speech in British society.

The class origins of Standard English, as it emerged in this period, explain the ideological difficulties it encountered. It claimed to speak on behalf of all, it claimed to be merely a question of correct language usage which transcended social divisions, but in reality it was the dialect of a narrow social layer. It was not just one English, but Good English, with the implication that other forms of speech were inferior. It became as it were 'embalmed', in Williams's memorable phrase (1961: 224).[15] It was presented as a mission to organize and control society, as part of an overall world view. However, nothing could hide the fact that its hegemony was exercised by a minority in the interest of that minority. This constituted a contradiction that the advocates of Standard English could not escape. However much Standard English was promoted, it came up against the reality that the majority of the population spoke differently and had different ideological concerns.

In society at large, in terms of language attitude and use, things were much more heterodox. While pronouncements were being made on the best English, regional and urban ways of speaking a common language blossomed and, as literacy increased, began to figure widely in written forms. Formal schooling, as the Educational Commissioners ruefully noted in the 1860s, was certainly not eroding dialect. There was a wave of dialect literature in Lancashire, Yorkshire and the North-East. Dialect appeared in popular literature, in serialized form, albeit sometimes not very realistically. This literature was immensely popular, with as many as 100,000 copies of serial fiction by Dickens and Reynolds being sold (Williams 1961: 165). Dialect almanacs flowered in the period 1860–1914 with a style and contents far removed from mainstream Victorian morality. As Joyce reveals, workers' journals, such as the textile operatives' *Cotton Times* recounted working-class life in local dialects (Joyce 1991: 278). Joyce's conclusions are that dialect constructs people's social identity, but the wealth of evidence he presents shows how social class shaped these workers' lives. The industrial cities brought forth distinctive dialects different to the rural areas around them and different from the standard prescribed from above. Class differences in life shaped class differences in language and this divergence testified to the limits of prescription.

Orwell and Demotic Speech

George Orwell, writing in the 1940s felt instinctively the snobbish obsolescence of Standard English and its 'stuffy' legacy from earlier prescriptivists. Standard English, 'salvaging obsolete words and turns of phrase which must never be departed from', was, for Orwell, the very opposite of what the defence of the English language should be. Orwell wrote a lot about language, partly because it was his trade perhaps, but also because he understood, amid the extremes of poverty and war in the 1930s and the 1940s, the intimate connection between politics and language. 'Politics and the English language' begins with an assumption that English is in decline. Orwell seems, thus, to be a traditionalist, defending, the language from the incursions of the new. Indeed, some of his views on language are traditionalist, for example his unproblematic rending of 'letting the meaning choose the word' (Orwell 1961: 336). But his concerns for a truly 'demotic speech' and his acute sensitivity to the interplay of class and language in Britain uncover, sometimes inadvertently, the limitations of the notion of Standard English.

In the twentieth century much continued to be done to buttress Standard English. Fowler's *The King's English* of 1906 had been followed by his *Dictionary of Modern English Usage*, which appeared in 1926. Compulsory education had seen Standard English copied from one blackboard to another with little questioning as to what it meant. Now style and usage became the model and seemed even more hedged about with laws and penalties than the old autocracy of the schoolmaster (Vallins 1953: 8). 'Public' uses of this socially accepted language, which Orwell variously called Standard English, Official English, Modern English, or more graphically, 'phrases tacked together like the sections of a prefabricated hen-house', signalled for Orwell a serious decline which reflected on all aspects of social life. He put it thus:

probably the deadliest enemy of good English is what is called 'standard English'. This dreary dialect, the language of leading articles, White Papers, political speeches, and BBC news bulletins is undoubtedly spreading. . . . The temporary decadence of the English Language is due, like so much else, to our anachronistic class system. 'Educated' English has grown anaemic because for long past it has not been reinvigorated from below. (Orwell 1970: 43)

Reinvigoration from below was, for Orwell, a question of returning to the principles of spoken speech. Standard English was aloof and stuffy because it was obsessed with flurries of words, empty-sounding phrases, and with supposed effect rather than transparency of meaning.

Orwell opposes this linguistic insincerity with 'demotic speech', language which accepts its connection with spoken speech. It would be a simple, concrete, everyday language, clear and popular, not the stilted, bookish language of broadcast speeches and what passed for political language.[16] It would contain regional and working-class features of speech. He held that '[t]he people likeliest to use simple concrete language and to think of metaphors that really call up a visual image are those who are in contact with physical reality' (Orwell 1970: 42). 'Language ought to be the joint creation of poets and manual workers', he claims, though, as things stood, the social gulf between them meant these two sorts of people would never meet (1970: 46).

Orwell's critique of Standard English summarizes, with rare intuition, the distance between the government and the people and how this distance is reflected in language, at a time when, during the war, there had been a surfeit of government broadcasts and, post-war, a feeling of disillusion. Orwell's comments often remain at the level of observations; he fails to develop his theory of language beyond generalities. In this respect, Williams is right to criticize Orwell for showing prejudices similar to those that he accuses others of. His branding of Americanism and certain phrases as 'ugly and inaccurate', for example, would seem to have more to do with personal taste than anything else. Moreover, his presentation of a series of linguistic guidelines, while invaluable, barely does justice to his theory of demotic speech (1961: 356–359). His understandable criticism of the unthinking style of contemporary communist leaflets (which he equates with the officialese of the BBC) should have been made on a political basis rather than a superficial stylistic one, especially from one so identified with socialist ideas. Nevertheless, Orwell's stressing of the degree to which the promotion of Standard English peremptorily brushes aside spoken language is important. Speech and writing, Orwell understands, 'are two different languages', with the former devalued, and he grasps the full political significance of this fact.[17]

The understanding of the role of spoken language in language development and use is highly relevant to the powers claimed for Standard English. In the present debate, writers have stressed that Standard English fails to take adequate account of spoken language (Milroy and Milroy 1985, Cheshire and Milroy 1993, Carter 1997: 94, Clark and Ivanic 1997: 187–216). The most codified forms of language are mainly those which are written down so the prescriptive tradition has relied heavily on the written language as its model. Yet writing and speaking are not, in Halliday's words, ' just alternative ways of doing the same thing: rather they are ways of doing different things' (Halliday 1989: xv). Written language cannot, in any practical sense, be held up as a model for spoken language, because it operates according to different ground rules. This fact highlights the ultimate flaw of the Standard English project. The desire to fix language, laying claim to an idealized form of language, the favouring of the written over the spoken, all these constitute a linguistic edifice whose principles disregard the fundamentally fluid and social nature of language. It is to the significance of spoken language that I now turn.

Standard English and the Marginalization of Spoken Language

Despite the fact that spoken language has been around over a million years longer than written language and inevitably has had the key role in the evolution and development of language, written language has always stolen the linguistic limelight, as Halliday (1989) has pointed out. This has an ideological dimension. Writing, from earliest times, was monopolized by those who controlled wealth; being able to write became an important manifestation of the division of labour in society. It was therefore associated with all that was powerful and prestigious – trade, religion, learning, affairs of state. Even when the needs of production required a more educated population, the ruling class stamped their mark on the mass educational process of acquiring writing. Spoken language was slighted, treated pejoratively as the vernacular, and presented as a debasement of written forms. Even those linguists who pioneered a focus on the spoken language attended exclusively to elements of pronunciation and, even there, tended to categorize according to a perceived yardstick. In imitation of correct forms in written language, the existence of 'acceptable' pronunciation was taken for granted.[18]

This written model (and sometimes a certain pronunciation) usually provides the framework for advocacy of Standard English.[19] Yet this framework is not appropriate for spoken language. 'Correct' has little place in the actual business of verbal interaction, since it is what is communicated that is important and successful communication in all its complexity the best arbiter. Spoken language is described as formless, disjointed, incomplete, as if how people express themselves and understand each other could actually be described in these terms. Such descriptions are indicative of the written prism through which spoken language is viewed. In fact, spoken language is highly intricate, with sophisticated grammatical and semantic structures that are often more complex because they are constructed across speakers, and with a complex awareness of the addressee (Halliday 1989: 76–92). Brazil also shows the degree to which contemporary grammar descriptions ignore speech and are still modelled on writing. He argues that the concept upon which grammar descriptions depend is the *sentence*, which is a basic functioning unit for written, but not for spoken, language. The 'sentencehood' of these grammars implies a self-contained object which links itself to other sentences to form a free-standing structural unit. Yet, Brazil maintains, the language of speaking has no need to operate in this structural, constituent-dependent way. Speech is an activity that takes place in time with elements added incrementally rather than hierarchically. The ongoing linear aspect of speech sharply marks it off from writing which can, to varying degrees, step outside the rush of time. Brazil shows that even some Discourse Analysis, with its purported

Grammar features found in spoken language	Examples
Ellipsis (omission of elements)	*Didn't know you used boiling water.* *Foreign body in there.*
Left dislocation (copying of preceding items)	*This friend of mine, her son was in hospital and . . .* *That couple we know in Portsmouth,, I don't hear of her for months and then . . .*
Reinforcement tags	*Good winter wine that.*
Indirect speech (use of continuous tenses in the reporting verb)	*I was saying to Mum earlier that . . .* *Maureen and Derek were telling me you have to get a taxi . . .*

FIGURE 1   *Examples of spoken grammar (after Carter and McCarthy 1995)*

concern with interaction, examines contextual aspects 'above the sentence', thereby taking sentence-grammar for granted. This two-tiered approach implies the existence of some kind of discontinuity between one level and the other (Brazil 1995).

In spite of the interest in spoken language in recent years, and computer and recording technology developments that have made the collection of speech much more manageable, grammars are still rooted in description of the grammar of written English. Carter and McCarthy (1995) have researched some of the grammatical features of spoken language. Their findings show how grammar is particular to speech functions, and how it is systematically, and widely, used by speakers (see Figure 1). Traditional grammars simply ignore the existence of such grammatical forms, even though these forms, as the table shows, are widely used, even in the supposed channels of Standard English, the radio and the television. He further shows that even modern grammars draw their language data mainly from quite restricted sources, 'the usage of university dons in a common room in the 1960s', to be precise. 'That restricted code is nevertheless used to illustrate and further reinforce definitions of what standard English grammar is' (Carter 1997: 58).

The value of the different contributions by Halliday, Brazil and Carter and McCarthy is that they show that grammar is not a fixed entity but a relative one, something that the Standard English concept does not accept. Far from grammar rules being 'natural and given', 'inherent, or intrinsic, or even inevitable' (Honey 1997: 67), they are a human invention, not the proof of the working of language to some prior design. Harris charts how the respect for rules has hung over grammatical studies in the Western tradition and grammar has almost been seen as part of the laws of nature. He underscores the fact that grammar is not a series of arbitrary laws which the language must obey, but rather a set of system-atized observations about how a language functions (Harris 1987: 99). He refers to Sapir's comment that 'no language is ever completely grammatical' and that 'unfortunately, or luckily, no language is tyrannically consistent'. Sapir's understanding that language emerges in the lap of society may have led him to some over-deterministic formulations, but it also led him to the shrewd observation that 'all grammars leak' (Sapir 1963: 38). Standard English, for the same reason, and luckily also, leaks badly.

The grammar of speech, the degree to which it varies and differs from a written norm, touches on a fundamental aspect of any social theory of language. For here, in embryo, can be seen the seeds of language change, rooted in actual speakers in a specific social context. This was a point that Volosinov insisted on and one which set the living language apart from the 'dead, alien' language presented by linguistic orthodoxy. We examined his view on these matters in Chapter 2 but in light of what I have said above, it is worth recalling the importance Volosinov attaches to 'utterance' as opposed to the abstract system of language.

> [L]inguistic thinking has hopelessly lost any sense of the verbal whole. A linguist feels most sure of himself when operating at the center of a phrase unit. The further he approaches the peripheries of speech and thus the problem of the utterance as a whole the more insecure his position becomes. He has no way at all of coping with the whole. (Volosinov 1973: 110; emphasis in original)

Similarly, Vygotsky's examination of the role of context in the spoken language, also shown in Chapter 2, uncovers social context as a key formative component of the understanding of language. Standard English as an overarching model is insecure because it fails to grasp this wholeness of language. Placing speech on the margins of language, Standard English leaves out its most essential and dynamic core.

Standard and Non-Standard: Varieties Apart?

Henry Newbolt, in 1921 chair of the committee whose findings set the tone for British education for five decades, in the report that bore his name made his views on non-standard dialects quite plain:

> It is emphatically the business of the Elementary School to teach all its pupils who either speak a definite dialect or whose speech is disfigured by vulgarisms to speak Standard English and to speak it clearly with expression. (Newbolt Report quoted in Crowley 1989: 245)

Elsewhere Newbolt refers to the powerful influences of the 'evil habits of speech contracted in home and street' (1989: 243). Disparagement of dialects was implicit in Standard English ideology in nineteenth-century Britain and was often extended to other languages as well (as we saw in Chapter 3). Today, it takes barely subtler forms. Marenbon tells us that modern-day dialects are as restricted 'in capacity as Chaucerian English', and dialects can only be used for 'the exchanges of everyday life, mainly among those unrefined by education' (Marenbon 1987: 22). Honey adds a variant of social Darwinism to this theme. All languages are not equal, is his claim. 'Not all languages appear to be able to adapt quickly in response to social change and 'speakers of some languages may be at a big disadvantage in handling certain types of knowledge' (1977: 21). In other words, for Honey there is a kind of league table of languages in which some languages have definitely come out on top. Once this happens, 'this dialect assumes a number of special characteristics which the others do not have'. Standard English has pride of place because it deserves it (1997: 28–30).

These views rest on a clear-cut ideology about ethnic and social class differences, which despite Honey's claims to the contrary, has always been held by staunch conservatives.[20] 'The most respected forms of language will be those seen to exemplify most clearly . . . characteristics of order, stability and control', as Honey unambiguously phrases it (1997: 143). Uniform Standard English becomes thus another mark of division for those who already hold that society should be divided. Class is not always openly referred to, but the understanding is that at the bottom of society lie evil, stupidity and philistinism. Honey, for example, sees non-standard dialects as the channels variously for 'tribalism', for the glorification of 'criminality, violence, and drug abuse', for physical intimidation, and, incredibly, for 'illiterates' who have language difficulties, defects that they share with 'very young children, the hearing impaired, and those who have lost their power of speech through brain damage' (1997: 33–35). His references to the supposed vernacular of the working class are as antagonistic as those of the Victorians, documented so fully by Crowley. They, too, recoiled in horror from working-class dialects and considered their speakers 'the enemies of every man who speaks the pure English tongue' (Crowley 1989: 157–158).

Venomous dislikes aside, Honey's arguments in support of the superiority of Standard English rest on two principal ideas. The first is that Standard English has the special characteristic of 'generality' or 'commonality', which is derived from its eminent history. Honey's explanation for the dominance of Standard English is that it was a natural evolution. Significantly, he dates standardization from the fifteenth century, giving Standard English a long lineage (despite the fact that no one explicitly referred to it until the mid-1900s). Standardization itself, in Honey's account, becomes a natural historical development, with no particular agent, a sort of organic process that grew up in response to the demands of British society and the British Empire (1997: 67–69).[21] Under these circumstances, not to claim that Standard English was better would be to turn one's back on history as well as linguistic complexity.

Yet history never does anything. It is people's activity, in specific times and conditions, that makes history. I have made the distinction in this chapter between the period when standardization involved the elaboration of functions, particularly written ones, which served the economic and political needs of the dominant class and the ideological promotion of Standard English in the nineteenth century, which was part of a process of wider ruling-class hegemony over the working class. In both processes, standardization did not just happen: it happened because of the priorities of a certain class. Honey glosses over the historical agent in much the same way as his Victorian forebears. Standard English thus becomes a spontaneous outgrowth of society, representing somehow language at its best; certainly not the conscious privileging of a certain dialect of English.

This is not to say that Standard English – or more exactly the East Midlands dialect – as result of its powerful promoters, did not come to monopolize, represent and record many of the areas of knowledge and culture which this same ruling class dominated. The material advantages conferred on it and the learned attention it received did indeed mean that this particular dialect became identified with science, power, politics, law, and often literature. Its selection for systematic codification, grammatical analysis and, crucially, for the printed word gave it a public prominence and history that other dialects, relegated usually (although not always) to spoken contexts, simply could not achieve. But to recognize this historical fact is not the same as to say that the Standard English variety had special qualities for its future role or that other dialects today bear witness to their lack of potential. Nor does it mean that once written, the history of a dialect is made. Gramsci's observation about grammar – that it is the photograph of a given phase of a language – is an apt metaphor for different dialects (Gramsci 1985: 178). Standard English is today a dialect which bears the imprint of its history, just as other dialects do, and, like them, it is continuously developing.

The second argument that Honey puts forward flows from the first: that Standard English intrinsically possesses greater powers of expression, particularly in abstract thought, than non-standard varieties. Of course the linguistic deficit theory is not confined to advocates of Standard English. Ever since Bernstein argued that working-class speech manifested aspects of a restricted code and that middle-class speech was in contrast an elaborated code, non-standard varieties have been seen to fall somewhere short of full linguistic expression. While Bernstein's categorisaton may have been prompted by the recognition that schools were failing the working class, and he repeatedly claimed that he was not valuing one code above another, nevertheless his ideas were taken up as giving some linguistic explanation for educational failure (Bernstein 1973). Language and disadvantage became an area of enquiry as if the two were causally linked.

Linguists have argued for at least three decades that non-standard varieties have just as elaborate powers of expression as standard varieties. In Labov's now famous 'Logic of non-standard English' the myth of language deficiency was refuted. Labov proved that the speech of black inner city children reflected a great deal of verbal stimulation, that they hear more well-formed sentences than middle-class children and that they participate fully in a highly verbal culture. 'They have the same basic vocabulary, possess the same capacity for conceptual learning and use the same logic as anyone else who learns to speak and understand English' (Labov 1972b: 179). Labov highlighted the expressive powers of non-standard varieties and showed that by comparison Standard American English could be verbose and imprecise. Labov's work is an important political landmark because he showed that the myth of verbal deprivation diverts attention from real defects of our educational system to imaginary defects of the child.

His research opened a wave of interest in and study of Black Vernacular English in the US and Black English in Britain, and of dialects in general. Trudgill's study of dialects and varieties in Britain, both geographical and those relating to social class, expanded on Labov's approach and his work has challenged the stereotypes that have so often disparaged non-standard varieties of English (Trudgill 1974, 1978, 1990, 1995). The effect of elaborate codification of Standard English, and the teaching of it in schools, has given rise to the idea that dialects are ungrammatical, unsophisticated, even 'incorrect'. Yet dialects and varieties of English are not just some quaint relic from rural times, with 'picturesque' vocabulary to be pulled out when, as Carter notes, wholemeal bread needs to be advertised (Carter 1997: 10). Like standard dialects, they have their own elaborate grammars, even if they don't have an army and a navy.

The studies that have described the grammars of dialects and varieties of English (Cheshire 1991, Milroy and Milroy 1993) have brought to light a number of points about non-standard dialects that it is important to bear in mind. First, there is considerable overlap between standard and non-standard dialects. Historically, the selection of one grammatical item as 'correct' was, in fact, quite an arbitrary, inconsistent affair. So that *broke* and *knew*, for example superseded *breaked* and *knowed*, even though the latter were more regular forms and had been part of the English language for centuries before. They continue to be used in some dialects today. Another example is the much-disparaged double negative as in *he never said nothing*. Following practice in French, this construction was widely used in Chaucer's and Shakespeare's time and would appear to conform to a pattern established in Latin. In other words, 'correct' forms are those which have been codified as such, in standard grammars, and become the convention, and are not inherently more correct or logical than forms to be found in other dialects.

Secondly, non-standard dialects exist in specific contexts, are used in specific situations and often coexist with standard varieties. Such variation according to situation is, as we have seen, part of the dynamic nature of language itself. Linguistic variation, far from being an alarming intrusion into correct speech as some would have it, is the very stuff of linguistic creativity. It is this that gives rise to innovation and the constant generative process of language. What we noted for the different grammar of spoken forms does not mean that automatically speakers begin to include these spoken forms within written language. On the contrary, speakers appear to be highly sensitive to context, to speech participants, and they channel and vary their speech accordingly. Research into speaking styles shows that people change their speech according to their addressees and that switching from one form to another constitutes part of natural linguistic competence (Bell 1997). The same applies for non-standard varieties, but non-standard varieties are seldom officially recognized. As a result, they are to be found mainly in spoken contexts, where they continue to be used because they provide a source of specific meanings to the speaker, side by side with other varieties.

This would seem to offer a more satisfactory explanation of the continuing range and diversity of non-standard forms than more functionalist accounts. For example, Milroy and Milroy ask why people continue to use low status varieties when they know that it may well be in their economic and social interests to acquire a variety of high prestige (Milroy and Milroy 1985: 57). The question thus posed assumes that social mobility is a realizable option for most people, and that if it does not happen, Milroy and Milroy imply, it is individual attitudinal factors that are the cause. These attitudes, they claim, are shaped according to the relative density of local networks which, if strong, may deter adoption of the standard form. They explain that if a boy begins to use *I saw* rather than *I seen*, he has to weigh up values of *status* as opposed to solidarity. More often than not, the Milroys' research in Belfast finds, people opt for solidarity rather than status (1985: 58). This is perhaps a too convenient way of explaining the absence of social mobility in the very unequal society of Belfast. Their view of society is one governed by *norms*, that individuals either conform to or resist, and they extend these concepts to language use. According to this model, use of standard forms reflect adherence to institutional norms and use of non-standard forms, adherence to another set of norms found within local social networks. This theory of competing norms underestimates the social factors that create these norms as well as reducing linguistic production to mere normative behaviour. Milroy and Milroy themselves seem to concede some of this in an observation that they make later. They claim that spoken English seems to manage to escape regulation by the ideology of standardization (1985: 59), not because of the pressure of norms but because spoken language itself seems to be subject to quite extensive variation and change.

The flourishing of non-standard forms in a more flexible pattern is shown by examples from Irish English in the Republic of Ireland. Harris in his account of the grammar of Irish English persuasively shows that forms of Irish English provide additional semantic distinctions. The example of the spoken Irish English form *youse* is a case in point. Where in Standard English *you* singular and plural are the same, in Irish English the addition of the *youse* form provides the distinction which exists in many other dialects and languages.[22] Its use is as systematic as the absence of it in Standard varieties (Harris 1993). In another study Kallen (1991) has shown that semantic forms specific to non-standard forms are embedded in specific social situations. The use in spoken Irish English of *after +ing*, expressing the recent past, as in *she's after leaving*, does not merely represent one aspect of tense, as has often been assumed. Instead it is a complex form which carries the full range of meanings normally associated with the perfect tense.[23] His analysis reveals this subtlety and how such vernacular forms are certainly not 'slipshod' or semantically imprecise. They carry the same multiple semantic distinctions as those found in standard varieties.

The position of Irish English in Ireland provides some interesting insights into ideology and attitudes to non-standard speech forms. Kallen's study reveals that spoken Irish English is used by all social classes although in different contexts. Working-class speakers were found to use *after +ing* in friendly contexts and some more public ones, whereas speakers from the middle class used the form only in friendly or family interaction. Non-standard forms of Irish English are regularly used on the national television and radio and are accepted quite widely in spoken contexts although not in written ones.[24] The English syllabus for Irish secondary education does not refer once to Standard English (Department of Education 1996). Equally, the national guidelines for teachers make no mention of Standard English, highlighting instead such things as 'a sense of register and audience' (Department of Education 1989). This contrasts with the welter of material in the British context that places Standard English at the centre of the curriculum. There are obvious ideological reasons why this contrast exists, not least that in Ireland, Irish, not English, has stolen the limelight for political controversy. The absence of the Standard English debate does not mean that social class is not an issue in English in Ireland. Certain accents are favoured for certain jobs and the 'Dublin 4' accent, or the 'South Dublin' accent evokes much the same social class as RP in Britain. What the Irish studies referred to here highlight, however, is that there is a greater flexibility about the use of Irish varieties of English which means that there appears to be no fully independent Irish English vernacular, there being instead a continuum of varieties ranging from the least to the most standard-like (Harris 1993).

The continuum between non-standard and standard varieties is an aspect of the process by which language changes and is a fundamental aspect of the nature of language itself. Traditionalists ¦ ave wanted to relegate non-standard varieties to quaint irrelevancy or historical contingency. Others, often in response to what they detect as the disparagement of non-standard varieties have, from a different viewpoint, sought to give non-standard dialects a separate status. Yet this last approach, far from combating the conservatism of the opposing view, actually relies on some of the same concepts.

The most highlighted case has been that of Ebonics in the US, in which a Californian school declared Black English to be a second language (McArthur 1998: 199).[25] The Oakland school's resolution had described 'Ebonics' as the 'primary language' but also as 'genetically based and not a dialect of English'. The demand for Ebonics, which incidentally did not emanate from the parents or the teachers but the school board, occurred at a time when failure to provide equal education to black students was reaching dire proportions.[26] As Labov noted, it was this that was more socially significant than any supposed linguistic claims for a black language. Demands for linguistic identity, far from liberating language from stigmatization, became in reality a freezing of inequality (Smith 1997).

Too sharp demarcations between different varieties tends to underestimate linguistic borrowing and overlap between varieties, thereby ghettoizing non-standard varieties further. It can be politically counterproductive. Bernstein's claims that working-class children have special ways of speaking is open to the same attacks as the Ebonics lobby. Conservatives have been quick to seize on Bernstein to give credence to their hierarchical leanings, a point made when Bernstein's elaborate and restrictive code distinction first appeared. Rosen criticized Bernstein for failing to indicate exactly what he meant by the social class system to which he so freely alluded (Rosen 1972). A later contribution of Bernstein's also refers to social class without ever really explaining it, despite the severity of the disadvantages claimed as its effects. Children of the working class are judged as having not only restrictive linguistic codes, but also mental ones.[27] Furthermore, social relations, for Bernstein, are taken to mean only those occurring within the school, as if the school were the whole of society in microcosm, with teachers and students constituting antagonistic social classes. Teachers are described as 'transmitters' and students as 'acquirers' of the 'message' (Bernstein 1981). Not surprisingly this over-focus on the status of the codes, like the overemphasis on Ebonics, means that the larger social reality of inequality becomes overlooked in the exclusive emphasis on what is termed 'symbolic power' and 'cultural capital', which now become the defining feature of class itself. This is a myopic view of language that mistakes the form for the content, the linguistic code for larger social relations.

It is also a functionalist view of language. The assumption in Bernstein's earlier and later view is that code representations condition mental processes and that restrictive linguistic codes are restrictive mentally. The educational upshot of this could be interpreted as being that a child with a 'restricted' code needs to adopt a new 'elaborated' code in order to reach higher mental planes. However, a continuum view of standard and non-standard varieties, as argued here, is that a child arrives at school not with a linguistic *handicap*, but with a linguistic *competence* that can be built on. Language production is a complex mental and social activity and this is true for all varieties not just the standard one. This valuable finding that Labov highlighted is equally important to remember in the non-standard/standard debate. It is a theoretical framework that allows the emphasis to be placed on enriching and expanding existing linguistic repertoires, not closing stigmatized ones down.

Conclusion

This chapter has surveyed the ideological nature of the Standard English debate. It has argued that the debate today has arisen because, in the context of certain changes in society, traditionalists have sought to present Standard English as the pillar of social stability and in doing so have obfuscated social inequalities. Standard English needs to be seen in its historical context and the roots of its emergence examined. Ideas about Standard English have not arisen from 'common sense' but from the specific history of social classes in capitalism. The history of Standard English has not been a smooth line: it has reflected the tensions within dominant ideology, different perceptions from those without access to the standard language and also the limitations of standardization itself to fix language. Standardization occurred as a result of an historical process in which a rising middle class came to need a standard language for the consolidation of its wealth and dominance. At the same time there was a popular demand for access to the written word. In the nineteenth century, the ideology of Standard English was part of a wider ruling-class project to extend its hegemony over a growing working class and to meet the demands of mass education on its own terms. However, this ruling-class ideology ran up against the narrowness of its social base, which, in the case of language, could be seen in the reality of the continued existence of non-standard forms used by the vast majority of society. The promotion of Standard English often meant in practice the marginalizing of spoken language and, through Standard English grammars, non-recognition of the grammar of speech. Yet the spoken language occupies a special place in the unfolding of the dynamic of language for it engenders change and variation, something that Standard English as a stable entity cannot encompass.

Standard and non-standard coexist linguistically on a continuum whose different features often relate to specific contextual features of which speakers themselves are only too aware. Over-rigid demarcations between non-standard varieties and standard dialects can lead to giving codes and varieties a causative role in inequality, whose roots lie in society not in language.

Notes

1 *English, Our English: The New Orthodoxy Examined* by Marenbon was published by the Tory think-tank, the Centre for Policy Studies in 1987.

2 Carter was on the receiving end of the political tensions as the LINC language project under his direction saw its materials effectively banned by the government in 1991 (Carter 1995: 6).

3 An example he gives is Estuary English. This includes the non-pronunciation of the 't' sound in *bit* or in *better* (what Honey calls the 'strangulation' of this sound). The adoption of such speech among 'even more educated people in Britain' is of deep concern to Honey (1997: 153).

4 Quoted in Ricks and Michaels (1990: xv). He said this in answer to a request that more foreign languages be taught in schools.

5 The example of the Irish, in close proximity to the pressure of Standard English, offers a clear contrast in this respect. Many Irish who have lived in

Britain have effected accent change whereas those in Ireland, who daily receive British programmes on their televisions, do not.

6 One of the many statistics provided by Adonis and Pollard in support of the widening social divide is that entry to higher education from state schools is 27 per cent and from private schools 88 per cent. When one considers that only 7 per cent of British school students attend private schools, the figure is even more startling.

7 This is not just a British phenomenon. Ireland, in the midst of a boom, had worse social inequality amongst entrants to higher education than Britain. Just 3.6 per cent of degree students come from socially deprived areas compared with 46.5 per cent from Dublin's middle-class areas, according to a report from the Higher Education Authority (*Irish Times* 4 December 1996).

8 The end of the eighteenth century is when the composition of the ruling class is in transition, when former merchants are becoming businessmen but also buying into the old gentry and investing in land and enterprises. Hobsbawm includes landlords, merchants, shippers, financiers and early industrialists amongst those who control capital at this time (Hobsbawm 1977: 67). Cole and Postgate describe how the landed class controlled the government 'but was salutarily supported by and admixed with the commercial interest' (Cole and Postgate 1961: 97).

9 Cave set up a spinning machine and carding machine and had one of Benjamin Franklin's lightning conductors in his office in Clerkenwell (Green 1996: 220).

10 As it turned out, history was harsher on Johnson than Johnson on working people. Many of the 800 words he deemed should perish have survived perfectly well (including such widely used words as *budge, glum, sensible* and *sham*). See Green (1996: 232).

11 Williams puts literacy levels at 58 per cent of the population in 1839 (Williams 1961: 166).

12 Harris claims that the first recorded use of the expression 'Standard English' was in 1844. It was taken up subsequently by the *OED* (Harris 1988: 20).

13 Harris explains the philosophical weakness of their reasoning. The statement 'I see the door' can only be judged 'correct' by taking into consideration, non-linguistic aspects, namely whether the speaker can actually see the door or not. Lifting the statement from its context, and assessing its correctness, is a procedure that fails to take account of how speakers actually use language.

14 See Chapter 2, pp. 26–28.

15 Williams, writing in the 1960s, describes the resentment that Standard English incurred. 'In its name, thousands of people have been capable of the vulgar insolence of telling other Englishmen that they do not know how to speak their own language. . . . And thousands of teachers and learners from poor homes became ashamed of the speech of their fathers' (Williams 1961: 224).

16 'That horrible plummy voice from the radio', ' a sort of over-fedness, a fatuous self-confidence, a constant bah-bahing of laughter' was how Orwell unceremoniously described upper-class accents (see Fowler 1995: 23).

17 See Williams for a discussion of the paradox of George Orwell (Williams 1983: 289). Despite his praise of the robustness of popular speech, Orwell also believed, as in his Newspeak of *Nineteen Eighty-Four* (1949), that people could be passively duped by language.

18 Wyld places 'Received Standard' at the centre of his description (Wyld 1921) and Jones takes for granted that some pronunciation is acceptable, others not (Jones 1964: 12–13).

19 Marenbon, for example, dismisses the need for special attention to spoken forms of language in school (Marenbon 1987: 19).

20 Honey claims he has been wrongly accused of being right-wing. He describes himself as a former member of the Labour Party and 'probably slightly to the left of Tony Blair' (1997: 215).

21 Honey's version of events equates imperial expansion with pushing out the boundaries of knowledge. The study of Sanskrit, which Honey claims was first researched by the British, had flourished long before the arrival of the British, from the fourth century BC to the sixth century AD.

22 Without the formality tag however of French, Spanish, etc.

23 Examples of its uses are:

- 'Universal' Perfect, linking the past to the present: *All the week is after being cold*
- 'Existential' Perfect, denoting the 'existence of past events': *The traffic is after being fierce*
- 'Hot news' Perfect, based on relative recency: *Glenn's just after being on to me*
- 'Stative' Perfect, indicating the direct effect of the past: *He's after taking the child up North* (Kallen 1991: 62–63)

24 Some uses of Irish English occur again and again. One of these is the recapitulative question tag, as in *You and your husband took over the farm three years ago, is it?* This is widely used in interviews because it manages to elicit confirmation both about the specific question and at the same time about the accuracy of the information in general.

25 'Ebonics', although used by some educators, was not a term much used before this. Black Vernacular English, Afro-American Vernacular English and Black English have been the terms used most widely by linguists.

26 Black students make up 53 per cent of all students but 71 per cent of students in special education classes and 80 per cent of students suspended from school (Smith 1997).

27 The experiment he quotes for this is unconvincing. In this, working-class children were found to categorize the presented food items according to which could be eaten together, rather than where they came from or from what they were made of. It was concluded that working-class children had less powers of classification than their middle-class counterparts who categorized according to origin or composition. Yet both mental steps – to the plate or to where they are produced – are abstractions from the present context of the item of food. When the objects used in the experiment are something so basic as food, it would be strange indeed if the material circumstances of the child did not affect how she categorized. If food is in plentiful supply, as it is in middle-class homes, it is surely easier to envisage it outside its eating context. (For an account of this experiement see Bernstein 1981: 327–332.)

6   Conclusion

Where people in England and America say slums,
Trinidadians say barrackyards. Probably the word
is a relic of the days when England relied as much
on garrisons of soldiers as on her fleet to protect
her valuable sugar-producing colonies. (C.L.R. James, *Triumph*)

In the 1990s, many have come to question the wisdom of theories about language which cut language loose from the world. It was a sure sign that postmodernist relativism had begun to run its course when Jacques Derrida, doyen of deconstructionism, revised his stance towards Marx. He told us that the spectre of Marx (or 'spectres', in a characteristic hedge) was still with us. 'Deconstruction' needed a certain spirit of Marxism 'so as not to flee political responsibility' (Derrida 1994). The point, amid the gruelling cruelties of Bosnia, Somalia and the ravages of the free market, struck home. For one who had claimed that there was no 'outside of the text', this turn back towards the real world was indeed significant. Derrida expressed his misgivings in terms of his own political pathway, which the collapse of the USSR allowed him the space to revise (Derrida 1994: 13–15).

Those from the Marxist tradition had already discerned the debilitating political wilderness represented by postmodernism. Callinicos had identified the current as an offshoot from radical politics and increased consumption, which applied particularly to those members of the new middle class in the academy – the children of Marx and Coca-Cola, as he dubbed them (Callinicos 1989). Eagleton, similarly, pointed out that, notwithstanding their radical pretensions, the postmodernists 'scoop up something of the material logic of advanced capitalism' and end up being part of the problem not the solution (Eagleton 1996: 133–135). Others from different political backgrounds, or none, have scathingly criticized postmodernists for their methodological paucity and absence of scientific rigour, as well as their throwing overboard of the ideal of justice: postmodern fads are simply intellectual impostures (Sokal and Bricmont 1998).

Those concerned with the politics of language have to take full account of this intellectual and political crossroads. This book has argued that the political nature of English derives from both views about language and how it is used in its specific social contexts. Views of language, in a rounded philosophical sense, are politically indicative because they tie in with a particular world view. Volosinov pointed out that Saussure's abstract objectivism reified language, thereby presenting it as an ahistorical construct, apart from society. Saussure's emphasis on the arbitrary nature of language and its enclosed autonomous linguistic system removed its connection with the social world and failed to take account of linguistic signs being infinitely changeable and adaptable. In brief, Saussure's *langue* left out human history. Volosinov, expressing his views in the late 1920s in Russia, attempted to bring Marxist historical materialism to bear on linguistics at a critical time. Against various strands of idealism, Volosinov sought to steer a path locating language as part of society, but in a dynamic and dialectical way. The view of language that emerged from his polemic then is starkly relevant for those who wish to challenge the notion that language is a cage which prevents access to objective reality.

Key to Volosinov's project was the return to Marx's view that language was part of ideology. For Volosinov, 'the domain of ideology coincides with the domain of signs' (1973: 10). He saw language as distillation of ideology. 'The word is the ideological phenomenon par excellence' (1973: 13). Postmodern approaches raced to jettison the term 'ideology' because it was linked to the economic foundation of society and social class, which they now rejected. Yet understanding that language is part of ideology is crucial to defining the political nature of language today, as it was for Marx and Volosinov.

I have argued that language is ideological in different ways. **Language is part of the social totality**. This is not to say that language *is* society, nor that language is material in the way that social forces are. The growth of English across the world, as I have attempted to show, illustrates the way in which language interrelates with social forces. Contrary to functionalist claims that English is neutral, World English is inseparable from the historical legacy of colonialism and from the internationalization of capitalism, both economically and politically. Nevertheless, it is not simply reducible to these. It is not either 'linguistic imperialism' nor, as postmodernism would have it, 'the world in English'. First, its reach and spread has been shaped by the limits of capitalism. It is not the case that everyone speaks English any more than it is true that everyone consumes capitalist goods or even enough food to keep hunger at bay. The actual spread of English while reflecting the greater internationalization of the world economy, also reflects its inequality. Second, where it is spoken, and even where it has been summarily imposed, it becomes transformed by new speakers in different social situations. While official versions of International English are promoted, Nigerian English, Indian English and even varieties spoken by relatively few speakers continue to flourish. A recent dictionary notes the contributions to new words provided by the media and the trading floor but it also notes the contributions of black slang which buzzes between Brooklyn, Trenchtown, Brixton and Soweto (Thorne 1997). Language is made from below as much as from above even if the two versions clash.

Language is part of our social being. Beaken captures the dynamic of the process involved when he writes: 'As we learn to speak we enter the world of social consciousness, a world created by others before us, to which our own consciousness can contribute' (Beaken 1996: 26). It is this dual character of language, language made and language in the making, that both sets limits and allows freedom. Discourse theorists tend to grasp language only as a disciplining mechanism. Yet, as Eagleton notes, language is a rather 'weightless way of carrying the world around with us' (1996: 73), an aspect of human potential rather than a straitjacket, part of the nature of human beings that allows us to intervene to shape the world about us.

Language is part of a social reality that is contradictory. Society is contradictory at root because it is divided into social classes. Society is also perceived in contradictory ways. Neither thought nor language forms a realm of its own but they are, as Marx put it, 'manifestations of actual life'. Consciousness arises from specific historical social conditions, not in a one-sided predictable way, but with all the contradictions of the social relations themselves. If in ideology people perceive their circumstances in contradictory ways, as in a *camera obscura* in Marx's phrase, this arises from the experience of class society itself (Marx and Engels 1974: 47).

Language is not ideological in itself through its system or its structure, but in its context of use. Different classes and different individuals will use the same language with different ideological meanings and it is this multivoiced nature of language that makes it such an arena of ideological struggle.

Thus feminist views which see language as 'man-made', or conversely, claim that women have their own language, are essentially determinist. The relationship between language and oppression is ideological, not essentialist. Sexism is an ideology that presents a distorted view of women in society and that arises, not innately in the minds of men, but for specific social purposes – mainly concerning the responsibility of childcare – which suits free-market capitalism. These are the social and material roots to sexism, not language. Women are not victims of language, nor does their verbal behaviour contribute to their discrimination – if it did they would be strangely complicit in their own oppression.

In this perspective, the concept of gender is an unsatisfactory theoretical framework for analysing women's oppression and language. On the one hand, it is asserted that gender is different to sex because it is socially constructed. On the other, studies concerning women and language take as their starting point *de facto* differences on the basis of sex. Feminist linguistics has taken women in their speech communities, the characteristics of all-women conversations, features of women's speech as the object of their study and has therefore often confirmed, in a self-fulfilling way, the principle of sexual difference rather than challenged it. The emphasis on *difference* tends to see sexism in language as a male/female dichotomy when the reality of speech, both men's and women's, is much more contradictory. The Vygotskian theme of language as social activity reminds us that it is cooperation between men and women for social purposes not competition that has a been decisive historically, and that social divisions are more significant than sexual ones. Yet there is widespread acceptance in the literature on women and language that gender is a social division in the same way as social class, though the causes for this are not often explained.

In the often uncritical adoption of this concept, gender analyses coincide, paradoxically, with dominant ideas of sexism which hold that the differences between men and women are natural and significant enough to warrant each being given different social roles. Gramsci once remarked that contradictory consciousness, if it does not move beyond the contradictions in society, feeds back into dominant ideas because it 'does not permit of any action, any decision or any choice and produces a condition of moral and political passivity'. It thus remains part of 'common sense' and fails to constitute a critical conception of the world (Gramsci 1971: 333). Feminism shares some of the political passivity to which Gramsci refers.

Language change reveals the social nature of language. The fact that language is in a constant state of change, in the making of new words and in the revising and creation of new structures, is one of its essential characteristics. It was this generative quality of language, which Volosinov discerned, that the Saussurean static emphasis of *langue* left out and that also was evidence of the social nature of language. Language is generative because it is embedded in the flux of social change. Views of Standard English, underestimate the generative nature of language partly because they do not focus on the most subtle indicator of change: spoken language. Spoken language has particular features which uncover its inherent dialogic and social nature.

The ideological nature of language is also the source of language change. Volosinov described words as having a Janus-like quality, looking different ways at the same time and for different speakers. 'Any current truth must inevitably sound to many other people as the greatest lie' (Volosinov 1973: 23). This he called the multi-accentuality of the ideological sign. This inner dialectic quality itself gave rise to language change, through contesting the meanings of words.

Language is part of ideology and is shaped by the material social world, by social relations. The influence of Foucault and the emphasis on discourse as social power in its own right, has resulted in a merging of the distinction between discourse and history, discourse and social change. This is most apparent in postmodernist commentaries which see language as the producer of inequality and counter-discourse as social change (Pennycook 1995). But even more eclectic renderings of discourse, including those that accept the role of social class and ideology, accord discourse a constitutive role. History is seen as so many different narratives, so many 'systems of intertextuality' (Hodge and Kress 1993: 211). Language has been used in the construction of 'historical formations such as nations, classes, genders and races' (Crowley 1996: 1). 'Social change is substantively constituted by changing discursive practices' (Fairclough 1996: 5). One version of the powers of language sees the English language as the carrier of a particularly virulent streak of 'fast capitalism' and non-English-speaking capitalist economies as less aggressive (Kress 1995: 23).

Yet the distinction between interpretations of history and history itself, between the power of discourse and social power, is crucial not only in the understanding of history but also in the understanding of language. Language is of a different order to historical events. Such a distinction was critical for Marx. Ideological things may appear as independent spheres but 'they have no history, no development; but men developing their material production and their material intercourse alter, along with this their real existence, their thinking and the products of their thinking' (Marx and Engels 1974: 47). Marxist dialectical materialism does not explain practice from the idea but the formation of ideas from social practice. 'Discursive practices' covers over and confounds this distinction by making discourse appear to construct the social world.

In my examination of the political aspects of English I have tried to show that it is precisely in the distinction between discourse and history that the political significance of language comes to the fore. History is not made through discourse but ideological interpretations, including language, may be critical in how ideas come to be accepted throughout society. Colonialism was the ruthless wresting of wealth from other lands and did not 'start with language', as one version has it (Ashcroft et al. 1995). The account given in Chapter 3 charts how imperial views of the world and English were constructed as ideological justification of the brutally expansion of Empire. These views attempted to justify Empires, they did not create them. I have tried to show that the hegemonic strength of these views depended precisely on the substantial and tangible wealth of the Empire. That most sure-footed opponent of Empire, CLR James, well understood the material underpinnings of imperial language, as the extract about Trinidadian English, at the beginning of this chapter shows. Similarly, Standard English cannot be understood without an appreciation of its origins in the rise of a certain merchant class in Britain, its promotion later by the Victorian bourgeoisie and its ideological embracing by the British ruling class. Indeed it is difficult to fully grasp the social significance of Standard English in Britain without accepting the primacy of social class over ideology. Ahmad has bemoaned the way in which through the enthronement of discourse power appears to have seeped into the pores of society and textuality, but has no origins and no object. The world appears as a 'wilderness of mirrors' in which representation is everything (Ahmad 1992: 185).The concept of ideology is vital because it secures the link between these two different orders of things: language and the economic foundation of society, and explains why one variety of English carries more weight than another.

The question of social change and agency becomes intractable for discourse theorists, as some recgonize (Mills 1997: 35). If discourse is constitutive of reality, then changing discourse and interpreting discourse are seen as ways to unlock social change. Indeed Discourse Theory and Critical Discourse Analysis have tended to focus more on analysis of individual texts than on a unified theory of language. This leads to an overemphasis on form with, in some cases, the form itself becoming defining of political content. The problem then becomes, in this form-determined world, where does the motive for change come from? How does one get out of discourse and what allows some to transcend it? As Marx remarked, such theories forget that it is people who change circumstances and that it is essential to educate the educator (Marx and Engels 1974: 121). The revolutionary practice proposed by Marx concerned the changing of society itself which hinged not on representations of society, but on the conflicting interests of social classes. That distinction moves beyond interpretation to actual social change and is one that a theory of language must embrace if it is not to remain locked within language itself.

Bibliography

Abbott, P. and Wallace, C. (1997) *An Introduction to Sociology: Feminist Perspectives*. London: Routledge.

Achebe, C. (1975) 'English and the African writer', in Mazrui (1975).

Achebe, C. (1977) 'An image of Africa', *Massachusetts Review*, 18 (Winter): 782–794.

Achebe, C. (1988) *The African Trilogy: Things Fall Apart, No Longer at Ease, Arrow of God*. London: Picador.

Adonis, A. and Pollard, S. (1997) *A Class Act: the Myth of Britain's Classless Society*. London: Penguin.

Ahmad, A. (1992) *In Theory: Nations and Literatures*. London: Verso.

Allen, K. (1990) *The Politics of James Connolly*. London: Pluto Press.

Angogo, R. and Hancock, I. (1980) 'English in Africa: emerging standards or diverging regionalisms?', *English World-Wide*, 1: 67–96.

Appignanesi, L. (1994) 'Liberté, Egalité and Fraternité: PC and the French', in Dunant (1994).

Ashcroft, B., Griffiths, G. and Tiffin, H. (eds) (1995) *The Post-colonial Studies Reader*. London: Routledge.

Assiter, A. (1983) 'Did man make language?' *Radical Philosophy*, 34 (Summer): 25–29.

Aufderheide, P. (ed.) (1992) *Beyond PC: Towards a Politics of Understanding*. St Paul: Greywolf.

Bakhtin, M. (1981) *The Dialogic Imagination*. Austin: University of Texas Press.

Bailey, R.W. (1991) *Images of English: A Cultural History of the Language*. Ann Arbor: University of Michigan Press.

Baldwin, J. (1995) *Notes of a Native Son*. London: Penguin.

Barker, M. (1994) 'A dialogical approach to ideology', in J. Storey *Cultural Theory and Popular Culture: A Reader*. New York: Harvester Wheatsheaf.

Baugh, A.C. and Cable, T. (1993) *A History of the English Language*. London: Routledge.

Bayart, J-F. (1993) *The State in Africa: the Politics of the Belly*. London: Longman.

Beaken, M. (1996) *The Making of Language*. Edinburgh: Edinburgh University Press.

Beezer, A. (1984) 'More on man made language', *Radical Philosophy*, 36 (Spring): 16–20.

Bell, A. (1984) 'Language style as audience design', *Language and Society*, 13: 145–204.

Bell, A. (1997) 'Language style as audience design', in Coupland and Jaworski (1997).

Berman, P. (ed.) (1992) *Debating PC: the Controversy over Political Correctness on College Campuses*. New York: Dell.

Bernstein, B. (ed.) (1973) *Class, Codes and Control* Vol. 2: *Applied Studies towards a Sociology of Language* (Foreword by M.A.K. Halliday). London: Routledge & Kegan Paul.

Bernstein, B. (1981) 'Codes, modalities and the process of cultural reproduction: a model', *Language and Society*, 10: 327–363.

Bickerton, D. (1995) *Language and Human Behavior*. Seattle: University of Washington Press.

Blake, N. (1996) *A History of the English Language*. London: Macmillan.

Bloom, A. (1986) *The Closing of the American Mind: How Higher Education Has Failed Democracry and Impoverished the Souls of Today's Students*. New York: Simon & Schuster.

Bolger, D. (1968) *Aspects of Language*. New York: Harcourt, Brace & World.

Bottomore, T., Harris, L., Kiernan, V.G. and Miliband, R. (1983) *A Dictionary of Marxist Thought*. Oxford: Blackwell.

Brazil, D. (1995) *A Grammar of Speech*. Oxford: Oxford University Press.

Brewer, A. (1980) *Marxist Theories of Imperialism: a Critical Survey*. London: Routledge & Kegan Paul.

British Council (1995) *English in the World: The English 2000 Global Consultation*. Manchester: The British Council.

Brittan, A. (1989) *Masculinity and Power*. Oxford: Blackwell.

Bryson, B. (1990) *Mother Tongue: The English Language*. Harmondsworth, Middlesex: Penguin.

Bukharin, N. (1972) *Imperialism and the World Economy*. London: Merlin Press.

Burchfield, R. (1985) *The English Language*. Oxford: Oxford University Press.

Burchfield, R. (1989) *Unlocking the English Language*. London: Faber & Faber.

Bureau of Education, India (1920) *Selection of Educational Records: Part I 1781–1839*, ed: H. Sharp. Calcutta: Superintendent of Government Printing.

Callen, T. and Wren, A. (1994) *Male–Female Wage Differentials: Analysis and Policy Issues*. Dublin: Economic and Social Research Insititute.

Callinicos, A. (1982) *Is There a Future for Marxism?* London: Macmillan.

Callinicos, A. (1987) 'Imperialism, capitalism and the state today', *International Socialism*, 2 (35), Summer: 71–115.

Callinicos, A. (1989) *Against Postmodernism*. Cambridge: Polity.

Callinicos, A. (1995) *Theories and Narratives: Reflections on the Philosophy of History*. Cambridge: Polity.

Cameron, D. (1984) 'Sexism and semantics', *Radical Philosophy*, 36 (Spring): 14–16.

Cameron, D. (1990) 'Demythologizing sociolinguistics: why language does not reflect society', in Joseph and Taylor (1990).

Cameron, D. (1992) *Feminism and Linguistic Theory*. London: Macmillan.

Cameron, D. (1994) '"Words, words, words": the power of language', in Dunant (1994).

Cameron, D. (1995a) *Verbal Hygiene*. London: Routledge.

Cameron, D. (1995b) 'Rethinking language and gender studies: some issues for the 1990s', in S. Mills (ed.), *Language and Gender: Interdisciplinary Perspectives*. London: Longman.

Cameron, D. (1997) 'Performing gender identity: young men's talk and the construction of hetereosexual masculinity', in Johnson and Meinhof (1997).

Cameron, D. and Coates, J. (1985) 'Some problems in the sociolinguistic explanations of sex differences', *Language and Communication*, 5 (3): 143–151.

Carter, R. (1995) 'Politics and knowledge about language: the LINC Project', in Hasan and Williams (1996).

Carter, R. (1997) *Investigating English Discourse: Language, Literacy and Literature*. London: Routledge.

Carter, R. and McCarthy, M. (1995) 'Grammar and the spoken language', *Applied Linguistics*, 16 (2): 141–158.

Chambers, J.K. (1995) *Sociolinguistic Theory: Linguistic Variation and its Social Significance*. Oxford: Blackwell.

Cheshire, J. (ed.) (1991) *English around the World: Sociolinguistic Perspectives*. Cambridge: Cambridge University Press.

Cheshire, J. and Milroy, J. (1993) 'Syntactic variation in non-standard dialects: background issues', in Milroy and Milroy (1993).

Cheshire, J. and Trudgill, P. (eds) (1998) *The Sociolinguistics Reader, Volume 2: Gender and Discourse*. London: Arnold.

Chomsky, N. (1970) *Current Issues in Linguistic Theory*. The Hague: Mouton.

Chomsky, N. (1972) *Syntactic Structures*. The Hague: Mouton.

Clark, K. and Holquist, M. (1984) *Mikhail Bakhtin*. Cambridge, Mass: Harvard University Press.

Clark, R. and Ivanic, R. (1997) *The Politics of Writing*. London: Routledge.

Cliff, T. (1984) *Class Struggle and Women's Liberation*. London: Bookmarks.

Coates, J. (1993) *Women, Men and Language: A Sociolinguistic Account of Gender Differences in Language*. London: Longman.

Coates, J. (1995) 'Language, gender and career', in Mills (1995).

Coates, J. (1997) 'One-at-a-time: the organisation of men's talk', in Johnson and Meinhof (1997).

Coates, J. (1998) 'Gossip revisited: language in all-female groups', in Cheshire and Trudgill (1998).

Cobbett, W. (1984) *A Grammar of the English Language* (Introduction by R. Burchfield). Oxford: Oxford University Press.

Cockburn, C. (1995) *Strategies for Gender Democracy: Women and the European Social Dialogue*. (Supplement 4/95). Luxemburg: Office for Offcial Publications of European Communities.

Cole, J.B. (1986) *All American Women: Lines that Divide, Ties that Bind*. New York: The Free Press.

Cole, G.D.H. and Postgate, R. (1961) *The Common People 1746–1946*. London: Methuen.

Conrad, J. (1926) *Last Essays*. London: Dent.

Conrad, J. (1990) *Heart of Darkness and Other Tales*. Oxford: Oxford University Press.

Coontz, S. and Henderson, P. (1986) *Women's Work, Men's Property: The Origins of Gender and Class*. London: Verso.

Cooper, R.L. (1989) *Language Planning and Social Change*. Cambridge: Cambridge University Press.

Coulmas, F. (1992) *Language and Economy*. Oxford: Blackwell.

Coupland, N. and Jaworski, J.A. (eds) (1997) *Sociolinguistics: A Reader and Coursebook*. London: Macmillan.

Crawford, M. (1995) *Talking Difference*. London: Sage Publications.

Crouch, I. and Dubois, B. (1975) 'The question of tag questions in women's speech. They don't really use more of them, do they?' *Language and Society,* 4: 289–294.

Crowley, T. (1989) *The Politics of Discourse.* London: Macmillan.

Crowley, T. (1991) *Proper English? Readings in Language History and Cultural Identity.* London: Routledge.

Crowley, T. (1996) *Language in History.* London: Routledge.

Crystal, D. (1987) *The Cambridge Encyclopaedia of Language.* Cambridge: Cambridge University Press.

Crystal, D. (1994) 'Which English – or English *Which*', in Hayhoe and Parker (1994).

Crystal, D. (1997) *English as a Global Language.* Cambridge: Cambridge University Press.

CSO (Central Statistics Office) (1996) *Social Trends 26: 1996 Edition,* ed. J. Church. London: HMSO.

Cummins, M. (1994) 'Is all this Peecee getting out of hand', *Irish Times,* 25 January.

Curtin, P.D. (1964) *The Image of Africa: British Ideas and Action 1780–1850,* Vol. 2. Madison: University of Wisconsin Press.

Daly, M. and Caputi, J. (1988) *Webster's First Intergalactic Wickedry of the English Language.* Dublin: Attic Press.

Darwin, C. (1930) *The Descent of Man.* (Part I). London: Watts.

Darwin, C. (1976) *The Origin of Species.* New York: Ameron.

Davis, T. (1974) *Essays of Thomas Davis,* ed. D.J. O'Donohoe. New York: Lemma.

Dennett, D.C. (1996) *Darwin's Dangerous Idea: Evolution and the Meaning of Life.* Harmondsworth, Middlesex: Penguin.

Dentith, S. (1995) *Bakhtinian Thought: An Introductory Reader.* London: Routledge.

Department of Education (An Roinn Oideachas) (1989) *The National Council for Curriculum Assessment: Guidelines for Teachers.* Dublin: Government Publications.

Department of Education (An Roinn Oideachas) (1996) *The Leaving Certificate: English Syllabus.* Dublin: Government Publications.

Department of Education and Science (1989) *English for Ages 5 to 16* (The Cox Report). London: HMSO.

Department of Equality and Law Reform (1997) *UN Convention on the Elimination of all Forms of Discrimination against Women (Ireland's 2nd and 3rd Report).* Dublin: Government Publications.

Derrida, J. (1994) *Spectres of Marx: the State of the Debt, the Work of Mourning and the New International.* London and New York: Routledge.

Dicker, S. (1996) *Languages in America: A Pluralist View.* Clevedon: Multilingual Matters.

Djite, P.G. (1992) 'The French Revolution and the French language: a paradox?' *Language Problems and Language Planning,* 16 (2): 163–177.

Douglass, F. (1995) *The Education of Frederick Douglass.* Harmondsworth, Middlesex: Penguin.

D'Souza, D. (1991) *Illiberal Education: The Politics of Race and Sex on Campus.* New York: Free Press.

D'Souza, D. (1992) 'Visigoths in tweed', in Aufderheide (1992).

Dua, H.R. (1994) 'Hindi language spread policy and its implementation: achievements and prospects', *International Journal of the Sociology of Language,* 107: 115–143.

Dumont, L. (1994) *German Ideology: from France to Germany and Back.* Chicago: University of Chicago Press.

Dunant, S. (ed.) (1994) *The War of the Words: The Political Correctness Debate.* London: Virago.

Eagleton, T. (1991) *Ideology: An Introduction.* London: Verso.

Eagleton, T. (1995) *Heathcliff and the Great Hunger.* London: Verso.

Eagleton, T. (1996) *The Illusions of Postmodernism.* Oxford: Blackwell.

Eckert, P. (1989) 'The whole woman: sex and gender differences in variation', *Language Variation and Change,* 1: 245–267.

Eco, U. (1995) *The Search for the Perfect Language,* trans. J. Fentress. Oxford: Blackwell.

Ehrenreich, B. (1992) 'The challenge for the Left', in Berman (1992).

Elyan, O., Smith, P., Giles, H. and Bourhis, R. (1978) 'RP – accented female speech: the voice of perceived androgyny?' in Trudgill (1978).

Engels, F. (1970) 'The part played by Labour in the transition from ape to man', in Marx and Engels (1970).

Engels, F. (1972) *Origins of the Family: Private Property and the State* (Introduction by E. Burke Leacock). London: Lawrence & Wishart.

Equiano, O. (1967) *The Interesting Narrative of the Life of Olaudah Equiano or Gustavus Vassa the African* (abridged and edited by P. Edwards). London: Heinemann.

Fairclough, N. (1989) *Language and Power.* London: Longman.

Fairclough, N. (1992) *Discourse and Social Change.* Cambridge: Polity.

Fairclough, N. (1995) *Critical Discourse Analysis.* London: Longman.

Fairclough, N. (1996) 'Border-crossings: discourse and social change in contemporary societies', in H. Coleman and L. Cameron, *Change and Language.* Clevedon, Avon: Multilingual Matters Ltd.

Fink-Eifel, H. (1992) *Foucault: an Introduction,* trans. E. Dixon. Philadelphia: Pennbridge Books.

Fishman, J.A. (1977) 'The spread of English as a new perspective for the study of "language maintenance and language shift"', in Fishman et al. (1977).

Fishman J., Cooper R.L. and Rosenbaum, Y. (1977) *The Spread of English: the Sociology of English as an Additional Language.* Rowley, MA: Newbury House.

Fishman, J. (1987) 'English: neutral tool or ideological protagonist? A 19th century East-Central Europe Jewish intellectual views English from afar', *English World-Wide,* 8 (1): 1–10.

Fishman, P. (1983) 'Interaction: the work women do', in Thorne et al. (1983).

Flaitz, J. (1988) *The Ideology of English: French Perceptions of English as a World Language.* Berlin: Mouton de Gruyer.

Foucault, M. (1970) *The Order of Things: An Archeology of the Human Sciences.* New York: Pantheon.

Foucault, M. (1972) *The Archeology of Knowledge and Discourse on Language,* trans. A. Sheridan-Smith. New York: Pantheon.

Foucault, M. (1979) *Power, Truth, Strategy,* ed. M. Morris and P. Patton. Sydney: Feral Publications.

Fowler, R. (1995) *The Language of George Orwell.* London: Macmillan.

Frank, A.G. (1978) *Dependent Accumulation and Underdevelopment.* London: Macmillan.

Fryer, P. (1993) *Black People in the British Empire.* London: Pluto Press.

Furfey, P. (1944) 'Men and women's language', *American Catholic Sociological Review*, 5: 218–223.

Gates, H.L. Jnr (1992) *Loose Canons: Notes on the Culture Wars*. New York: Oxford University Press.

Genovese, E. (1991) 'Heresy, yes – sensitivity, no', *New Republic*, April: 30–35.

Geras, N. (1995) 'Language, truth and justice', *New Left Review*, 209 (Jan.–Feb.): 30–35.

German, L. (1981) 'Theories of patriarchy', *International Socialism*, 2 (12): 33–51.

Gerratana, V. (1973) 'Marx and Darwin', *New Left Review*, 82 (Nov.–Dec.): 60–83.

Givon, T. (1979 *On Understanding Grammar*. New York: Academic Press.

Goodman, S. and Graddol, D. (1996) *Redesigning English: New Texts, New Identities*. London: The Open University/Routledge.

Goodwin, M. (1990) *He-Said-She-Said: Talk as Social Organisation among Black Children*. Bloomington: Indiana University Press.

Gordon, L. (1991) 'On difference', *Genders*, 10: 91–111.

Gorlach, M. (1988) 'English as a world language: the state of the art', *English World-Wide*, 9 (1): 1–32.

Graddol, D. (1996) 'Global English, global culture?' in Goodman and Graddol (1996).

Graddol, D. and Swann, J. (1989) *Gender Voices*. Oxford: Blackwell.

Graddol, D., Leith, D. and Swann, J. (eds) (1996) *English: History, Diversity and Change*. London: The Open University/Routledge.

Gramsci, A. (1971) *Selections from the Prison Notebooks*, ed. Q. Hoare and G. Nowell Smith. London: Lawrence & Wishart.

Gramsci, A. (1985) *Selections from Cultural Writings*, ed. D. Forgacs and G. Nowell Smith. London: Lawrence & Wishart.

Green, D. (1983) *Great Cobbett: The Noblest Agitator*. Oxford: Oxford University Press.

Green, J. (1996) *Chasing the Sun: Dictionary Makers and the Dictionaries They Made*. London: Jonathan Cape.

Greenbaum, S. (1988) *Good English and the Grammarian*. London: Longman.

Greenbaum, S. (1990) 'Whose English?' in Ricks and Michaels (1990).

Grimshaw, A. (ed.) (1992) *The CLR James Reader*. Oxford: Blackwell.

Gumperz, J.J. (ed.) (1982) *Language and Social Identity*. Cambridge: Cambridge University Press.

Gumperz, J.J. and Levinson, S.C. (1996) *Rethinking Linguistic Relativity*. Cambridge: Cambridge University Press.

Halliday, M.A.K. (1978) *Language as Social Semiotic: the Social Interpretation of Language and Meaning*. London: Edward Arnold.

Halliday, M.A.K. (1989) *Written and Spoken Language*. Oxford: Oxford University Press.

Halliday, M.A.K. and Hasan, R. (1989) *Language, Context and Text: Aspects of Language in a Social-semiotic Perspective*. Oxford: Oxford University Press.

Hardy, T. (1992) *Tess of the d'Urbervilles*. Ware, Hertfordshire: Wordsworth Editions.

Harman, C. (1992) 'The return of the National Question', *International Socialism*, 2 (56): 3–61.

Harman, C. (1994) 'Engels and the origins of human society', *International Socialism*, 65 (special issue): 83–143.

Harris, J. (1993) 'The grammar of Irish English', in Milroy and Milroy (1993).

Harris, R. (1987) *The Language Machine*. London: Duckworth.

Harris, R. (1988) 'Murray, Moore and the Myth', in R. Harris (ed.), *Linguistic Thought in England (1914–1945)*. London: Duckworth.

Hasan, R. and Williams, G. (eds) (1996) *Literacy in Society*. London: Longman.

Hayhoe, M. and Parker, S. (eds) (1994) *Who Owns English?* Buckingham: Open University Press.

Haynes, M. (1985) *Nikolai Bukharin and the Transition from Capitalism to Socialism*. London: Croom Helm.

HEA (Higher Education Authority/An tUdaras um Ard-Oideachas (1997) *Reports, Accounts and Student Statistics 1992/93 and 1993/94*. Dublin: Government Publications.

Heller, D. (1994) 'The problem of Standard English', in *English Journal* (NCTE Secondary Section), September: 17–18.

Hentoff, N. (1992) '"Speech codes" on the campus and problems of free speech', in Berman (1992).

Hindley, R. (1990) *The Death of the Irish Language*. London: Routledge.

Hiro, D. (1992) *Black English, White English: a History of Race Relations in Britain*. London: Paladin.

Hobsbawm, E.J. (1977) *The Age of Revolution 1789–1848*. London: Abacus.

Hobsbawm, E.J. and Ranger, T. (1983) *The Invention of Tradition*. Cambridge: Cambridge University Press.

Hodge, R. and Kress, G. (1993) *Language as Ideology*. London: Routledge.

Holborow, M. (1996) Review of *Cultural Politics of English as an International Language*, *ELT Journal*, 50 (2): 172–175.

Holmes, J. (1992a) 'Women's talk in public contexts', *Discourse and Society*, 3 (2): 131–150.

Holmes, J. (1992b) *An Introduction to Sociolinguistics*. London: Longman.

Holmes, J. (1995) *Women, Men and Politeness*. London: Longman.

Honey, J. (1983) *The Language Trap: Race, Class and the 'Standard English' Issue in British Schools*. Kenton, Middlesex: National Council for Educational Standards.

Honey, J. (1997) *Language is Power: the Story of Standard English and its Enemies*. London: Faber & Faber.

Houston, M. and Kramarae, C. (1991) 'Speaking from silence', *Discourse and Society*, 2 (4): 387–399.

Hughes, R. (1993) *Culture of Complaint: the Fraying of America*. New York: Oxford University Press.

Hymes, D. (1981) *In Vain I Tried To Tell You*. Philadelphia: University of Pennsylvania Press.

Hymes, D. (1986) 'Models of the interaction of life and social life', in J.J. Gumperz and D. Hymes, *Directions in Sociolinguistics: the Ethnomethodogy of Communication*. Oxford: Blackwell.

Irigaray, L. (1993) *Je, tu, nous: towards a Culture of Difference*. London: Routledge.

Jackson, J., Piper, T. and Yildiz, N. (1997) 'A Chinese initiative', in Kenny and Savage (1997).

Jameson, F. (1974) Review of *Marxism and the Philosophy of Language*, *Style*, 8 (3): 535–543.

Jenkins, S. (ed.) (1992) *The Times Guide to English Style and Usage*. London: Times Books/HarperCollins.

Jespersen, O. (1922) *Language: its Nature, Development and Origin*. London: Allen & Unwin.

Jespersen, O. (1938) *Growth and Structure of the English Language*. Oxford: Blackwell.

Johnson, P. (1996) *To Hell with Picasso and Other Essays*. London: Weidenfeld & Nicolson.

Johnson, S. (1768) *Dictionary of the English Language*. Dublin: W.E. Jones.

Johnson, S. (1997) 'Theorizing language and masculinity: a feminist perspective', in Johnson and Meinhof (1997).

Johnson, S. and Meinhof, U.H. (eds) (1997) *Language and Masculinity*. Oxford: Blackwell.

Jones, D. (1964) *An Outline of English Phonetics*. Cambridge: Heffer & Sons.

Jones, P.E. (1991) *Marxism, Materialism and Language Structure, Part I: General Principles*. Sheffield: Centre for Popular Culture Series No. 6.

Joseph, J.E. and Taylor, T.J. (eds) (1990) *Ideologies of Language*. London: Routledge.

Joyce, J. (1992) *Portrait of the Artist as a Young Man*. Harmondsworth, Middlesex: Penguin.

Joyce, P. (1991) *Visions of the People: Industrial England and the Question of Class*. Cambridge: Cambridge University Press.

Kachru, B.B. (ed.) (1982) *The Other Tongue: English across Cultures*. Urbana: University of Illinois Press.

Kachru, B.B. (1983) *The Indianization of English*. Delhi: Oxford University Press.

Kachru, B.B. (1985) 'Standards, codification and sociolinguistic realism: the English language in the outer circle', in Quirk and Widdowson (1985).

Kachru, B.B. (1986a) 'The power and politics of English', *World Englishes*, 5 (2–3): 121–140.

Kachru, B.B. (1986b) *The Alchemy of English*. Oxford: Pergamon Press.

Kallen, J. (1991) 'Sociolinguistic variation and methodology: *after* as a Dublin variable', in Cheshire (1991).

Kanyoro, M.R.A. (1991) 'The politics of the English language in Kenya and Tanzania', in Cheshire (1991).

Kelly, A.C. (1988) *Swift and the English Language*. Philadephia: University of Pennsylvania Press.

Kenny, B. and Savage, W. (eds) (1997) *Language and Development*. London: Longman.

Key, M.R. (1996) *Male/Female Language*. Lanham, MD: The Scarecrow Press.

Kiberd, D. (1996) *Inventing Ireland: the Literature of the Modern Nation*. London: Vintage.

Kiernan, V.G. (1969) *The Lords of Human Kind: Black Man, Yellow Man and White Man in an Age of Empire*. New York: Oxford University Press.

Kimball, R. (1990) *Tenured Radicals: How Politics Has Corrupted Our Higher Education*. New York: Harper & Row.

Kollontai, A. (1977) *Selected Writings*, trans. A. Holt. London: Allison & Busby.

Kosulin, A. (1990) *Vygotsky's Psychology: a Biography of Ideas*. Hemel Hempstead: Harvester Wheatsheaf.

Kramarae, C. (1985) 'Beyond sexist books', *Women's Review of Books*, 11: 15–17.

Kramarae, C. and Treichler, P. (1985) *A Feminist Dictionary*. Boston: Pandora Press.

Kress, G. (1995) *Writing the Future*. Sheffield: National Association for the Teaching of English.

Labov, W. (1966) *The Social Stratification of English in New York City*. Washington, DC: Center of Applied Linguistics.

Labov, W. (1972a) 'The study of language in its social context', in J.B. Pride and J. Holmes (eds), *Sociolinguistics*. Harmondsworth, Middlesex: Penguin.

Labov, W. (1972b) 'The logic of non-standard English', in P. Giglioli (ed.), *Language and Social Context*. Harmondsworth, Middlesex: Penguin.

Labov, W. (1998) 'The intersection of sex and social class in the course of linguistic change', in Cheshire and Trudgill (1998).

Lakoff, R. (1975) *Language and Woman's Place*. New York: Harper & Row.

Lapping, B. (1989) *End of Empire*. London: Grafton.

Leacock, E. Burke (1981) *Myths of Male Dominance: Collected Articles on Women Cross-culturally*. New York: Monthly Review Press.

Leith, D. (1983) *A Social History of English*. London: Routledge & Kegan Paul.

Leith, D. (1987) 'Standardisation in English', in B. Mayor and A.K. Pugh (eds), *Language, Communication and Education*. London: Croom Helm.

Leith, D. (1997) *A Social History of English* (second edition). London: Routledge.

Leith, D. and Graddol, D. (1996) 'Modernity and English as a national language', in Graddol et al. (1996).

Lenin, V.I. (1947) *The Right of Nations to Self-Determination*. Moscow: Progress Publishers.

Longman (1991) *Dictionary of the English Language* (foreword by Prof. R. Quirk). Harlow, Essex: Longman.

Lorde, A. (1996) *The Lorde Compendium: Essays, Speeches and Journals* (Introduction by A. Walker). London: HarperCollins.

Lovenduski, J. and Rendall, V. (1993) *Contemporary Feminist Politics: Women and Power in Britain*. Oxford: Oxford University Press.

Luria, A. (1981) *Language and Cognition*. New York: John Wiley & Sons.

Macaulay, R.K.S. (1978) 'Variation and consistency in Glaswegian English', in Trudgill (1978).

Maccoby, E.E. and Nagy, J.C. (1974) *The Psychology of Sex Differences*, Vol I. Stanford, CA: Stanford University Press.

Major, B.M. and Pugh, A.K. (eds) (1987) *Language, Communication and Education*. London: Croom Helm/Open University Press.

Maltz, D.N. and Borker, R.A. (1982) 'A cultural approach to male–female miscommunication', in Gumperz (1982).

Marenbon, J. (1987) *English, Our English: the New Orthodoxy Examined*. London: Centre for Policy Studies.

Martin, F.M. (1954) 'Some subjective aspects of social stratification', in D.V. Glass (ed.), *Social Mobility in Britain*. London: Routledge & Kegan Paul.

Marx, K. (1971) *The Grundrisse*, ed. and trans. D. McLellan. New York: Harper Torchbooks/Harper & Row.

Marx, K. (1975) *Early Writings*. Harmondsworth, Middlesex: Penguin.

Marx, K. (1976) *Capital: Volume 1*. Harmondsworth, Middlesex: Penguin.

Marx, K. and Engels, F. (1959) *On Colonialism*. Moscow: Progress Publishers.

Marx, K. and Engels, F. (1963) *Theories of Surplus Value (Part I)*. Moscow: Progress Publishers.

Marx, K. and Engels, F. (1969) *Selected Works: Volume 1*. Moscow: Progress Publishers.

Marx, K. and Engels, F. (1970) *Selected Works: Volume 3*. Moscow: Progress Publishers.

Marx, K. and Engels, F. (1973) *Manifesto of the Communist Party*. Beijing: Foreign Language Press.

Marx, K. and Engels, F. (1974) *The German Ideology*, ed. C.J. Arthur. London: Lawrence & Wishart.

Matejka, L. and Titunik, I.R. (1973) Appendix 1 in Volosinov (1973).

Mazrui, A.A. (1966) 'The English language and political consciousness in British colonial Africa', *Journal of Modern African Studies*, 4 (3): 295–311.

Mazrui, A.A. (ed.) (1975) *The Political Sociology of the English Language: An African Perspective*. The Hague: Mouton.

McArthur, T. (1996a) 'English in the World and in Europe', in R. Hartmann (ed.), *The English Language in Europe*. Oxford: Intellect.

McArthur, T. (1996b) *The Oxford Companion to the English Language*, abridged edn. Oxford: Oxford University Press.

McArthur, T. (1998) *The English Languages*. Cambridge: Cambridge University Press.

McCallan, B. (1989) *English: a World Commodity* (The International Market for Training in English as Foreign Language). London: The Economist Intelligence Unit.

McCashin, A. (1996) *Lone Mothers in Ireland: a Local Study*. Dublin: Oak Tree Press/Combat Poverty Agency.

McClintock, A. (1995) *Imperial Leather: Race, Gender and Sexuality in the Imperial Contest*. London: Routledge.

McConnell-Gillet, S., Borker, R. and Furman, N. (1980) *Women and Language in Literature and Society*. New York: Praeger.

McCrum, R., McNeil, R. and Cran, W. (eds) (1986) *The Story of English*. London: Faber & Faber/BBC Books (revised edition 1992).

McMahon, A.M.B. (1994) *Understanding Language Change*. Cambridge: Cambridge University Press.

Mengham, R. (1993) *The Descent of Language: Writing in Praise of Babel*. London: Bloomsbury.

Mey, J.L. (1985) *Whose Language? A Study in Linguistic Pragmatics*. Amsterdam and Philadephia: John Benjamins.

Mey, J.L. (1997) *Pragmatics*. Oxford: Blackwell.

Miller, C. and Swift, K. (1976) *Words and Women*. New York: Anchor Press/Doubleday.

Miller, C. and Swift, K. (1989) *The Handbook for Non-Sexist Writing for Writers, Editors and Speakers*. London: The Women's Press.

Miller, J. (1993) *The Passion of Michel Foucault*. London: HarperCollins.

Mills, S. (ed.) (1995) *Language and Gender: Interdisciplinary Perspectives*. London: Longman.

Mills, S. (1997) *Discourse*. London: Routledge.

Milroy, J. (1991) 'Variation in Belfast English', in Cheshire (1991).

Milroy, J. and Milroy, L. (1985) *Authority in Language: Investigating Language Prescription and Standardisation*. London: Routledge & Kegan Paul.

Milroy, J. and Milroy, L. (eds) (1993) *Real English: The Grammar of English Dialects in the British Isles*. London: Longman.

Modleski, T. (1991) *Feminism without Women*. New York: Routledge.

Molyneux, J. (1994) 'The "politically correct" controversy', *International Socialism*, 2: 61, Spring: 42–74.

Moody, T.W. (1982) *Davitt and the Irish Revolution 1846–82*. Oxford: Oxford University Press.

Morris, D. (1997) *The Human Sexes: a Natural History of Man and Woman*. London: Network Books (BBC Books).

Naysmith, J. (1987) 'English as imperialism?' *Language Issues*, 1 (2): 3–5.

Negroponte, N. (1995) *Being Digital*. London: Hodder & Stoughton.

Nelson, B.J. and Chowdhury, N. (1994) *Women and Politics Worldwide*. New Haven: Yale University Press.

Newman, E. (1974) *Strictly Speaking: Will America be the Death of English?* London: W.H. Allen.

Newman, F. and Holzman, L. (1993) *Lev Vygotsky: Revolutionary Scientist*. New York: Routledge.

Newmeyer, F.J. (1986) *The Politics of Linguistics*. Chicago: University of Chicago Press.

Newmeyer, F.J. (1991) 'Functional explanation in linguistics and the origins of language', *Language and Communication*, 11: 3–28.

Ngugi wa Thiongo (1985) 'The language of African literature', *New Left Review*, 150 (March/April): 109–130.

Ngugi wa Thiongo (1993) *Moving the Centre: the Struggle for Cultural Freedoms*. London: James Currey.

Nichols, P.C. (1978) 'Black women in the rural South: conservative and innovative', in B.L. Dubois and I. Crouch (eds), *The Sociology of the Languages of American Women*. Texas: Trinity University Press.

Oakley, A. (1972) *Sex, Gender and Society*. New York: Harper & Row.

Oakley, A. (1997) 'A brief history of feminism', in A. Oakley and J. Mitchell (eds), *'Who's Afraid of Feminism?'* Harmondsworth, Middlesex: Penguin.

O'Barr, W. and Atkins, B.K. (1980) 'Women's language or powerless language?' in McConnell-Gillet et al. (1980).

O'Connor, P. (1996) 'Organisational culture as a barrier to women's promotion', *The Economic and Social Review* (Dublin), 21 (3): 205–234.

Ohmann, R. (1995) 'On PC and related matters', in Williams (ed.), 1995.

O'Leary, E.O. and Ryan, M.M. (1994) 'Women bosses: counting the changes or changes that count', in M. Tanton (ed.), *Women in Management: a Developing Presence*. London: Routledge.

Orwell, G. (1961) 'Politics and the English language', in *George Orwell: Collected Essays*. London: Secker & Warburg.

Orwell, G. (1970) *The Collected Essays, Journalism and Letters of George Orwell, Volume 2: My Country Right or Left 1940–43*, ed. S. Orwell and I. Angus. Harmondsworth, Middlesex: Penguin.

Oxfam (1995) *Oxfam Poverty Report*. Oxford: Oxfam UK and Ireland.

Paglia, C. (1995) *Vamps and Tramps: New Essays*. London: Virago.

Parrington, J. (1997) 'In perspective: Valentin Volosinov', *International Socialism*, 75 (Summer): 117–150.

Pattanayak, D.P. (1985) 'Diversity in communication and languages: predicament of a multilingual nation state: India, a case study', in Wolfson and Manes (1985).

Penelope, J. (1990) *Speaking Freely: Unlearning the Lies of the Fathers' Tongues*. New York: Pergamon Press.

Pennycook, A. (1990a) 'The diremptive/redemptive project: postmodern reflections on culture and knowledge in international academic relations', *Alternatives*, 15: 53–81.

Pennycook, A. (1990b) 'Critical pedagogy and second language education', *System*, 18 (3): 303–313.

Pennycook, A. (1991) ' A reply to Kanpol', *Issues in Applied Linguistics*, 2 (2): 305–312.

Pennycook, A. (1994a) *The Cultural Politics of English as an International Language*. London: Longman.

Pennycook, A. (1994b) 'Incommensurable discourses?' *Applied Linguistics*, 15 (2): 115–138.

Pennycook, A. (1995) 'English in the world/the world in English', in Tollefson (1995).

Phillipson, R. (1992a) *Linguistic Imperialism*. Oxford: Oxford University Press.

Phillipson, R. (1992b) 'ELT: the native speaker's burden?' *ELT Journal*, 46 (1): 12–18.

Pierce, B.N. (1989) 'Toward a pedagogy of possibility in the teaching of English internationally: people's English in South Africa', *Tesol Quarterly*, 23 (3): 401–420.

Pinker, S. (1995) *The Language Instinct*. Harmondsworth, Middlesex: Penguin.

Pratt, M.L. (1992) *Imperial Eyes: Travel Writing and Transculturation*. London: Routledge.

Quirk, R. and Widdowson, H. (eds) (1985) *English in the World: Teaching and Learning the Languages and Literatures*. Cambridge: Cambridge University Press/The British Council.

Quirk, R., Greenbaum, S., Leech, G. and Svartvik, J. (1972) *A Grammar of Contemporary English*. London: Longman.

Rainbow, P. (ed.) (1987) *The Foucault Reader*. Harmondsworth, Middlesex: Penguin.

Ranger, T. (1983) 'The invention of tradition in colonial Africa', in Hobsbawm and Ranger (1983).

Ricento, T. (1995) 'A brief history of language restrictionism in the US', in TESOL (1995).

Ricks, C. and Michaels, L. (eds) (1990) *The State of the Language*. London: Faber & Faber.

Rose, S., Lewontin, R.C. and Kamin, L.J. (1984) *Not in Our Genes: Biology, Ideology and Human Nature*. Harmondsworth, Middlesex: Penguin.

Rosen, H. (1972) *Language and Class: A Critical Look at the Theories of Basil Bernstein*. Bristol: Falling Wall Press.

Rutherford, J. (1997) *Forever England: Reflections on Masculinity and Empire*. London: Lawrence & Wishart.

Said, E. (1992) 'The politics of knowledge', in Berman (1992).

Said, E. (1993) *Culture and Imperialism*. London: Chatto & Windus.

Sanday, P.R. (1981) *Female Power and Male Dominance: on the Origins of Sexual Inequality*. Cambridge: Cambridge University Press.

Sapir, E. (1963) *An Introduction to the Study of Speech*. London: Rupert Hart-Davies.

Sapir, E. (1985) *Selected Writings: in Language Culture and Personality*, ed. D. Mandelbaum. Berkeley: University of California Press.

SarDesai, D.R. (1997) *Southeast Asia: Past and Present.* Boulder, CO: Westview Press.

Saussure, F. de (1971) *Cours de linguistique générale.* Paris: Payot.

Schmied, J. (1991) *English in Africa: an Introduction.* London: Longman.

Schiffrin, D. (1994) *Approaches to Discourse.* Oxford: Blackwell.

Schulz, M. (1975) 'The semantic derogation of women', in Thorne and Henley (1975).

Scott, J.W. (1995) 'The campaign against political correctness: what's really at stake', in Williams (1995).

Scott, J.W. (1996) *Feminism and History.* Oxford: Oxford University Press.

Scruton, R. (1990) 'Ideologically speaking', in Ricks and Michaels (1990).

Seaton, I. (1997) 'Linguistic non-imperialism', *ELT Journal,* 51 (4 October): 381–382.

Showalter, E. (1989) *Speaking of Gender.* New York: Routledge.

Smith, O. (1986) *The Politics of Language 1791–1819.* Oxford: Clarendon Press.

Smith, P.M. (1985) *Language, the Sexes and Society.* Oxford: Blackwell.

Smith, S. (1997) 'Mind your language', *Socialist Review,* 206 (March): 15.

Sokal, A. and Bricmont, J. (1998) *Intellectual Impostures.* London: Profile Books.

Spender, D. (1985) *Man-made Language.* London: Routledge & Kegan Paul.

Spender, D. (1995) *Nattering on the Net: Women, Power and Cyberspace.* Melbourne: Spinifex Press.

Spolsky, B. (1998) *Sociolinguistics.* Oxford: Oxford University Press.

Sweet, H. (1908) *The Sounds of English.* Oxford: Oxford University Press.

Tannen, D. (1990) *You Just Don't Understand: Women and Men in Conversation.* London: Virago.

Tannen, D. (1991) 'Response to Senta Troemel-Ploetz's *Selling the Apolitical* (1991)', *Discourse and Society,* 3 (2): 249–254.

Tannen, D. (1995) *Talking from Nine to Five: How Men and Women's Conversational Styles Affect Who Gets Heard, Who Gets Credit and What Gets Done at Work.* London: Virago.

Tanner, N.M. (1981) *On Becoming Human.* Cambridge: Cambridge University Press.

Taylor, B. (1983) *Eve and the New Jerusalem: Socialism and Feminism in the Nineteenth Century.* London: Virago.

TESOL (1995) *Official English? No! TESOL's Recommendations for countering the Official English Movement in the US.* Alexandria, VA: TESOL.

Thompson, E.P. (1980) *The Making of the English Working Class.* London: Victor Gollancz.

Thorne, B. and Henley, N. (eds) (1975) *Language and Sex: Difference and Dominance.* Rowley, MA: Newbury House.

Thorne, B., Kramarae, C. and Henley, N. (eds) (1983) *Language, Gender and Society.* Rowley, MA: Newbury House.

Thorne, T. (1997) *A Dictionary of Contemporary Slang.* London: Bloomsbury.

Todd, L. (1974) *Pidgins and Creoles.* London: Routledge & Kegan Paul.

Tollefson, J.W. (ed.) (1995) *Power and Inequality in Language Education.* Cambridge: Cambridge University Press.

Troemel-Ploetz, S. (1991) 'Selling the apolitical' (review essay), *Discourse and Society*, 2 (4): 489–502.

Trotsky, L. (1971) *In Defence of the October Revolution*. London: New Park Publications.

Trudgill, P. (1974) *Sociolinguistics: An Introduction to Language and Society*. Harmondsworth, Middlesex: Penguin (revised edition (1995).

Trudgill, P. (1978) *Sociolinguistic Patterns*. London: Edward Arnold.

Trudgill, P. (1990) *The Dialects of England*. Oxford: Blackwell.

University of Strathclyde (1994) *Non-Sexist Communication: Guidelines for Staff and Students*. Glasgow: University of Strathclyde.

University of Western Australia (1993) *A Guide for the Use of Non-Discriminatory Language*. Nedlands: University of Western Australia.

Utting, D. (1995) *Family and Parenthood: Supporting Families Preventing Breakdown: a Guide to the Debate*. York: Joseph Rowntree Foundation.

Vallins, G.H. (1953) *Better English*. London: Pan Books.

Viswanathan, G. (1989) *Masks of Conquest: Literary Study and British Rule in India*. New York: Columbia University Press.

Volosinov, V.I. (1973) *Marxism and the Philosophy of Language*, trans. L. Mahejka and I.R. Titunik. New York: Seminar Press.

Volosinov, V.I. (1976) *Freudianism: a Marxist Critique*, trans. I.R. Titunik. New York: Academic Press.

Vygotsky, L.S. (1962) *Thought and Language*, trans. E. Haufmann and G. Vakar. Cambridge, MA: MIT Press.

Vygotsky, L.S. (1978) *Mind in Society: the Development of Higher Psychological Processes*, ed. M. Cole, V. John-Steiner, S. Scribner and E. Souberman. Cambridge, MA: Harvard University Press.

Vygotsky, L.S. (1986) *Thought and Language*, trans. and ed. A. Kosulin. Cambridge, MA: MIT Press.

Walby, S. (1990) *Theorizing Patriarchy*. Oxford: Blackwell.

Wang, W.S-Y. (ed.) (1991) *The Emergence of Language, Development and Evolution (Readings from Scientific American)*. New York: Freeman.

Wenner, A.M. and Wells, P.H. (1990) *Anatomy of a Controversy: the Question of a 'Language' among Bees*. New York: Columbia University Press.

Wenner, A.M., Meade, D.E. and Friesen, L.J. (1991) 'Recruitment, search behavior and flight ranges of honey bees', *American Zoologist*, 31: 768–782.

Wertsch, J.V. (1985) *Vygotsky and the Social Formation of Mind*. Cambridge, MA: Harvard University Press.

Whorf, B.L. (1956) *Language Thought and Reality: Selected Writings*, ed. J.B. Carroll. New York: The Technology Press of MIT/John Wiley & Sons.

Williams, G. (1992) *Sociolinguistics: a Sociological Critique*. London: Routledge.

Williams, J. (ed.) (1995) *PC Wars: Politics and Theory in the Academy*. New York: Routledge.

Williams, R. (1961) *The Long Revolution*. London: Chatto & Windus.

Williams, R. (1976) *Keywords*. London: Fontana.

Williams, R. (1983) *Culture and Society*. New York: Columbia University Press.

Wilson, C. (1997) 'The politics of information technology', *International Socialism*, 74 (Spring): 41–72.

Wilson, E.O. (1991) 'Animal communication', in Wang (1991).

Wolf, N. (1994) *Fire with Fire: the New Female Power and How It Will Change the 21st Century*. London: Chatto & Windus.

Wolf, N. (1997) *Promiscuities: a Secret History of Female Desire*. London: Chatto & Windus.

Wolfson, N. and Manes, J. (eds) (1985) *Language of Inequality*. Berlin: Mouton.

Woolfson, C. (1982) *The Labour Theory of Culture*. London: Routledge & Kegan Paul.

Wright, S. (1996) 'Accents of English', in Graddol et al. (1996).

Wyld, H.C. (1907) *The Growth of the English Language*. London: John Murray.

Wyld, H.C. (1921) *A History of Colloquial English*. London: T. Fisher Unwin.

Yemgoyan, A. (1977) Review of *Marxism and the Philosophy of Language* (V. Volosinov), *American Anthropologist*, 79 (3): 700–701.

Zimmerman, D. and West, C. (1975) 'Sex roles, interruptions and silences in conversation', in Thorne and Henley (1975).

Index

The letter n *following a page number indicates a reference in the notes*

Abbott, P., 111
abstract objectivism, 26–7, 190
academic institutions, women's participation in, 98
accent: class and, 156–7; *see also* dialects
Achebe, C., 65, 94; *No Longer at Ease*, 90
Africa: colonialism, 63–6; use of English in, 58
African languages, 64, 87, 93
Afrikaans, 91
Ahmad, A., 53, 62, 67, 89, 91–2, 195
alien word, 35–9, 47, 87, 89
Angogo, R., 59
Applied Linguistics, 27, 45–6, 47, 76, 81
Arnold, M., 3
Atkins, B. K., 124

Bailey, R. W., 57, 58
Bakhtin, M., 49–50n, 109
Baldwin, J., 87, 94
Barker, M., 27, 30, 35
Bayart, J-F., 77, 93
Beaken, M., 68, 191
beehive analogy, 18, 49n
Beezer, A., 105
Bell, A., 127
Bentham, J., 82
Berman, P., 97
Bernstein, B., 178–9, 183
Bickerton, D., 47, 51n
biological determinism, 105–6, 114–15, 147n
Birnbaum, N., 71
Black English, 88, 179, 183
Bloomfield, L., 49n
Bolger, D., 102
Brazil, D., 173–4
British Council, 53, 55, 74
British government, role of in ELT, 74–5
Bryson, B., *Mother Tongue*, 67
Bukharin, N., 78–9
Burchfield, R., 67
Burke, E., 159–60
Bush, G., 113

Callinicos, A., 10, 85, 189
Cameron, D., 70, 100, 112–13, 117, 140, 141, 142
capitalism, 57–8, 118, 143, 191; global, 76–9, 83; and spread of English, 56–7, 75
Carter, R., 150, 174, 179

centre/periphery model, 76–9, 82
Chambers, J. K., 115
changes in language, 47–8, 100, 129–30, 146, 153–4, 193; social change and, 18, 26, 34, 35, 68, 108–13, 146
childcare, and speech of children, 130
children: egocentric speech, 43; language and social interaction, 136–7
Chomsky, N., 13, 75
civilizing mission, 63–4
Clark, K., 49–50n
class, 46, 77, 78, 155, 162; Marx and, 21, 23; meaning and, 30, 37–8; power and, 9–10; pronunciation and, 127, 128; Standard English and, 165–70, 195; and standard written language, 157–60; and use of English in India, 61–2; and use of English in Malaysia, 83; and use of Irish English, 182; Volsinov and, 36, 37–8; women and, 125–6, 130, 135, 144
Coates, J., 131–3, 135–6, 139, 142
Cobbett, W., 162; *Grammar of the English Language*, 163–5
Cole, G. D. H., 186n
Cole, J., 144
colonialism, *see* imperialism
Connolly, J., 92
Conrad, J., *Heart of Darkness*, 65
consciousness, 4, 137, 191–2, 193; Marx and, 8–9, 16–19, 23; Volsinov and, 25, 31–2; Vygotsky and, 39, 40
Conservative Centre for Policy Studies, 149
context, 32, 44; meanings and, 28–9, 48, 175
conversational styles, gender and, 115–16, 117, 119–120, 121, 131, 132, 139, 142
Coulmas, F., 71–3, 87
Coupland, N., 130
covert prestige, 125, 128
Crawford, M., 123, 140–1
creoles, 87, 95n, 131
Croce, B., 26
Crowley, T., 177, 194
Crystal, D., 55, 56, 57, 58–9, 76, 96n
Curtin, P. D., 63

Dante, 37
Darwin, C., 19, 49n, 147n
dead language, 38–9

demotic speech, 170, 171–2
Dentith, S., 24, 50n
Derrida, J., 189
developmental role of language, 41–2, 46
dialectics, 86–94
dialects, 37, 154, 169–70; class and, 157–9, 162; Cobbett and, 163–4; disparagement of, 176, 177; East Midland, 158–9; non-standard, 179–84, 185
dialogue, 32
dictionaries: Johnson, 160–1; and language production, 111–12; and Standard English, 168
differences, *see* verbal differences
direct/indirect speech, 33
disadvantage; language and, 178–9; of women, 135–6
discipline, 5, 82
discourse, 4, 10, 193–4; Foucault and, 5–6; postmodernism and, 80–6; and reality, 6–7
discrimination against women, 98–9, 117–18
Douglass, F., 7, 88
Dua, H. R., 89

Eagleton, T., 6, 38, 189, 191
Ebonics, 183–4
Eckert, P., 133–5
Eco, U., 68
economic factors, in spread of English, 57–8, 62–3
economics, language likened to, 72–3
education: in Africa, 64; English used in India, 61–2; policies for in developing world, 78; Standard English used in, 168, 169, 170, 173
EFL (English as a Foreign Language), 56, 59
egocentric speech, 43
Ehrenreich, B., 100
EIL (English as an International Language) 59, 95n
ELT (English Language Teaching), 74, 75, 76, 80
Engels, F., 22, 46, 85; *Introduction to the Dialectics of Nature*, 19–20
English, 46–7, 47–8; as alien word, 36–7, 38; history of, 69; world-wide spread of, 53–60; ENL (English as Native Language), 59
Equiano, O., 88–9, 96n
ESD (English as a Second Dialect), 59
ESL (English as Second Language), 59
essentialism, 140–1
EWL (English as World Language), 59, 95n

Fairclough, N., 14, 121, 194
feminism, 98–9, 101, 111, 138, 141, 192–3
Fishman, J., 69–70, 71, 120
Flaitz, J., 68
Ford Foundation, 74, 75
Foucault, M., 4–6, 7, 14, 81, 82; and ideology, 7–8; and power, 5, 9
Fowler, H. W., 170
France/French language, 3, 68, 91, 109–10
Frank, A., 7
Frank, A. G., 96n

Fryer, P., 109
Furfey, P., 114

Garrick, D., 160
Gates, H. L., 99, 113
gender, 131, 134, 138–46, 192; and verbal differences, 114–16, 119, 125–7, 129, 131–7
generative view of language, 28, 48, 180, 193
Genovese, E., 98
Geras, N., 85
Giroux, A., 85
globalization, 1, 55, 58, 76–9, 83
Goodwin, M., 136–7, 146
Gordon, L., 143
Graddol, D., 57, 119, 120
grammar, 174–5; Cobbett and, 163, 164, 165; evolution of, 32–4, 47–8; of non-standard dialects, 179–80; speech and, 173–4, 175
Gramsci, A., 3, 37, 86, 122, 149, 151, 157, 178, 193
Green, J., 112, 161

Halliday, M. A. K., 172
Hancock, I., 59
Hardy, T., 168
Harman, C., 19, 93–4
Harris, J., 153, 166–8, 175, 181
he/man generic, 103, 106, 107
Hentoff, N., 98
history, 27, 68–9, 194; English and, 86–94, 157–8; and standardization, 157–8, 177–8; Vygotsky and, 39
Hobsbawm, E., 186n
Hodge, R., 194
Hodgkin, T., 63
Holmes, J., 143
Holquist, M., 49–50n
Honey, J., 149, 152, 155, 156, 164, 176–7
Humboldt, W. von, 21, 26
Hume, D., 57, 94–5n

ideology, 4, 7–9, 109, 118, 190–4; dictionaries and, 112; of imperialism, 79; Marx and, 21–4, 26, 46–7; and Standard English, 149, 157, 185; Volsinov and, 24–6, 38, 46–7, 190
imperialism, 78–9, 84, 91, 191, 194–5; English and, 53, 60–6, 74; Marx on, 83
India, use of English in, 58, 61–2, 89
Indian languages, 60–1, 93
information technology, and spread of English, 57, 58–9
inheritance of language, 27, 38
inner speech: Volsinov and, 31–2; Vygotsky and, 42–5
international organizations, use of English in, 55
Internet, 55, 111
Ireland, 96n, 109, 186n; English language in, 92; Irish English in, 181–2; Irish language, 77, 89, 92, 93; Marx on, 83
Irigaray, L., 101
Italy/Italian language, 3, 37, 109–10

Jakobson, R., 24
Jameson, F., 50n
Japanese, 34
Jaworski, J. A., 130
Jenkins, S., 110
Jespersen, O., 67–8, 114
Johnson, P., 97
Johnson, S., 158, 160–2
Jones, D., 152–3, 156
Jones, P. E., 15
Joyce, J., 36–7, 38
Joyce, P., 169

Kachru, B. B., 54, 59, 60, 89
Kallen, J., 181–2
Kiberd, D., 93
Kipling, R., 66, 95n
Kirkby, J., *Grammatical Rules*, 103, 106–7
Koestler, A., 7
Kollontai, A., 145
Kosulin, A., 41, 44–5
Kramarae, C., 111, 148n
Kress, G., 194

Labov, W., 125, 126, 128, 129, 130, 131, 179, 183
Lakoff, R., 107, 122–4
language, 10; origins of, 16, 18, 45–6; as site of struggle, 84; social nature of 29–32, 34; social production of, 16–20; society and, 18, 19, 23, 25, 34–5, 40, 91–2, 191
language change, *see* changes in language
langue/parole, 4, 27, 167
Leith, D., 153, 156–7, 158
Lenin, V. I., 87
Levi, P., 7
linguistic determinism, 86, 102–6
linguistic imperialism, 73–80, 90
linguistic rights, 79, 87
Lorde, A., 144, 145
Luria, A., 39

Macaulay, Lord, 3, 60–1, 166
McArthur, T., 59
McCallan, B., 73
McCarthy, M., 174
Maccoby, E. E., 135
McCrum, R., 69, 88, 150, 161
Malaysia, 93; use of English in, 83, 89
males, and creation of language, 103–4, 107, 111–12
Marenbon, J., 149–50, 176
Marx, K./Marxism, 8–9, 9–10, 46, 83, 120, 194, 195; *Das Capital*, 17–18; and consciousness, 15–19; and colonialism, 91; on language, 15, 16–19, 21–2; Pennycook and, 82–3
materialism, 15, 16, 62–3
Mazrui, A. A., 84
Mead, M., 147n
meaning/s, 28, 30, 43, 85; changes in, 103, 106; class and, 30, 37–8; ideology and, 109
Mengham, R., 164

Mey, J. L., 110
Mill, J. S., 95n
Miller, C., 107, 108
Mills, S., 6, 7
Milroy, J. and L., 180–1
Molyneux, J., 98
Moore, G. E., 166, 167
Morris, D., 113–14
multilingualism, 73
Murray, J., 154, 166, 167, 168
myths about Standard English, 151–7

Nagy, J. C., 135
nationalism, 77–8, 92, 93–4
Naysmith, J., 74
Negroponte, N., 147n
neo-marxism, 80–1, 82
neutrality, 69–73
Newbolt, H., 176
Newmayer, F. J., 14, 15, 16–17
Ngugi wa Thiongo, 53, 88, 90
Nichols, P. C., 130–1
Nigeria, 77
non-sexist linguistic guidelines, 97, 101, 102, 108, 112–13
non-standard/standard pronunciations, 124–5, 126–7, 128, 131

Oakley, A., 138
O'Barr, W., 124
oppression, 6, 7, 110, 145; linguistic, 36, 78, 79, 87, 93, 142–3; and spread of English, 89, 90–1; *see also* women's oppression
Orwell, George, 2, 170–2
Oxford English Dictionary, 168

Paine, T., 159–60
Parrington, J., 50n
patriarchy, 105, 139–40
Pattanayak, D. P., 58
Penelope, J., 142, 147n
Pennycook, A., 80–6
Phillipson, R., 70, 74–8, 79
pidgins, 87, 95n
Pinker, S., 13, 50n
political correctness, 1–2, 97–100
polysemy, 123
Postgate, R., 186n
postmodernism, 1, 6–7, 10, 189–90; and discursive practices, 80–6
poststructuralism, 13–14
Powell, E., 154
power, 3, 5, 81, 84, 85, 128, 132, 146; alien word and, 36; Foucault and, 5, 9; male, 105, 106; Marx and, 9–10
Pratt, M. L., 66
prestige forms of speech, 124–31
production, relations of, 22–3, 26
progress, English and, 64–5, 81
pronunciation, standard/non-standard, 124–5, 126–7, 128, 131

quantitative sociolinguistics, 70
question tags, 123–4

race/racism, 63, 89, 109
Ranger, T., 66
reality, 4; discourse and, 6–7; signs and, 25
Received Pronunciation (RP), 127, 156–7
reported speech, 32–4
revolution, and linguistic change, 109–10
Rose, S., 114
Rosen, H., 183
RP (Received Pronunciation), 127, 156–7
ruling class, 23–4, 77, 78, 92–3; and Standard
    English, 158–9, 166, 173, 178, 185
Russia/Russian language, 33, 79, 110

Said, E., 62, 98
Sapir, E., 47, 68, 175
Saussure, F. de, 13, 26–7, 167, 190
Schmied, J., 87–8
Scott, J. W., 145
Seaton, I., 74
sexism, 99, 100–1, 123, 141, 192; in language,
    101, 103, 112, 146
sexual division of labour, 120, 132
Sidney, P., 152
signs: Volsinov and, 25, 34–5, 37–8; Vygotsky
    and, 41
Singapore, 76, 77
slavery, 87–9
Smith, O., 159–60
social change, 3, 56–7, 91, 165–6, 194, 195; and
    linguistic change, 18, 26, 34, 35, 68, 108–13,
    146
social conduct, and standards of speech,
    152–3
social division, 64, 75–6, 119, 128, 177
social inequality, 58, 59, 80, 93, 117, 156, 184
social mobility, 70, 129, 181; Standard English
    and, 155–7
social norms, 126–7, 128, 181
social organization, 35, 36, 137, 141
social relations, 16, 29, 36, 37, 38, 120, 121, 136,
    141, 183, 193–5
South Africa, English in, 91
speech codes, 108, 110
speech genres, 35
Spender, D., 147n; *Man-made Language*, 101–7
spoken language, 155, 161, 171–2, 180, 185;
    Johnson and, 161–2; marginalization of,
    172–6
Spolsky, B., 72
Standard English, 2, 3, 149, 184–5, 193; as class
    dialect, 165–70; debate on, 149–51; evolution
    of, 157–9, 177, 195; and marginalization of
    spoken language, 172–6; myths about, 151–7;
    and non-standard dialects, 176–84, 185;
    Orwell and, 170–2
style, and grammar, 33–4
superiority of English, 66–9
Swann, J., 119, 120

Sweet, H., 168–9
Swift, J., 152, 154
Swift, K., 107, 108

Tannen, D., 115–18, 142
theme, 30
Thorne, B., 133
thought, 21, 22, 102; Vygotsky and, 40–2, 48
trade, and spread of English, 58, 64–5
Trevelyan, G. M., 61, 95n
Troemel-Ploetz, S., 118
Trotsky, L., 110
Trudgill, P., 114, 125, 127, 128, 129, 130, 154, 179
truth, 5, 8, 9

United States of America: anti-PC crusade, 99;
    promotion of ELT, 75
universities, guidelines for non-sexist
    language, 108

varieties of English, 2, 191
verbal differences, sex and, 114–15, 119, 125–7,
    129
verbal interaction, 28–31, 133
Viswanathan, G., 61–2
Volosinov, V. I., 4, 14–15, 106, 175, 193; and
    alien word, 35–9, 89; and context, 28–9;
    critique of Saussurean linguistics, 26–8;
    'Discourse in life and discourse in art', 29;
    and grammar, 32–4; and ideology, 24–6, 38,
    46–7, 190; and inner speech, 31–2
Vygotsky, L. S., 31, 46, 48, 175; and inner
    speech, 42–5; *Thought and Language*, 39–42

Walby, S., 139
Wallace, C., 111
Wallerstein, I., 82
Wertsch, J. V., 39
West, C., 119, 120
Whorf, B. L., 102, 104
Williams, G., 70, 96n
Williams, R., 151, 158–9, 171
Wolf, N., 99
women: educational disadvantage, 135;
    speaking differently, 114–18, 119, 131–7, 192
women's language, 104, 105, 111, 122–4, 134,
    140; accents and, 124–31; use of language,
    119
women's oppression, 108–9, 134, 139, 140, 141,
    142; language as cause of, 102–8, 119, 192;
    social relations and, 143–4
women's studies courses, 143
working-class language, 126, 129, 155, 177,
    178–9, 183
World English, 57, 191
written language, 154–5, 172–3; class and,
    159–60
Wyld, H., 156

Zimmerman, D., 119, 120